Somebody Stole My Game

CHRIS LAIDLAW

SOMEBODY STOLE MY GAME

Hodder Moa

National Library of New Zealand Cataloguing-in-Publication Data

Laidlaw, Chris, 1943-

Somebody stole my game / Chris Laidlaw.

Includes index.

ISBN 978-1-86971-192-4

1. Rugby Union football.

796.333-dc 22

A Hodder Moa Book

Published in 2010 by Hachette New Zealand Limited

4 Whetu Place, Mairangi Bay

Auckland, New Zealand

Designed and produced by Hachette New Zealand Limited

Printed by 1010 Printing International Ltd., China

This book is dedicated to all those loyal rugby fans around the world who are wondering what's happening to their game.

Contents

Introduction 9

Somebody Stole My Game 13
From Chump to Chic in One Generation 33
Upstairs and Downstairs: Unity and Division 49
Riding the Money-go-round 57
The Salvation of Sanzar 65
Lord Ranfurly's Hospital Pass 69
Marching to the Beat of the Broadcasters 73
The Weight of the Winner's Burden 81
The Quicksands of Correctness 87
Nasty, Brutish and Short 101
The Cup that Underflows 111
Nothing Short of Perfection Will Do 119
Dosh or Glory 127
The Thoroughly Modern Player 139
This Sporting Life 143
The Last Hurrah and the Mid-term Break 153
More Brawn, Less Brain 159
Is Brown the New Black? 163
Of Poachers and Gamekeepers 169
Tatou Tatou 177
The Cultural Calling Card 185
Uncomfortable Bedfellows 189
Climbing the Stairway to Heaven 199

The Magic of Seven 205
Sibling Rivalry 211
Being There 217
Under England's Skin 229
England Expects 235
The Beastly Beatitudes of European Union 241
Whatever Happened to the Hwyl? 247
Is Life Worth Living Without the Lions? 253
Le Beau Jeu to the Rescue 257
Finding Gold at the End of the Rainbow 261
Wallaby Wannabe 269
The Slowly Rising Sun 275
Going Global 281
Conclusion 287
Postscript 293

Bibliography 295
Index of Names 299

Introduction

RUGBY HAS a problem. It's now more than a decade since the game went professional and there are growing signs that it isn't sustainable. Everywhere it is played there is a growing sense of unease about this and it is becoming more and more obvious that some fairly radical changes are needed.

It is not the first time I have had that feeling. I last wrote a book about the game in the early 1970s as a thoroughly disgruntled ex-player, when rugby had run into another crisis. Unlike the present runaway pace of change, what happened back in the 1960s and 70s was a crisis of inactivity. Rugby had become stuck in the mud.

I wrote *Mud in Your Eye* for the very reason that to do so as an amateur was considered an act of rebellion. Anyone who appeared in print was treated in much the same way as a member of Al-Qaeda or, equally treasonous, a defector to rugby league. Any suggestion of commercial gain from amateurism immediately defined you as a professional, an outcast, on the wrong side of a very forbidding fence. Ironically, if you're not on the professional side of the fence today you're a loser.

Rugby has meant a lot to me. I played it at every level and in several countries. I owe it a huge debt. It took me round the world, opening new horizons and awakening a personal awareness of politics and the meaning of democracy and discrimination. The friends I made then — among club, provincial and All Blacks teams, at Oxford and in France or Fiji where I played and coached in the early 1970s — are friends for life. Many of them are as anxious about the game as I am. Most are realists. They know that the professional game is here to stay but they wonder what sort of game it will be if the amateur dimension — its heart and its soul — just withers away and dies. They have reservations about letting market forces completely determine every aspect of the game's future. Those reservations are justified.

With professionalism has come a cloying bureaucracy, a suffocating mass of red tape, the stunting of player lifestyles and a hundred other challenges that threaten to drown rugby in its own politically correct pea soup.

A few years ago, fascinated and at times horrified by the new professional revolution, I found myself getting involved with my old game again. I started writing about it, talking about it on television, and became a director of the Hurricanes professional franchise. I discovered that it wasn't just a game any more. It was a business too — a business like many others in an unforgiving world in which costs rise inexorably and income is very uncertain.

Every crisis has its particular motif. For me, the most compelling hint that rugby had a problem was the extraordinarily crass attempt by the New Zealand Rugby Union to persuade its fans to pick up part of the new professional tab in the late 1990s via a television commercial featuring All Black Justin Marshall asking for donations. This was trickle up economics, the same madness we saw a decade later that brought the world economy to its knees. It was the first ominous hint of unsustainability in the new commercialised game. That hint has now turned into a loud scream.

This book is inspired by rugby's colourful story of evolution and revolution; its eccentric origins, its often turbulent politics and its powers of exclusivity and inclusiveness in the many countries in which it is played. There is of course a danger of excessively romanticising the past. Nostalgia has blinded many of today's critics to the inevitability of progress and the importance of coming to terms with the fact that the game is never going to return to the good old days. And just how "good" were the good old days anyhow? The game was played on appallingly muddy surfaces for much of the time. The ball was actually in play about half the time it is today. We kicked for touch as a first rather than as a last resort. Our speed, strength and skills were modest compared to those of today's best players. Spectators were uncomfortable and there were no television replays.

There is much mythology in rugby's history and some of the present discontent is fuelled by this. It is important to filter out the irrational and to focus on what actually needs attention.

A lot of what follows might seem unduly critical. I make no apology for that. There is much to be critical about as the game lurches this way and that in search of its place in the world. But it is important to remember that the momentous challenges that it now faces weren't exactly of its own making. They are the product of unforeseen circumstances rather than any real incompetence or mismanagement. The market invaded a fiercely amateur sport before it even knew it was coming let alone being prepared for an orderly transition. Rugby, as it always has been, is blessed by many genuine and talented people whose overriding desire is to do the best by their sport, from the chairman of the NZRU, all the way through to those who wash the jerseys of the under-9 team in the smallest rural town. There is no shortage of commitment. The problem is they have become hostage to forces beyond their control.

The game is once again at a crossroads. It will either continue relentlessly down the path to total, soulless professionalism with the amateur dimension quietly dying in an impoverished ditch, or it will adapt, and reinvent itself as the one great international sport that didn't mindlessly succumb to the black magic of the market. A worrying question persistently nags away at rugby's conscience. Is the very soul of the game itself being leached out in pursuit of profit? How safe are all those precious traditions, myths and legends now that money rather than pleasure or companionship is the driver? How sustainable is a game that is ever more bloated at the professional top and slowly starving to death at the amateur bottom?

There is obviously no going back now that the game's foot is enmeshed in the voracious machinery of the market. It's far too late for that. The question is: can enough of the essential spirit of the game embodied in the clubs, the provinces and the minds and memories of rugby enthusiasts be preserved alongside the commercial dimension or are they destined to part company forever? Let us try to find out.

Somebody Stole My Game

RUGBY IS no ordinary game. With deliciously perverse origins and an idiosyncratic set of rules, it has delivered up untold pleasure and pain to those involved with it over nearly two centuries. Its character is born out of a jumble of historical facts and a large body of stories, garnished by hugely entertaining folklore. All this "belonged" to the rugby community. For over 100 years this intangible treasure has been the most precious possession of the game.

A shabby antique that was suddenly wrapped up in shiny new packaging, rugby isn't really just a game at all any more. These days the All Blacks are more than just a team. They are a brand. The most saleable brand in the game. A match isn't just a match. Rugby is now referred to as "product". Product is the word the sponsors, the broadcasters and even the rugby union use these days without a trace of self-consciousness. The product that is manufactured by dutiful teams is then suitably packaged and hawked off to the highest bidder.

Where does rugby now take its cue from? Not any longer from its colourful origins, still less from those who continue to derive pleasure from watching it. The game is steadily drifting away from those precious connections, not intentionally, or with any evident desire to break free from its past. On the contrary it is trying mightily to keep the past and the present within the same purview. But the past is slowly slipping into obscurity. It is another country, a primitive and irrelevant one.

The many loyal rugby fans who thought that rugby was *their* game, something to which they assumed they had some measure of proprietory right, are now beginning to realise that maybe it doesn't belong to them any longer.

Somebody stole it. It now belongs to the multinational corporate sponsors, the media companies who dictate what gets played, where, and when, and the heavily corporatised national unions that run it as a business.

Where before there was a fierce sense of egalitarianism, professionalism has ushered in a new form of elitism. Now, there are three classes of participant: those at the top who get paid a lot, those who are on the way up who get paid a little, and all the rest whose only return is the buzz they get from playing. The ranks at the top are expanding, in the middle they are stagnant, and at the bottom they are in decline. Rugby's accumulated folklore, its history and its infectiousness, for so long lodged in the bloodstream, are in danger of being killed off by the antibiotics of professionalism. Some of it has already gone, lost in the exhaust fumes of modern consumerism.

A generation ago the rugby establishment worldwide had lapsed into a kind of evolutionary coma: frozen solid while the world washed over it, leaving it behind as a fossilised relic of a gentlemanly age that had gone. Yet, within a relatively short time much of what was wrong with rugby had been transformed. The game took a great jump-shift forward. It extricated itself from under the rotting carcass of apartheid in South Africa. A more business-like approach was taken to the game's finances and its often appalling public relations. In New Zealand the administration was radically restructured. The large, unwieldy NZRU council — an unruly parliament of all the country's provincial unions — gave way to a new executive board as the primary decision-making body. Rugby took its first few steps towards becoming a business, but few of us realised just how far that would go, or how quickly and destructively. We do now.

Rugby is in crisis mode once again because the market has got its hands firmly round the game's throat. Markets, being markets, bring a confusing mixture of wealth and suffering. In rugby those two conditions can be neatly equated with the two dimensions of the game, the professional and the amateur. One is consuming like there's no tomorrow, while the other is sitting outside with a begging bowl. Trickle down isn't working.

The market certainly needs to have a place in rugby but must it always be the only determinant? As the eminently pragmatic Chicago economist Charles Kindleberger so pithily put it, "Where the market doesn't work, don't use it." That lesson is being painfully learned by governments and businesses all over the world as they come to terms with the devastation wreaked by free market greed, yet it seems to be passing rugby by. As in the 1970s, rugby needs a revolution.

Many of those in the corporate sector who now effectively call the tune are equally convinced they are doing the right thing by the game and their sincerity is, mostly, very real. But the interests of their own organisations and those of rugby don't always coincide. They see it purely as a business and they want it run as a business. They just don't have any other frame of reference and all too often they push the game further out towards potential disaster without the slightest awareness of the risks. It is the clash of those corporate interests with rugby's community spirit that has caused the crisis that the game now faces.

The most worrying thing about it all is that there seems to be no particular wish to come to terms with what all-out professionalism really means for rugby.

Rugby is now like the organ grinder's monkey. It dances to the tune of a new owner: the market. In many ways the new owner has been remarkably beneficent. It has enabled rugby to gain a foothold in a variety of new countries, something that wouldn't have happened if the old amateur Commonwealth regime had continued to hold sway. In some countries, like the United States, soccer mums have been joined by rugger mums.

The new owner has showered gifts upon those who play it best but that beneficence doesn't filter all the way down to those who still play it for pleasure. In many ways it is now a case of trickle up. The game is divided into the haves and the have-nots and the two dimensions are drifting inexorably apart. In New Zealand this is having a highly corrosive effect. Experience shows that this is what always happens when the market is given free rein anywhere. Rugby will be no exception unless it takes radical steps to secure its sovereignty.

In New Zealand that contest is as acute as anywhere on earth. There is a risk that the All Blacks will lose touch with ordinary people simply by virtue of money. Can a game that was a foundation stone of our egalitarianism retain its mythical place if it no longer practises egalitarianism itself? The situation is alive with ironies. While the All Blacks haggled with the union over their salary levels in the later 90s, one of their number appeared in a TV ad urging the public to make donations to keep the clubs afloat. It caused such an uproar that the ad was hastily shelved. A lesson was learned. The rugby public would only tolerate so much crass exploitation.

This frustration was illustrated vividly in 2009 when the NZRU warned a number of pubs and restaurants that they couldn't legally use the words "All Blacks" on their advertising boards outside inviting fans in to watch a Bledisloe Cup match on the big screen. "Those words are copyrighted," announced an NZRU brand lawyer sniffily. "Bollocks!" shouted 1000 restaurateurs in unison and tens of thousands of rugby fans echoed this. There erupted a public debate over who actually "owns" the All Blacks. People began to realise that they might think they own their national team but they sure as hell don't have the law on their side when it comes to using the words commercially. People are incensed by this. If the words "All Blacks" don't belong to them then, presumably, neither does the game. They are of course right to be incensed because, as one pub owner put it, "the NZRU thinks that it owns the All Blacks but it doesn't. They belong to all of us."

If only somebody from the NZRU had at the time stepped up to explain that ownership of a trade mark doesn't confer exclusive rights to a commodity as emotionally symbolic as an All Blacks team. Alas, the moment was missed and yet another gripe was stored away in the collective consciousness. The silver fern is now jealously protected intellectual property. The NZRU will sue the pants off anybody who tries to coat-tail on its precious imagery and the reasons for that are not sentimental: they are commercial.

The trade mark issue is illustrative of the way that throughout the rugby world a whole new commercial layer has been superimposed over the existing structure. Two seemingly incompatible cultures are in combat with each other. The culture of the corporate has seized control of the cash flow and little permeates through to the game at the grass roots. Huge sums are siphoned off in player, managerial and support staff salaries and other professional operating costs, while ageing grandstands rot in the smaller towns and local clubs resort to bring and buy sales to pay for laundering the players' jerseys. In such places the only risk to the local turnstiles is rust.

There is much enthusiastic talk about the "globalisation" of rugby, as if this particular mantra, chanted loudly enough, will deliver untold riches. The IRB, after an unconscionably long gestation, has begun to come to grips with the post-professional challenges and much of what it is trying to achieve is in what the IRB sees as the interests of the game as a whole. But is it? The IRB has become steadily more blinded by the need to raise more and more money in its almost obsessive desire to turn the game into a genuinely global one that can compete with soccer. Nobody has yet paused to ponder the implications of that.

The IRB's otherwise commendable efforts to grow the game in new markets might, ironically, lead to the amateur game in older member countries dying for want of investment. The game's resources are being pumped increasingly into Asia, the Gulf states, Africa and other frontier zones at the same time as the professional game vacuums up more and more of the resource base in traditional rugby playing countries. There is a crucial dilemma here.

Is the relentless pursuit of new markets a zero sum game? Will the rugby club in New Plymouth finish up more impoverished than its counterpart in Nairobi? That might seem an unlikely prospect now but it may not by 2020. The IRB pumps out statement after statement about expansion. Quantity is the watchword. Quality will presumably follow. In the rush to expand the market for the international rugby brand there isn't time to waste.

At the same time, the IRB has enormous difficulty in asserting any real authority in an environment in which it holds only some of the cards. Former IRB chairman Syd Millar confessed as much on a visit to New Zealand a few years ago. The game, internationally, he said, is hostage to a coterie of commercial interests and it is these forces that are driving it into this next phase of restructuring. His successor, Bernard Lapasset, has said much the same thing. He feels like a hostage, caught between a large army of xenophobic European clubs on the one hand and a bunch of voracious corporate backers on the other.

There is now a real danger that another sudden jump-shift in the commercialism of the game could result in one or more rebel competitions which, if enough money was thrown at them, could swamp the establishment. All the preconditions for it are present, just as they were for the rebel Twenty20 cricket circus that has brought such misery to cricket. If one or more of the billionaires who are looking to buy their way into rugby decide to back a rebel competition and set out to poach the most exciting players from around the world, there isn't much, other than the dragging entrails of loyalty to something that once was, to stop it.

And how much loyalty can one expect from today's players? What do they really owe the rugby establishment? Most of them are contractors who will sell to the highest bidder. They have been brought up to believe in the market and have only the vaguest appreciation of the game's historical roots. Can they be expected, now, to be driven by sentiment? Who can blame them for that? They have been brought up to believe that what they are engaged in is a business.

It isn't hard to shift from Auckland to Leicester or from Transvaal to Toulouse any more, or even to play for another country. Why then should it be hard to play for another competition if one suddenly appears? Remember the so-called Cavaliers? A quarter of a century ago most of the All Blacks squad went off to South Africa in a flash — thumbing their noses at the rugby establishment and for peanuts compared to what's often on the table now — and fully aware that they could have been drummed out of the game for life. That incident showed all too clearly how fragile the loyalty of a player can be when he catches a sniff of the folding stuff. So it proved a decade later.

The dumbing down of professional sportspeople is one of the great features of the modern age. It's the same everywhere you look. Few of the players are genuinely educated. They don't have the time. Most have only the faintest idea what's going on in the world around them or, it seems, the faintest interest. Where, once, it was possible to study and play, that option is fast disappearing in most sports. College football or basketball in the United States retains the figleaf of academic attachment through the scholarship system. It is an elaborate charade behind which athletes are able to sign on for a minimal number of classes, which they generally fail or don't complete, in return for handsome fee payment deals and a crack at a senior pro contract. This is happening in rugby too. Even at Oxford University there is a scholarship system which enables talented rugby players to play for the university and simply go through the motions of academic study. Without it, Oxford rugby would be sunk. University rugby worldwide is mostly sunk already.

Globalisation also breeds monotony. A generation ago playing in France, Italy or Argentina was a radically different experience for a player from the Anglo-Saxon world. Their players, officials and spectators thought differently, acted differently and interpreted rugby's Byzantine laws in their own idiosyncratic way. Now it is like going to play in an adjoining suburb. Rugby has been gathered up by the primal forces of homogenisation. New Zealand historian Jamie Belich observed, "Global integration leads to the convergence of prices, products and services; everywhere becomes more similar — eventually, perhaps, even the same."

Any form of cultural individuality is seemingly powerless in the face of this onslaught. As Benjamin Barber, the author of *Jihad vs. McWorld,* put it: these forces "demand integration and uniformity and mesmerise peoples everywhere with fast music, fast computers and fast food — MTV, Macintosh and McDonald's — pressing nations into one homogeneous global theme park, one McWorld tied together by communications, information, entertainment and commerce." To the fast music, fast computers and fast food you can now add fast sport. Rugby finds itself somewhere between Babel and Disneyland these days. It is being dug out from its roots by the interests of McWorld and flaunted as a new entrant in a vast new sporting music hall.

The game bends over backwards to try to stay in touch with its roots. Tenuous connections are maintained between the amateur and the professional game and between the older generations of All Blacks and today's stars. Strenuous efforts are being made to preserve the game's sense of its own history and the loyalty of so many of its followers and former players. The NZRU's decision to revive the tradition of awarding international caps, and to formally cap all those All Blacks who had missed out from the post-war years right up till a few years ago, is a case in point. It was a genuine and very well received effort to bridge the history gap.

The Community Rugby Programme, run inspirationally by "Buck" Anderson, is, likewise, a highly significant initiative. But somehow it still isn't enough.

This same struggle to link the past with the present is being waged wherever rugby is a dominant sport. In places like Wales and South Africa they are responding in similar ways. But in those countries the same doubt about the game's sustainability lingers as the unforgiving powers of the marketplace abandon sentiment and tradition in their wake.

Business gurus like Kevin Roberts of Saatchi and Saatchi travel the world extolling the corporate virtues and values of the All Blacks as a brand demonstrator for business itself. Sport at the level of excellence practised by the All Blacks has become a metaphor for successful enterprise of almost every kind. Rugby, having borrowed its techniques and management practices from the business world, has now turned into a poster boy for good business. The frantic promotions of rugby's merchandise feature the hot properties of the moment, but the proceeds of this activity are not available to the game at the grassroots level. The national unions are charging such a premium for international matches that ordinary fans simply can't afford to go any longer. This was vividly illustrated when the British and Irish Lions toured South Africa in 2009. The price of a ticket was so high the three test matches simply didn't sell out. In all three Sanzar countries patrons are voting with their feet.

There was a time when, if you couldn't actually go to the game, you simply stayed home and watched it on television. But even there exclusivity reigns. The game is no longer consistently free to air. If you want to watch it on television you have to buy a subscription from the commercial rights holder. Sorry about that. TVNZ can't afford it any more and successive governments have lacked the courage to intervene, as their counterparts did in Britain and Australia, to require key matches to be available free to air.

By professionalising rugby at its top end we have unleashed a whole new set of forces that are going to be hellishly difficult to control in future. There is now a thriving but badly regulated market for the services of young rugby players. It is not so much a market as a casino that has run dangerously out of control. There was an opportunity in the late 1990s to consider just how far down rugby's food chain the issue of player payments should go, but the opportunity was never taken up. As a result the commercial ethic filtered all the way down, through the provincial unions to the clubs, where it quickly became standard practice to use money as an inducement to players. Thus began a corrosive competition for talent among rugby institutions who simply couldn't afford it. Provincial unions are going to the wall because they are forced to buy talent in order to stay competitive. The strongest clubs and unions increase their dominance and the weaker go under and we all wonder what's wrong with the system.

At the same time the volume of top rugby matches just keeps getting larger — not because the governing bodies want that, but because they have to provide more and more to satisfy the voracious appetite of their commercial backers. Sky TV wants wall to wall rugby. In New Zealand its rugby channel blasts out games all day and all night. It was great for a while, but people soon began to suffer from too much of a good thing.

The broadcaster dictates when a game will start in accordance with its international scheduling and ratings interests, not the convenience of those who go along to watch it. Afternoon test matches are but a pleasant memory. Halftime breaks are lengthened to accommodate more television advertising. Soon we will probably have quarter time breaks officially instituted, for no other reason than the marketability of the game to advertisers. Then what?

All over the world the same complaint can be heard. We can't take any more. There's too much. Test matches have ceased to have any enduring meaning. Lesser matches are now ignored unless they feature local, tribal rivalries. But the broadcasting deals impose more, not less. Rugby has been obliged to stretch its season to the point where summer, the time when the game used to take a welcome breather, has been more or less abolished. Rugby isn't a winter game any more. It's played right through spring and autumn and, during the last World Cup in France, it was played in high summer — not because the players wanted it that way, but because that's the way the broadcasters insisted on having it in return for their largesse.

The sponsors want it all faster, fiercer and more full-on. The advertisements now feature massive doses of biff and bash. Watching a *Terminator* movie ad and an ad for an upcoming rugby test is much the same. Surreal images, forbidding figures, absurd analogies abound.

Overstatement is piled on hyperbole. According to Adidas, Richie McCaw is only partly human. You want violence, big hits and high drama? Rugby will deliver. The ads promise it.

The same pattern is being repeated among other traditional team sports. Cricket, once the most sedate of games, has succumbed more or less completely to the spirit of the sound bite. How long will five day tests, said to be the essential cornerstone of the game, survive? The one day game is already under pressure from Twenty20, a madcap, helterskelter version that is over in a few hours — including ad breaks. Someone will no doubt invent a version of cricket that can fit neatly into a one hour TV schedule. Other traditionally leisurely games are also under the hammer. Golf now has a running version of itself called, imaginatively, Speed Golf, in which participants race each other round the course in an absurd mockery of the very essence of the game. What's next? Netball is speeding up. Only soccer, the beautiful game, seems capable of avoiding the speed-it-up, change-the-format impulse. Do they know something we don't know?

International rugby before the professional era might have been button down but it was a breeze compared to the stilted lifestyle of the modern professional. I played it as intensively as any other player in the 1960s all the way from club to international level. Yes, the strictures surrounding an All Black of the 1960s were pretty irritating. They were a product of the times. But as an amateur I could walk away after a test match and indulge in a thoroughly liberated lifestyle compared to that of the contemporary full-time professional and relatively safe from the prying eyes of the media. All that has changed radically in less than a generation. What is it doing to those who do nothing else but train for it and play it?

The player is now a full-time employee, a virtual hostage to whoever pays his salary. In return, he must obey the rules. He must always be available for duty. He has little or no opportunity to lead a balanced lifestyle. He is hounded mercilessly by a media with a permanent taste for blood. Most of today's professionals are becoming unidimensional personalities, amassing a maximum of income in as short a time as possible to compensate for a life after rugby that promises to be uneventful, probably unfulfilling and very likely plagued by chronic health problems.

Many of them seem to be aware of this reality already.

All that old international mateship is but a distant memory. There is now virtually no fraternisation between professional teams and it is a very rare thing to see international players enjoying each other's company after a test match. It's not as if they don't want to. Occasionally, as for instance when New Zealand played Portugal in the 2007 World Cup, there is a joyful sharing of rugby's core values at a party afterwards. That, significantly, was an afternoon game. Now, with night rugby, it is invariably midnight before players emerge from the locker rooms and the debriefing and the press conference. The nightlife of the contemporary player, such as it is, is confined to the wee small hours. A troublesome time.

I suspect that without the vital ingredient of mateship rugby will soon become a colourless commodity. It might be more spectacular than it used to be and the players may be bigger, faster, stronger and with more overtly controlled aggression, but the contemporary game is slowly leaching out the asymmetry, the oddities and the curiosities. Now it has become machine-like, repetitive like rugby league, with defences lined up like picket fences and the gradual disappearance of backlines running at each other. There are growing complaints about the seemingly impossible business of trying to make the scrum work even tolerably well and to make lineouts a genuine contest as they were in the past before the lawmakers laid such a heavy blanket of regulation over them that players are scared to even touch an opponent while the ball is thrown in. And as for the breakdowns, the rule makers have tied them up in knots. Variety of action and of incident, rugby's perennial trump card, is itself now being trumped by the dreaded threat of monotony.

The rules have become a dense jungle of cloying complexity, constantly being tampered with and argued over, causing confusion and frustration everywhere. At a time when we should be simplifying we are adding further layers of complication. The rules need a revolution. They need to be reassessed from a single perspective: what can be done to better enable the referee to keep his whistle in his pocket and to maximise the contest for possession. As things stand we seem to be unconsciously devising ways to require the referee to stop play rather than encourage it to flow. If we can't get this right in an age of limited tolerance of inaction, the game is sunk.

As a result of this onrush of complexity one referee isn't considered to be enough any longer. Now the touch judges are in on the act, calling the shots, waving their flags like self-important signalmen on a busy railway siding. They are joined by Him Upstairs, the third eye, the TMO, the television match official whose job it is to have the defining say on whether or not a try has been scored. Some of the dialogue between the referee and TMO could be mistaken for an episode of *The Goon Show*.

But it isn't just referees who are proliferating. The field today is cluttered with waterboys, physiotherapists, message carriers from the coach and various other hangers-on who rush on to dispense liquids, instant treatment or strategic advice at every stoppage while the spectators, presumably on the assumption that they cannot cope with more than a few seconds of inactivity, are regaled with deafening bouts of rock music which drowns out the conviviality of conversation that sports events were once a focus for.

Behind the scenes is an extraordinary array of specialisation. Every professional outfit has a growing cast of characters. There are head coaches, assistant coaches, defence coaches, attack coaches, kicking coaches, scrumming coaches, lineout coaches, conditioning coaches and technical advisers. There are fitness experts, team doctors, dietary specialists, lifestyle advisers, baggage men, physiotherapists, technical analysts, video analysts, communications officers, team managers and operations managers along with the usual cast of lawyers and accountants lurking in the shrubbery. The supporting cast threatens to outnumber the players. Perhaps it already does. Every match now features a posse of waterboys who are on and off the field like flies on a bull's backside. A professional franchise is starting to look like a small government. There are now more people employed by the NZRU than by the entire government of Tuvalu. Are they all really indispensable?

And while we're talking about simplification, a machete needs to be taken to rugby's judicial system. While we weren't watching, the administrators of the game turned it from a sport with its own forms of justice — in which the referee decided what to do about anyone who transgressed — into the equivalent of a corrections ministry with its own court, battalions of lawyers, citing commissioners and even its own judiciary. This ridiculous legal overlay illustrates all that is worst about the ballooning out of the game's administration and its seriously impaired sense of proportion.

There are wider social implications. New Zealand is just beginning to come to terms with the full force of the professional era. Will sport that is essentially stratified end up causing more social division or less? We don't yet know for sure. One thing we do know is that it's having some very interesting social effects, some of them on the face of it surprisingly positive. Because the professional game is by its very nature designed to be more openly spectacular and surrounded by non-stop entertainment, the spectator catchment has actually widened. Big matches are gilded with music, supporting acts, fast food, shapely cheerleaders and all the trimmings now found necessary to capture and keep the dwindling attention span of the modern audiences.

Women, who earlier would have shunned rugby or cricket as ridiculous backwaters of male machismo, are now warming to the colour and drama of it all. Women play it in rapidly increasing numbers, with a frightening new display of aggression. A third of all Super 14 patrons are female. They go to the sevens to party. They are less interested in the rules or the subtleties of the game. They go along because it is an occasion. They go as groups these days and the marketers feverishly encourage them. Rugby is growing steadily more dependent on women, particularly younger women, but are they permanent devotees or just fair weather friends? It rather depends on the level of pre- and post-match entertainment that can sustain their interest. And a production line of seductive stars to titillate them. There are ominous signs in the Southern hemisphere, as crowds steadily decline, that all this isn't enough to get the fans through the gate. So what's plan B?

Old and very deeply embedded provincial or community identities have been overlaid with new regional brand values in the push to promote support for the professional dimension. The way in which the Super 14 franchises in New Zealand, South Africa and Australia, or the Heineken Cup teams in Europe, have superimposed themselves over entrenched club or provincial identities has, at least until recently, been remarkably successful, thanks largely to the efforts of the marketers. The market homogenises the product by gaining control of all the components — the teams, the TV rights and the sponsorship clout — and the brand label is advertised as the local point of difference. It's as simple as selling cars or cornflakes.

Imagery is the issue. The Hurricanes have skilfully turned a stiff breeze from a negative to a positive, helping the Hurricanes franchise to brand itself as a team of movement and energy. The Stormers cottoned on to the same imagery in Cape Town. The Highlanders have drawn successfully on southern Scottish identity but the imagery underpinning the Crusaders, Blues and Chiefs has always been muddled and indeterminate. In reality the regional franchises have had to flog themselves ever more relentlessly to persuade people to buy in.

Young and old, rich and poor: anyone can identify with the brand. Anyone can go along in support so long as they can afford a ticket. If they can't afford it they simply watch it on TV, if they can afford the pay-TV fee. If they can't, they watch it at a pub or community centre.

So far, it hasn't seemed to matter where the players come from any more. They are now drafted to and fro around the country with bewildering speed each season, and as often as not there are very few home town boys in any of the major provincial or Super 14 teams. It is the brand that matters. Convince them of the brand and they won't care where the players come from. Yet, at the same time, many people in the provinces would rather have local boys to represent them. Is there a limit to this representative merry-go-round? And is there a difference between the amateur and professional games? Do the punters accept that professional franchises will recruit from all over the country but object when it comes to their own provincial team? There are some intriguing psychological subtleties here that we are only beginning to understand. The surge in turnouts to the 2009 Air New Zealand Cup suggested very strongly that local identity is fighting back. People in the provinces are growing tired of highly paid mercenaries from somewhere else. They want their local boys up front.

Labels are everything these days. It is no longer fashionable to call a team by some humdrum geographical name. Now it's all imagery, as rugby slavishly adopts the same silly lexicon of macho names that American sports teams have established as the norm. Even in Japan, where local resistance to such silliness has been strongest, they too have succumbed. Whether Hurricanes or Stormers, or Bulls, Chiefs, Cowboys, Raiders,

Sharks or Steelers, the pattern is familiar. The nametags are lifted straight out of the McWorld sporting lexicon. Rugby, without pausing to think, has been swept along mindlessly by this irresistible urge to homogenise, to do it the same way as its elder neighbours in the professional sports world. Yet, at sub-professional level, provincial spectators prefer to have the geographical name up front and this tells us something very compelling about their preferences.

But there are bigger issues at stake as the professional game matures. Whether it likes it or not, rugby is now becoming obliged to provide more "product" for less dosh. How does it do that? So far it has simply expanded the international calendar. Thus the serious bloating of the Sanzar tournaments. We get more Tri Nations games. The Super 12 becomes the Super 14, then 15; then what? The number of internationals featuring the leading Northern versus Southern hemisphere teams creeps inexorably up. Meaningless but revenue-rich test matches are being staged in third world rugby countries, ostensibly with a view to stimulating the game in those places but, in reality, to pay the bills back home.

Organisationally, rugby is in a state of almost permanent ferment. Common ground when it comes to the international playing season is hard to find. There just aren't enough months in the year. Northern hemisphere and Southern hemisphere interests clash. Rugby, the winter game, becomes a game for all seasons in order to fit in all the fixtures. The Sanzar countries have struggled to settle on a format or timing for the Super 15 or the Tri Nations. Japan and the Pacific Islands have for years wanted a part of the Sanzar action but can't seem to get a foot in the door. Instead, Argentina gets the nod.

The International Rugby Board and the national unions are at war with privately owned European clubs as to the availability of players. Players are at war with their unions over terms and conditions. When it comes to talent, the rich are poaching from the poor and nobody seems able to come up with a formula that can stop, or even moderate, this.

One of the greyest areas is that of salary caps. Is there any real hope of an international set of protocols on salary levels? If recent experience is anything to go by, then this is probably a lost cause. The escalation of elite salaries is the greatest single threat to rugby union today. This is richly ironic when you consider that a generation ago, the fact of no salaries at all was arguably the greatest threat to the game. Should restraint of trade laws, particularly in Europe, be allowed to dictate to an international sport as to where and when a national union can expect to call upon a player to represent his country? A generation ago that would have been unthinkable. Now it is the norm.

There has been much talk of bringing back the traditional rugby tour — the total immersion by one country's team in another's, rather than the new approach of parachuting a team in for one game only. There certainly seems to be a market for that. The British and Irish Lions are fighting their way back onto the international schedule much to the pleasure of their Southern hemisphere hosts. Almost everyone in the rugby world wants them but can the crowded international calendar be adjusted to accommodate longer tours again? Only by dropping something else.

Then of course there's the World Cup. It's an inspirational concept and it's given the game an extraordinary boost over the last 20 years. But it has its problems, not the least of which is its propensity to set countries against each other. It seriously damaged the relationship between Australia and New Zealand in the débâcle over the 2003 hosting rights. It has led to tensions between England and France, feelings of exclusion in Japan, and an aggressively uncooperative attitude in South Africa. New Zealand won it for 2011 on the merits of its slightly cheeky claim to be a "stadium of 4 million", something that caused not a few in New Zealand to cringe with embarrassment at the time. As things stand, New Zealand will never be able to afford to host it again after 2011. More importantly, can the All Blacks ever win it again? And if they don't, what does that imply for the status of rugby as New Zealand's national sport?

Other longer term strategic questions demand answers. Will rugby union ever find a *modus vivendi* with its estranged cousin, rugby league? The traditional antipathy born of class conflict seems to be waning. Once upon a time, union had all the class and league had all the money. Now the two are virtually indistinguishable. Will the market eventually force them to merge?

The lamentable way that New Zealand and other major rugby powers have responded to the needs of the Pacific Islands over the years is a sorry story. One way or another these remarkable rugby talent factories must be given a better deal. The IRB, after years of indifference, has started that process, but there is a long way to go and a lot of problems to be solved along the way. We owe these societies so much, but return so little. Sooner or later a restructured Sanzar will have to do something about this. The fact that Argentina is now part of the Sanzar mix makes this even more unlikely in the immediate future and it is hardly any wonder that all three of the Pacific unions are bitterly disappointed with the treatment they get.

And what about Japan? The story of rugby's emergence there is a wonderfully romantic one and Japan offers New Zealand in particular an almost perfect partner as the commercial dimension of the game intensifies. Yet, somehow, the NZRU — and most others for that matter — seem to shrink from real engagement.

Other issues pluck persistently at the game's sleeve. What future is there for Maori rugby as a feature on the international stage? Why is the All Blacks haka so controversial? And why has New Zealand rugby generated such hostility in Britain since 1905? The history of this relationship is a tortured one and although the professionalisation of the game has reduced that tension somewhat as the ranks of British teams slowly swell with New Zealanders, the sharp edge is still there. They still don't like being beaten by the boys from the colonies.

Rugby has always been associated with political conservatism and the entrails of this are still evident. Rugby became entrenched as the national game in South Africa and apartheid very nearly brought the world game to its knees. Now South Africa is finding its feet again, ominously, and the rest of the rugby world, particularly New Zealand, is rather nervous about that. Is South Africa destined now to go on and become the world's single rugby superpower? Or will domestic politics eventually cripple it? Surely France and England, with more players and more money than the rest of the rugby world put together, should already be dominant international forces, yet neither seems capable of asserting itself for more than one season or even one game at a time. We heave a sigh of relief in the Southern hemisphere every time we beat these two brooding giants and wonder how much longer it will be before they finally impose themselves.

For reasons nobody can quite put their finger on Welsh rugby hit the doldrums 20-odd years ago but has miraculously found its feet again after many of its supporters had given it up for dead. Similarly, Irish rugby, against all expectations, has literally risen from the grave in recent years, buoyed by a virile Irish economy, but Scotland seems headed in the opposite direction, a victim of its deeply conservative history.

The elite players are on the move, inducements are being waved about with reckless abandon and we now have an international marketplace for rugby talent. What does all this movement foreshadow? Will the time come when the sport is totally dominated by a bunch of privately owned professional franchises and the amateur game just dies away? That prospect is real and it is imminent. One look at the way pro basketball, baseball and football in the United States has killed off the amateur roots of those sports is surely enough to persuade us of that.

There are fears, too, for the future of the international matches, those great country-to-country contests that have given rugby so much of its drama and its folklore. Players, especially in Europe, don't "belong" to their national unions any more. They dance to the tune of the private owners of the franchises who are all too willing to shelter behind the laws of competition designed for markets far removed from sport.

And, of course, the most intriguing question of all: how sustainable is the lifestyle of the thoroughly modern full-time rugby player? How much physical punishment by 120kg human cannonballs can any modern player endure? Is rugby headed for freakshow status as players get bigger and more musclebound with every passing year? Will it become WWF on grass? And does that gladiatorial obsession spell ultimate doom for a game that once catered for all physiques?

Rugby in the 21st century still remains in the emotional grip of its own history. Without an understanding of the way that history has unfolded it is impossible to appreciate the state of the present dilemma. Oscar Wilde once said of American society that it had gone from barbarism to decadence without the usual intervening period of civilisation. In 15 years rugby has made much the same leap. And it shows.

Could rugby have possibly held its place as a major sport without handing the game over lock, stock and barrel to commercial interests? The question has become rhetorical. It's too late to go back. The trick from here on is to try to manipulate the tiger we have by the tail in the interests of preserving what's left.

A Perfectly Simple Game

Rugby is a perfectly simple game where the forwards pass the ball back to the backs, and the backs run forward while passing it back until they make progress forward.

If they pass it forward, instead of back, then it's a forward pass even if the player passing it forward is a back or even a halfback.

When the backline gets the ball over the tryline, which is also known as the goal-line, they don't get a goal; they get a try. But if they don't quite get it over the tryline, but only try to get it over the tryline to get a try then they don't get a try and the try doesn't count, however hard they try, and it's not a try even if they try to persuade the referee that it is a try.

If they do get a try then they try for a conversion. But that's called a goal. If they get that over, the try plus the goal is called a goal. If they get that over, the try plus the goal is called a converted try, except in the UK where the whole thing is called a goal, conversion being something that happens to cars or people susceptible to religious persuasion.

Rugby is a game of two halves, especially outside New Zealand where there are no five eighths. In New Zealand we play the percentages. There are two five eighths and three threequarters — that's a total of 28 eighths per team which when you add the four eighths for the halfback and another eight eighths for the fullback you get 40 eighths which doesn't add up to seven backs which should add up to 56 eighths, so maybe somebody's playing an extra man.

But even in the other half of the rugby world — namely the Northern hemisphere — it's just as simple. The inside half, or scrumhalf, even though he's not in the scrum, plays inside the outside half who's also an inside back. Sometimes the outside half is known as the flyhalf if he has trouble with his trousers. In England he's known as the outside half in spite of the fact that he's an inside back. Outside the outside half is the inside centre who plays outside the outside half but inside the outside centre. The inside centre, like the outside half, is also an inside back while the outside centre is an outside back who is inclined to cut back inside, being an inside back by instinct.

Normally, the outside centre plays outside the inside centre and inside the other outside backs but on occasions the inside and outside centres swap sides and play inside out.

If you find this hard to follow all you have to remember is that both sides play outside, except in Dunedin where it's inside, or in Cardiff where it's inside or outside, right up till no-side.

— with acknowledgement to New Zealand poet, ad-man and wit, John Ansell.

From Chump to Chic in One Generation

IN ANY debate about rugby's future it is important to have at least an appreciation of where it came from because it is this rich accumulation of folklore and fantasy that makes us so suspicious about where it seems to be headed today.

Conventional wisdom has it that a momentarily anarchic public schoolboy picked up a more or less round football one day and ran with it. Nobody knows why, or what happened next. All we do know is that somehow the identity of rugby football began to emerge, like an amoeba, from the clutter of all those old games involving kicking a ball or kicking an opponent, or both. Nobody could possibly have imagined that a century and a half later rugby would be a world game festooned with all the trappings and gaudy pretensions of the entertainment business.

William Webb Ellis, elevated since to patron sainthood, is a shadowy figure. Jed Smith, the Rugby Football Union historian, is convinced that it wasn't Ellis but a chap called Jem Mackie who established the habit of running forward with the ball. Jem hasn't made it to the history books, however. He became the Richard Pearse of rugby. Pearse, the pioneer New Zealand aviator, missed out on eternal fame because the Wright brothers had a better publicist. Jem probably didn't get around to taking his particular credit. But then neither was William Webb Ellis an attention seeker. He obviously didn't know that what he was doing was revolutionary. He was probably intent only on avoiding a caning for bending the rules. And he hardly basked in any particular glory from his achievement later in life. Quite the reverse. He died in penury and obscurity in southern France. There's a moral in there somewhere for today's prematurely rewarded professionals but it's unlikely any of them will get it.

And, anyway, who cares who invented the game? The obscurity of it all is an asset not a liability. Running with an approximation of a football through a defensive line of would-be opponents was invented a very long time before Rugby School began making a habit of it. Running around with a pig's bladder, a stone, a loaf of bread or a human head recently acquired on the battlefield was nothing revolutionary. Wandering nomads on the Caucasian Steppes probably enjoyed pastimes which bore a closer resemblance to the modern game than anything dreamed up at Rugby School. They were certainly more accomplished when it came to head high tackles.

It all sounds very obscure when you think about it but we can conclude with the utmost certainty that the English gave the game its eventual shape, and, for better or for worse, dominated its codification and regulation for a long time thereafter. Some say far too long.

Over the years there has been a sense of wonderment that a game, ostensibly the product of the English public school system, invented as a means of getting public school boys' minds off subversive things like sex and socialism and more or less ignored by the great unwashed, should take root in so many radically different social contexts and become the national barometer of wellbeing in societies like Wales, New Zealand and South Africa.

But it did and it went on to become a global game with all the trappings of professionalism, commercialism and multiculturalism that are the essential hallmarks of big-time sports in the 21st century. The story of that transformation is a fascinating one. From a dowdy, deeply conservative, blinkered beginning it was led, at times dragged like a reluctant mule, into modernisation and it is richly ironic that that very modernisation has produced a new kind of strait-jacket, as the deadening weight of commercialism slowly suppresses individuality and expression in the game. Rugby was slow to enter the 20th century but, no sooner had it done so, than it had to face the 21st and it has been stumbling along trying to catch up ever since.

Rugby has always been a fairly basic sort of game. If you strip away all the modern layers of complexity it is remarkable how much the endearing simplicity of purpose has remained. Anyone who had seen it a century ago and who by virtue of some Rip Van Winkle miracle was to see it again today would certainly recognise it.

This simplicity of purpose has often intrigued social and political thinkers who watched it. P G Wodehouse, something of a spokesman for the original values of the game, summed it all up rather nicely half a century ago. He said, "The main scheme is to work the ball down the field somehow and deposit it over the line at the other end." Exactly. Even the dimwitted Bertie Wooster would have grasped that much. But P G Wodehouse knew at least a little more about it than that: enough to put his finger on the most distinctive feature of the game. As he described it, there was a certain licence extended to players of this game, befitting its status as the world's most patently contact sport. "Each side," said P G, "is entitled to put in a certain amount of assault and battery and do things to its fellow man which, if done elsewhere, would result in fourteen days without option, with some strong remarks from the bench."

Much of what is done on a rugby field would result in a good deal more than 14 days if it happened out there on the street. But what happens on a rugby field has tended to remain confined to that arena. This is legalised assault and battery and the difference, if not all that apparent to the more squeamish of critics, is rather important. To be sure, there has been the odd prosecution for an assault that took place on a rugby field but these have been extremely rare and generally frowned upon by those in the game.

A "certain amount of assault and battery" has in more recent times, however, come to be severely circumscribed. Nowadays, the slightest hint of unregulated violence, a raised fist or an errant boot, or the mere suggestion of a high tackle, is a guarantee of retribution. If it looks serious enough there's the guarantee of an appearance before rugby's bench, surrounded by lavishly remunerated QCs carefully reconstructing the scene of the crime, weighing the evidence and contributing to a judicial outcome that has every appearance of a scene from *Alice Through the Looking Glass*.

The *New Zealand Punch*, 1888

A little assault and battery and not a referee to be seen.

There is a fundamental question here. How do you make rational judgements about relative intent in a game in which the intent to take the wind out of your opponent's sails lies at the very centre of the whole enterprise? Players don't kick each other very much at all these days and that is the one area where more vigilance has yielded positive results. But you might argue that a 120kg body, arriving in collision with another at terminal velocity, has far graver health implications than a flick of a boot. The tackle is what sets rugby apart from all other sports. It is what excites and appals those who watch.

The tackle, the art of stopping the ball carrier, is the game's most primeval action, but as the players get bigger and the collisions become steadily more deadly, those who govern the game become more and more determined to proscribe what a player can and can't do on the field as if to compensate somehow for all that extra brawn on display.

This is a nice idea in principle. In practice it is a flirtation with the absurd when it comes to a sport like rugby. It is characteristic of the obsessively risk-averse way we think these days. The impulse to regulate behaviour is something that bedevils post-modern western democracy as a whole and it is a real worry. There is a working assumption that individuals and groups must be constantly more controlled to save them from themselves, to eliminate risk; to stop people getting hurt and to absolve those who administer the rules from failures of accountability. Sport has been sideswiped by this tidal wave of correctness and sometimes it seems we are drowning in it. The relentless drive for player safety is slowly draining the very lifeblood from the physical confrontation.

But this instinct to constrain in the name of decorum and risk aversion has something of a history in rugby. From the very beginning of contact between teams from New Zealand, Australia or South Africa and those in Britain it was evoked in protest at the unrestrained physicality of the colonials. It was invariably called for in England whenever the All Blacks toured and tended to rough up the gentlemen they faced on the field.

New Zealand and South Africa, where the game was far more robustly played than it ever was in Britain in the earlier days, raised the bar of physicality in rugby last century and were obliged to pay a price for that whenever they played in Britain. Squeamish referees were pressured into imposing strict discipline on unruly colonials, generating an ill feeling that has never really gone away.

But even the English were sometimes criticised by their own for going too far on the physical front. It was rugby, particularly as played by upper middle-class gentlemen who rather liked a little anarchy on the field as an antidote to the strict limits of decorum everywhere else, which reputedly inspired George Orwell to declare that "serious sport has nothing to do with fair play. It's bound up with hatred, jealousy, boastfulness, disregard of all rules and sadistic pleasure in . . . violence". It was, in other words, *Animal Farm* on a footy field. Heaven knows what George Orwell would have made of the mayhem of a club game in Invercargill or Bloemfontein at the time.

But Mr Orwell was a noted pessimist, a killjoy who didn't approve of the jolly ruling-class antics that characterised the rugby community. He lacked a sense of proportion and it's a sense of proportion, an ability to accept the highs and lows, the unpredictable outcomes of a game built around unpredictablity, which gives rugby its peculiar character. With a ball shaped like an egg what else would you expect?

Actually, it isn't quite egg-shaped. According to the rulebook, that vast compendium of laws most of which have only passing relevance to the game, the ball can be any shape other than round. The rugby ball is, according to a scientist who was asked to describe it, a "prolate spheroid" which sounds rather more like an unpleasant medical condition than a piece of sporting equipment.

The seemingly brutal side of rugby might attract criticism and if that was all there was to the game then the criticism might be justified. But rugby is multi-dimensional. It combines brute strength with artistry. It juxtaposes organisation with a large measure of chaos. It provides for both the carefully planned and the outrageously instinctive. It caters for the large and the small, the fast and the slow, the smart and the dumb.

Rugby has always generated polemics. Those who don't understand it are sceptical that it can be anything other than semi-organised mayhem. Those who watch it for the first time are appalled at its apparent violence. But those who can see past the biff and the bash can also see that the violence is tempered by a certain elegance, an aesthetic quality to go with all the gladiatorial stuff. And a curious code of civility. It's a very perplexing mix.

But there's something else too. Right from the very beginning rugby was injected with an ethical serum. Players have known instinctively that there is more to it than mere physicality. They might trample on each other with apparent disdain for the consequences but there is another dimension which sets it apart from most, if not all, other sports. It is hard to pin down and it always sounds trite when somebody talks about it. But it's still there, a kind of code of respect, of honour, a working assumption that when the rough stuff on the field is finished, friendship and conviviality immediately take over. The French call it *camaraderie* and so, too, have generations of Anglo-Saxons, cheerfully mangling the pronunciation of the word in doing so.

There are other labels for what amounts to a recognition that somehow the game is the bigger thing; that the *bonhomie* is more important than the biff. That "rugby should always be the winner" as the old cliché goes. The essence of the game is in fact all about the essence of getting on in real life. It is this dimension that has given it the quality that really stands out. It is said that rugby is the game played in heaven. They even have a website to prove it. What they should be saying is that rugby is an ideal preparation for life on earth.

As the great Irish player Tony O'Reilly once put it, "It's an odd mixture of your own talent and skills and a total dependence on other people. It requires you to meet triumph and disaster. It requires you to come up smiling and it requires you to show grace under pressure." That quality of grace under pressure is what Ernest Hemingway saw as the ultimate measure of a man. If there's a better form of apprenticeship for the rigours of adulthood then I'd like to know what it is.

Not many people know that the hoary old song "On the Ball" actually has several verses, the last of which is a deeply philosophical one:

This life's but a scrummage we cannot get through
But with many a kick and a blow,
And then to the end, though we dodge and we fend
Still that sure collar "death" takes us low.

Nobody would of course be seen dead singing something like that publicly these days but it still represents the unspoken essence of rugby. One can only hope that this quality can continue to shape the behaviour of today's full professional for whom life, in occupational terms, is rugby and nothing much else.

Perhaps the only real constant is the phenomenon of teamwork. After a year or two in the game any player will realise that he is crucially dependent on those around him. It's something that has been recognised for a very long time in world sport. Last century the great American baseball star Babe Ruth made the point: "The way a team plays as a whole determines its success. You may have the greatest bunch of individual stars, but if they don't play together the club won't be worth a dime." And that was baseball where they only have limited physical reliance on one another. In rugby that reliance is almost total. When you think about it the cliché that there is no "I" in "team" probably applies more in rugby than any other sport.

Many people have remarked over the last century or more on rugby's peculiar combination of demands. British sports journalist Adam Nicholson for instance put it this way. "Rugby," he said, "is exceptionally difficult to play well — it demands a boxer's depth of resolution in the service of the skills of a watchmaker."

The erratic bounce of the ball gives rugby a wonderfully unpredictable, almost perverse character. You never know precisely what will happen next. The round ball in soccer has a kind of inevitability about the way it rolls, regularly, over and over. Beckham might be able to bend it but beyond that it doesn't do anything really unpredictable. The rugby ball is all angles and corners. It will never do what you want it to do no matter how talented a ball-player you might be. A Jonny Wilkinson or a Daniel Carter might get close, but that's as close as anyone will ever get.

This contrariness mirrors the inherent contrariness of life. Rugby teaches you to accept life's bounce of the ball. It is as good a metaphor for the real world as you will ever get. Tony O'Reilly was right. Coping with unpredictablity is character forming. Interestingly, there is quite a literature on rugby's higher virtues. Pope John Paul II is recorded as saying it taught him to deal with adversity. One would have thought praying was sufficient but praying, plus rugby, was obviously unstoppable. Che Guevara, an Argentine, played enthusiastically till he became preoccupied with liberating Latin America. The game's cohesive nation-building nature appealed to darker spirits as well. Nicolae Ceausescu, Oswald Mosley, Idi Amin and Albert Speer all remarked on its disciplinary virtues which is a bit of a worry, or at least it would have been if Hitler or Stalin had decided to patronise the game and turn it into a quasi-military form of nation building. The Japanese toyed with the thought in the 1930s but concluded it was a bit too anarchic to work. The Chinese have shown interest in it as a way of generating greater *esprit de corps* among their military.

Weekly News, 1933

Democracy must have had a very good fullback.

Even the Americans are slowly realising the obvious truth that the more professional sport you have the less sport has to offer by way of socialisation. In recent years a number of prominent American sports writers have been beating this particular drum and some have discovered the virtues of amateur rugby as an antidote to the venal, cash-obsessed fringe world of American football. No less an authority than the *New York Times* commented that "all sports can help break down racial and cultural barriers, but certain elements of rugby make it especially suited. With its raw physicality and traditional post-game bonding, rugby forces an intimacy among opponents not found in many other sports." The *Times* wasn't of course talking about professional rugby. It probably didn't know there was such a thing. It was lauding the virtues of the amateur game.

That amateur game was hugely successful in promoting its broader sense of fellowship but it was in fact a rigidly hierarchical outfit. For more than a century the game was effectively ruled by a single entity — the Rugby Football Union in London. The RFU, the Old Farts as they later became known, made the rules and changed them over a few sherries at RFU headquarters. When the International Rugby Board was formed it immediately became a cautious, exclusive little coterie of core Anglo-Saxon countries, the four Home Unions of Britain together with Australia, New Zealand and South Africa. Astonishingly, France, which had been a major rugby power since the 1950s, couldn't break into the club for decades. Nor was the IRB interested in opening the inner sanctum to any of the numerous other rugby unions around the world clamouring for admission. It was an old Commonwealth white man's game, more obviously than any other on earth and this bigoted exclusivity was nearly its downfall.

In 1971 the Rugby Football Union, in a fit of unaccustomed expansiveness, hosted a centenary congress to which all the aspiring rugby nations were invited. Pleas were issued for more contact, for help, for new competitions, for a measure of equity in the rugby world. They were ignored. What was particularly galling was the fact that the Southern hemisphere countries were entirely complicit in this exclusivity. We went along with it all, compliant dominions, happily taking orders issued from the rotting leather armchairs of the East India and Sportsmen's Club in St James's Square in London. Rugby was in grave danger of dying of its own self-inflicted wounds.

Players were mere incidentals, like the labourers who built the pyramids under the watchful eye of the Pharoahs or the armies of extras in *The Lord of the Rings*. Spectators were a necessary evil. The administrator was king. Rugby was stuck in a cul-de-sac. It imposed its own unique brake on social progress. As late as the 1970s and 80s the New Zealand Rugby Union was a secretive organisation with monopolistic powers that appeared to have no limit. The NZRFU Council was the guardian of a moral code of forbidding austerity. Keep your hair short and your mouth shut. Step out of line at your peril.

The Council was the sporting equivalent of the Vatican — suspicious, conservative, all seeing and all knowing, the dispenser of favours and punisher of those who strayed from the faith. Rugby's administration was a feudal society in which, like the Catholic Church, the greater the seniority one possesses, the less chance one ever has of being wrong. I was convinced that the game needed a bomb under it. As it turned out a succession of incendiary devices went off, the biggest of which was to be the virtual *coup d'ëtat* inflicted by professionalism.

The same quiet revolution was happening elsewhere. Rugby extricated itself finally from the nasty swamp of apartheid, with some honour in the end, and many of those who had abandoned it in frustration during the 70s and early 80s began to return. The International Rugby Board began to look rather less like a college of cardinals and slowly became a more visibly democratic institution. The hoary old patronage exercised from the East India and Sportsmen's Club gave way to a new political framework and new members were brought into the fold. Even the French were admitted.

The players began to get a say in things, albeit still very much at the margins, and the game began to prosper again. A World Cup was introduced in the 1980s. Women were no longer relegated to cutting the cucumber sandwiches or washing the jerseys but were actually permitted, almost encouraged, to play the game. Countries in Eastern Europe, the Pacific, Asia and Africa finally began to receive material support instead of being treated with patronising indifference. Democracy began to break out in St James's Square.

And then, just as things seemed to be reaching a nice, modern and comfortable equilibrium, along came the greatest revolution rugby had ever faced. Professionalism hit the game like a tsunami in the mid-1990s.

It was sudden, unexpected and unwanted. It was provoked by a realisation among the players, abetted by a bunch of opportunistic entrepreneurs and some less than scrupulous coaches, that they could make small fortunes out of the game if they played their cards right. Most of them played their cards horribly wrongly as the Trojan horse of a private world rugby circus was wheeled up outside the game's castle gates and almost certain destruction loomed. Revolution was once again in the air.

Needless to say the rugby establishment in London had a panic attack. They weren't at all ready for this kind of Ned Kelly surprise raid. Privatisation was averted at the last moment but professionalism wasn't. The game stumbled along, trying to come to terms with what professionalism actually meant, led by the nose by its new corporate partners, constantly asking itself, "Have I got this right?" and living in perpetual fear of the future.

There has been a tendency to forget how tumultuous that transition from game to business has been. New Zealand arguably handled the convulsions better than any other country. Appointments to the governing body were no longer based on longevity of service but on relative merit. At last a semblance of real competency began to appear in the decisions that the NZRFU took. The relations between players and administrators converged. They began to realise that everyone was in this together and if they got it wrong the game could be irreparably damaged. Living in each other's pockets, tied to a business enterprise, they actually began to cooperate effectively.

The NZRFU board of directors, by then composed almost entirely of businessmen convinced that the corporate model was the only way forward, managed to forge a new set of creative relationships with Australia and South Africa on the one hand, and with major commercial sponsors like News Ltd, Lion Breweries and Adidas on the other. Given the circumstances, they did a pretty good job. A new Southern hemisphere competitive structure, SANZAR, was ushered in, replacing the old disorderly programme of test matches between the three protagonists. It was backed by television rights sales and other sponsorship revenue. There didn't seem to be much choice at that stage, particularly with a bunch of money-hungry entrepreneurs poised to muscle in with their own private rugby circus given half an opening.

The South led the way. The North, dominated by its deeply conservative Home Unions, prevaricated, harrumphed in irritation and tried to wish it all away. The IRB blanched, then acquiesced. France was delighted. The other members of the five nations in Europe followed suit, some — like Scotland — considerably less enthusiastically than others.

Gradually, the weight of professionalism, with all its corporate trappings, attendant legalism and commercial conformity, began to bear down on the game ever more heavily. Now, it is crushing it. Now, we are seeing the transformation of rugby into fashionable entertainment. A generation ago rugby players were to fashion what bulls are to china shops. But now it's chump to chic in less than a generation. Today, they are to be seen at every fashion opening and every celebrity party. They are social A-listers selling their stories to women's magazines and auctioning off exclusive pictures of their weddings to the highest bidder. It is virtually impossible to trawl through a Sunday newspaper without encountering the knowing smile of Ali Williams somewhere.

Popular culture is building sports imagery into just about everything that is marketable because it's cool. Athletes and football players are icons. They wear the right gear, tote the right sunglasses at just the right angle on the forehead and listen to the right music on the right iPod. Daniel Carter sets the standard when it comes to promoting goods and services. He is now better known in fashion circles as a Jockey model than a footballer and he carries off the dual personality with considerable skill, partly by adopting an almost sheepish attitude. It's as if he's saying to the rugby community, "Look, don't take this fashion stuff too seriously. I'm a footy player, not really a model."

Others, if not quite so mercantile, are equally adventurous. Ma'a Nonu started using eye liner, and interesting haircuts — dreadlocks, mullets and Mohawks, along with tints, are all the rage. Where once the only available boot colour was black we now see white, yellow, lime green and several indescribable shades in between. Lote Tuqiri's boots were a veritable kaleidoscope. An opponent could see him coming at 50 metres in pitch darkness, not that that would be much help in trying to stop him. Other fashion conscious players are following suit. So long as the boots are from the right manufacturer — the sponsoring one — then anything goes.

All of this imagery reinforces rugby's new-found position in show business and there's nothing inherently wrong with players making the most of their new status. Yet, beneath that shallow layer of glitz the bulk of the rugby community remains relatively unchanged. Provincial and club players are conspicuously absent from all this. Rugby's great public support base is slightly embarrassed by the antics of the elite and sternly disapproving of the flightiness of their lifestyles. As the top tier drifts slowly apart from the stolid ranks of the also-rans the gulf becomes increasingly unbridgeable.

The game has even begun to attract literary attention. Traditionally, rugby seems to have caused fiction writers to stampede off in a panic in the opposite direction. Until lately that is. The literary world is waking up to the drama that elite sport generates and sports novels are flourishing. We are even seeing the emergence of successful fiction built around rugby, something that 10 or 20 years ago would have been laughable.

Astonishing as it may seem after 100 years of determined decorum the English Rugby Football Union signed up a deal with Mills and Boon to promote a series of steamy touchline tales starring famous footy players. Heaven only knows what the old farts at the East India and Sportsmen's Club would make of this.

RFU marketing manager Jane Barron announced without, apparently, even a hint of tongue-in-cheek, that rugby "has always been a game enjoyed by women," something that will come as a bit of a surprise to the vast numbers of women who are repelled by it. "A deal with Mills and Boon is a fantastic way to encourage even more women and their families to get involved with rugby," she assured us. Given the likely content of the fiction that will be served up, the appeal will largely be confined to the ranks of the new ladettes and sundry nymphomaniacs, neither of which group is particularly fussy about its choice of male company. If this is the target audience of rugby's new marketers we're in for some interesting times.

Inevitably, this has provoked a spirited debate about how the game somehow isn't what it used to be. But how rational is that? Ever since it went professional, rugby has begun to gaze back at its past through spectacles that are ever more rose tinted. That past is full of contradictions, counter-currents and curiosities but, somehow, those have been ironed out of the public memory. None of this has been seriously examined over the last generation and the myths tended to morph into reality. Recently, a group of enterprising academics devoted their energies to turning over some of these sacred standing stones to see what really does lie beneath them and they came up with some very interesting conclusions.

New Zealand rugby, our popular history tells us, grew out of the rural pioneering spirit of the settler, but in *Tackling Rugby Myths* Greg Ryan and his colleagues demonstrated that, from the very beginning, rugby was essentially an urban game, played by far more townies than gaunt, taciturn farmers. And they backed this up with an impressive array of statistics to give the proposition some scholarly biff. Even in the late 1960s it was being maintained that the core of the All Black team was rural in character, whereas it was obvious to anybody who did the numbers that the national team was an overwhelmingly urban one.

Rugby did not take hold as the national game in quite the way that history would have it. Frequently, it has been a divisive and divided activity, frowned upon by certain sectors of society and far from the classless vehicle for national unity that historians have tended to perpetuate. The book also drew attention to a growing contemporary assumption that somehow rugby has been taken away from the masses as a result of professionalism; that the game has been "eroded, perhaps even sabotaged, by forces acting contrary to the best interests of the game". Happily, the authors stopped short of labelling this a myth for the very good reason that it isn't.

So, what has actually changed? Off the field, just about everything seems to be different. Yet on the field hardly anything has changed if you set aside the relatively trivial tampering with the rules that just seems to go on and on in the interests not of those who play it but of those who want it to earn more and entertain more. The game remains steadfastly the same in outward appearance even if mud and slush and oranges at halftime are just a happy memory. P G Wodehouse would recognise it. It's still a matter of working the ball down the field by one means or another and depositing it over the goal-line. And there's still a reasonable amount of assault and battery along the way. It's better as a spectacle of pace, power and physicality. The skillsets are more or less the same as they ever were. But is it any better as a contest of brains, will and character? And, more important still, can it still lay claim to being a force for healthy social inclusion?

Because of its profound influence at almost every level of society, professional sport is starting to be taken seriously by many of those who would never have done so before and rugby has its full share of this sort of attention. Academic careers are being fashioned from it. Medical science is fascinated by it. Business is bedazzled by its sales potential. Universities are beginning to realise the potential for analysis of sports issues as a significant indicator of cultural trends. Doctoral theses are now being written on the social and psychological as well as the physiological dimensions of sport.

Robin McConnell, senior lecturer in sports management and coaching at Massey University's Albany campus, produced a book from his PhD thesis on life inside the All Blacks. It is an intriguing mixture of voyeurism, academic objectivity and personal passion and it represents a stamping ground for sociological analysis. There are many careers being built around the statistical analysis of rugby matches, the physiological requirements of players, the psychological pressures that full-on professionalism imposes and even on the intricacies of team "cultures".

A whole industry has sprung up servicing this. A few years ago, a touring team would have a manager, a coach and a locally appointed baggage man; today the entourage is enormous. One coach has given way to three or four, plus doctors, psychologists, physiotherapists, video analysts, tactical advisers and all the others judged to be indispensable to a modern professional rugby team.

When the All Blacks tour it seems like a cast of thousands trundles along with them. When the British Lions came to New Zealand in 2005 they didn't just bring three teams. They brought enough officials to man the *QE2*. It was the biggest British expeditionary force to land here since the redcoats came to quell rebellious Maori. And it was rather less successful.

Was that ridiculous extravaganza a high water mark? Or will rugby continue to ape its more affluent cousins among the football codes of the world and keep opting for bigger, brighter and bolder. What will it take for a sense of proportion to finally reassert itself? It all rather depends on your view as to growth. At the moment most of the emphasis is on raw, quantitative growth, just as it is when economists talk obsessively about the national economy, ignoring the fact that growth for its own sake is meaningless. But just like the national economy, rugby's future depends rather more on qualitative growth and that's the hard bit. It implies that less can sometimes be more.

Upstairs and Downstairs: Unity and Division

RUGBY ISN'T just any old game. It's a social phenomenon in its own right. It has become embedded in the psyche of many of those who play it, run it or watch it. You might be inclined to say the same of many other sports. Yet, perhaps because it has mattered so much to national identity in a number of countries, rugby has actually altered the course of social and political history and for a while in the late 20th century it was the focus of intense global attention as it found itself carrying the poisoned chalice of racial discrimination in South Africa.

One of rugby's most distinctive attributes is its seemingly contrary capacity to unite and to divide, to provide a beacon for national aspirations and a stick for others to beat it with. Over a century and a half it has had its full share of both and the scar tissue still remains.

The most distinctive characteristic the game perennially exhibited — the exclusivity of class distinctions — has given way to a democratisation which in turn has opened the way for professionalism and, ironically, a new form of class distinction based, not on a player's heritage or his colour, but on his earning power. In other words elitism to elitism in one generation.

In Britain it served to divide for a very long time. The exclusive preserve of the English public schools, it was one of those sports like croquet or polo: unimaginable to those beneath the upper middle classes. The *hoi polloi* took to soccer instead and it, too, developed its own kind of exclusivity. Class dictated the future of both games and that's the way it stayed until relatively recently. It was class that caused the schism with rugby league as well. As rugby began to spread to other parts of Britain it became apparent that the Rugby Football Union might have to begin selecting ungentlemanly players from beyond the Home Counties and that prospect didn't appeal to the Old Farts at all. They resisted such temptations with extraordinary resilience. Thus the breakaway in the north of England that gave rise to rugby league. And so it was that league and union settled into their own comfortable class-defined armchairs, rugby upstairs and league downstairs.

The exception to this pattern in Britain was of course Wales where rugby's ability to wash over class divisions had been fully accomplished by the time the 1905 All Blacks arrived and began an historical dialogue that has continued to fascinate people from both societies ever since. All of Wales became impassioned. Welsh peers would proclaim its virtues in the House of Lords. Welsh miners celebrated it in corner pubs after a long day underground. Rugby became a talisman for Welsh identity, a stick with which to beat the English in particular and anyone else in general. It has stayed that way ever since.

But class remained a formidable obstacle elsewhere in Britain. Amazingly, the RFU, locked into a "home counties" exclusivity, was still resisting the rugged charms of northern players as late as the 1960s. Take the famous case of Ron Jacobs. For years he had been the best prop in England but couldn't ever seem to get an international cap as a player from beyond the social walls of the home counties until there was such an almighty outcry from all around the country that the England selectors simply had to swallow hard and pick him. Needless to say the England scrum prospered thereafter.

These days that class division is much more muted, as it is within society as a whole. Sure, the game in the southeast remains stalwartly middle, if not upper middle-class in complexion, but it is flourishing in other parts of the country where class distinctions count for much less and where rugby increasingly goes head to head with soccer for affiliation and patronage.

In the colonies where it took root most firmly, rugby rapidly became a social cornerstone of almost every community. All other leisure activities were relegated to insignificance by comparison. In South Africa and New Zealand its grip on the national identity by the late 19th century was vice-like. The game slowly became a national barometer of feelgood. If the national team won, the mood would be buoyant and jaunty. If they lost, a pall of gloom would settle like a depressive cloud. Nobody who was around when New Zealand finally beat the Springboks in 1956, or when Wales beat New Zealand momentously in 1953, or when South Africa won the World Cup in 1995 would be under any illusion as to the collective high that those moments brought to a whole nation.

In no country has rugby been more primal than in New Zealand. Rugby has been to New Zealanders what football is to Brazil, or cricket to India. It transcends the mundanities of life. It has filled a cultural gap — and an identity gap — in ways that have brought great satisfaction to almost everybody in the country at one time or another.

Although some people would hotly deny it, rugby, remarkably, has so far managed to retain its relative primacy in the New Zealand consciousness. In spite of decades of political buffeting and, for far too long, a thoroughly inept response from those who ran it, and in spite of the fact that the All Blacks cannot quite seem to win back the World Cup, the game keeps bouncing back after each reversal of fortune. It does that because we still seem to need it; maybe not as much as we once did, but the need remains. It might sound trite but there is still no more telling barometer of the average Kiwi's sense of wellbeing than the fortunes of the All Blacks.

That isn't difficult to understand. It may even have an explanation in science. The Oxford biologist Richard Dawkins identified a genetic-like transfer of beliefs and understandings, which he called "memes", by which cultural tendencies are spread and intensified in particular societies. It is perfectly possible that the rugby meme has been working away in New Zealand, transferring an extraordinary passion for, and insights into, the game from person to person and from generation to generation. Some would say it's far simpler than that. There was so little else to do in New Zealand when rugby began to assert its primacy that it was simply a case of no contest. Rugby just got out front and never really had to look over its shoulder.

For better or for worse the national psyche has been caught up in the chain that drives this game and notwithstanding many disturbing signs of fatigue at being overdosed on the game, there isn't any question that rugby — for the moment at least — remains unchallenged as the national sport.

In spite of all the other ways in which New Zealand manages to stand out in the world, rugby still provides a rallying cry for a nationalism that otherwise has difficulty in finding ways to express itself. Nationalism is a curious commodity. It can be very easily manipulated by self-serving opportunists and history is littered with examples of whole populations being led by the noses, often up the garden path, by self-serving despots. In the Anglo-Saxon world relative social stability has meant that nationalism became increasingly expressed through sport, with the fortunes of a single team becoming an expression of a country's particular personality.

But whether or not that chosen sport unites or divides rather depends on the morality of the moment. In New Zealand, rugby has been a Jekyll and Hyde ever since it arrived. It started out as an unseemly impediment to good order and moral rectitude, played by ruffians. It soon became very much a town game effectively reserved for the urban middle classes, then began to weave a kind of egalitarian spell all over the population and all around the country.

When apartheid reared its serpentine head rugby became the meat in a racist sandwich and divided a nation possibly more than at any time in the history of sport. It was a division that astonished social scientists and forced the people of New Zealand to take a long hard look at themselves and their attitudes. Although the wounds have largely healed, the lingering message is that excessive devotion to sport at the expense of wider social or political considerations is the mark of a pretty dumb society.

Rugby was something of a slow learner when it came to matters of race, but then every sport that had its origins in the British colonial diaspora suffered from the same racial myopia. Rugby and cricket stood out as the most extreme examples and the legacy of that is still with both of them today.

Cricket has had its own turbulent history. It too was transported to the colonies and established as an urban, middle-class pastime. Perhaps it was too slow for the indigenous peoples, too arcane, too idiosyncratic. Yet, oddly, it became an extraordinarily powerful expression of emancipation in, of all places, India. Cricket's role in the political evolution of India and in the breaching of caste barriers in that country is perhaps the most compelling example in history of a sport becoming a vehicle for political change.

Ramachandra Guha's magnificent evocation of that process, *A Corner of a Foreign Field*, sets out how the power of a single sport can substantially impact on the course of a country's social and political history. Now, of course, cricket is the most distinctive unifying force in India and it has often proved to be a valuable political safety valve in the tortured relations between India and Pakistan where they are equally besotted with the game. It is played by tens of millions at the amateur end and by a tiny, elite and exceedingly well remunerated group at the professional peak.

In its own way rugby has been almost as culturally pivotal in many of the countries in which it has taken root. As an "establishment" sport for the most part it has mirrored the gradual democratisation of society and now, notwithstanding a severe attack of the hiccups along the way, it can genuinely claim to be a game that is open to all classes and all races. And that is no mean claim.

Many historians and sociologists have marvelled at the role rugby has played in reconciling Maori and Pakeha in New Zealand. From the very beginning rugby instantly appealed to Maori and it can legitimately lay claim to being a fundamental nation-building block. But that didn't come naturally, and thereby hangs a fascinating tale.

Despite popular mythology, rugby began every bit as urban and middle-class a game as anywhere else and that made it rather hard to accommodate Maori, the vast majority of whom lived outside the towns. Nor was the performance of the European rugby fraternity particularly honourable towards Maori. It was made clear from the beginning that if Maori wanted to play they could have their own competitions out of town and out of sight. That is what they did until formal recognition of Maori rugby as a viable entity was forced on the New Zealand union in 1910. That too was a distinctly pragmatic act because a number of upwardly mobile Maori had begun to infiltrate the provincial teams and it was becoming apparent that they were almost perfectly suited to the game. In other words the Pakeha administrators realised that it would be rather dumb to kick that particular gift horse in the mouth. A fear also developed, prompted by the mercantilist instinct of many Maori, that this great untapped store of indigenous talent might be lured off to Australia or Britain to the reviled competitor, league.

And so, in the best traditions of self-interest, and with little grace it must be said, the Pakeha rugby establishment opened its door to Maori but maintained a separate Maori rugby entity just in case. Let us, they thought, have our cake and eat it. But the cake was not available to Maori when it came to playing against the Springboks in South Africa and there too hangs another tale of equal if not greater disrepute.

Rugby was too pervasive for white sensitivities to prevail. Slowly but surely Maori and Pakeha conjoined. The gates of even the most exclusive private schools were thrust open by the barnstorming talents of young Maori where, otherwise, those gates would have remained firmly shut. New Zealand folklore is rich in stories of racial misgivings being swept away on the footy fields of provincial towns and, in time, all the cities.

More recently, the game has become a fascinating point of convergence for Maori, Pakeha and Pacifica: one of the few real bridges between this otherwise tentative set of relationships. The romance, the legends, the folklore of the great matches and the great players are not a Pakeha monopoly. They belong to all. Happily, that spirit of inclusiveness has survived the onset of professionalism. It is now so embedded that the game has reached a stage where it provides a working example of comfortable multiculturalism. In an odd way professionalism in sport removes class or race barriers by superimposing another culture — that of the team — over every other difference. Professional rugby has unquestionably served to strengthen the imagery of three cultures working in visible harmony. The All Blacks set an example that has no parallel in this respect.

The same forces of unity have been at work in other rugby-playing communities. In Ireland the game has, from the very beginning, floated above the vicious sectarian divisions that wrecked that deeply troubled island. North and South, Protestant and Catholic have always joined forces in the Irish rugby team, in the most eloquent reminder to those who sought to drive the communities apart that sport can sometimes outflank war and provide a telling metaphor for peace.

The spectacle of Ulster Protestants alongside the Catholics of the republic unselfconsciously taking on the rest of Europe and the world would warm the hearts of the ancient Irish kings who tried so hard to unite the tribes of Ireland but never quite succeeded. Those regal Irish hearts would be particularly warmed by the spectacle of Ireland delivering a beating to the English hordes on their own home battlefield of Twickenham. Shades of the rather less successful Irish invasion of England by the forces of the Boy King in the 12th century.

But history tends to repeat itself. The English forces were too great for the Irish invaders eight centuries ago just as they tend more often than not to be too great for the gallant united Irish these days. Ireland might not always win but the Irish rugby community can always be secure in the part they played in demonstrating the madness of sectarianism.

In November 2008 a curiously symbolic moment occurred. The Irish government agreed to let the fabled home of Gaelic football, Croke Park, be used for a game of rugby, a test match between Ireland and New Zealand. For a very long time public stadiums in Ireland were prevented by law from allowing any English game to be played there. You might think this a rather antiquated attitude in the 21st century but it had been rigidly applied beforehand. Rugby might have been an English game but by 2008 its conflict-resolving credentials were good enough to see off the remnants of an anomalous prejudice.

But rugby's role at the cutting edge of reconciliation has had other dimensions as well. Rugby, after becoming a painfully visible expression of the problem of apartheid, eventually became part of the solution. That too is something that is little appreciated by all those who have dismissed the game as blimpish and bigoted. The story of how rugby, led by Springbok Tom Bedford and others, played a pivotal role in bringing down the pillars of apartheid has never been fully or effectively told. It is rather more subtle than the "rugby was the bad guy and the anti-apartheid movement was the good guy" mantra chanted ever since.

The imagery of Nelson Mandela dressed in a Springbok jersey joining the World Cup victory celebrations in 1995 certainly helped. Shortly after he was released from prison in 1990, Mandela said, prophetically, in handing a lifetime achievement award to Pelé, the Brazilian soccer star, "Sport has the power to change the world. It has the power to inspire, the power to unite people that little else has . . . it is more powerful than governments in breaking down racial barriers." In South Africa he set in train a process that, had it not been for rugby, would have produced a very different South Africa today.

Yet, paradoxically, for all its socially healing qualities, rugby has always had a remarkably militant persona. Traditionally, it is associated with war rather than peace and the warrior tradition is what underpins the contemporary game. Rugby and war are the most comfortable of bedfellows. Rugby and its variants, American football, the curious kick and punch offshoot of Gaelic Football known as Australian Rules, and of course rugby's errant sibling, rugby league, are tailor-made for the warrior without a war but a ready-made arena in which to test his courage, tactical deployment and physical prowess against the enemy. An international tour is a campaign. Each test match is a set-piece battle. Prisoners were not to be taken. Quarter was neither asked for nor given. Cover defence was a second front. Forwards were the heavy artillery; backs the bayonet thrust administering the *coup de grâce*. The injured were casualties. Reinforcements would be called up off the bench. The dressing-room in the aftermath of a hard fought game would resemble a field hospital.

The great tours to the other side of the world that took place in the amateur era were the equivalent of a peacetime expeditionary force. A Lions tour to the Southern hemisphere was the modern equivalent of a crusade. All that was missing was the religious bigotry.

It's quite understandable really. War and sport are the only means by which the people of one community can match themselves physically against another. Rugby and war may have been locked in mutual dependence for a century or more but will that powerful emotional bond survive? It's unlikely. First, because war has become a good deal less honourable in the public consciousness; and, second, as the game progressively becomes a business, owing nothing to history and everything to future profits, who will give a toss about all those old romantic notions? Thus, another of rugby's most important taproots will be severed.

Riding the Money-go-round

FINDING WAYS of keeping an umbilical cord intact between the amateur and professional arms of rugby has become a primary preoccupation of most of the world's rugby unions. That cord represents the only means by which the traditional integrity of the game can be kept alive. It is, in effect, a life and death struggle.

In some countries, New Zealand in particular, the professional end subsidises the amateur game. But as costs relentlessly rise that subsidisation is wearing thin. As a result, the game at provincial and club level is slowly withering away. In Europe, in particular, the big clubs who attract sponsorship or patronage on a grand scale have parted company with those who can't. The rift is almost permanent. Two societies have been created, each with different philosophies and objectives. The clubs and provinces who have been left behind are angry and resentful. Again, they see things in terms of trickle up rather than trickle down. They have become more militant in their demands for a better slice of the cake. Whether it's England, France, South Africa, New Zealand or Australia the picture is depressingly similar. Clubs are either forced into amalgamation to survive or they simply close down.

At the top end the market has invaded with electrifying speed. Professional clubs in Europe are the hallmark in this respect. They are fully fledged businesses with ambitious objectives. Within a few years we will almost certainly see professional rugby teams traded on the stock exchange in spite of the fact that nobody has yet devised a way of making them a secure investment.

The private ownership of a football team is a long established phenomenon in the United States and Europe and now the virus is spreading to rugby. Wealthy individuals seem to derive more of an ego boost from owning a football team than from having a Raphael or a garage full of Bugattis. Elton John brought it to the front pages of the tabloids in Britain in the mid 1970s with a very cheeky purchase of his hometown football club in Watford. The whole process has gathered momentum throughout Europe since then but one thing has stood out: it is the increasing dominance of media-related companies as owners. Headstrong British and French tycoons have been tripping over each other for a slice of the Harlequins, Stade Français, Cardiff, the Saracens or the Wasps, pouring megabucks into a seemingly bottomless hole. The only dividend that these ventures pay is in terms of ego.

What's driving this? Nobody in their right mind would normally invest in a British rugby team. Nobody is ever expected to make a profit doing so. Most of them are teetering on the brink of insolvency. The same can be said, with a few exceptions, of France. Investors have been losing their shirts on rugby teams but they just don't seem to mind.

A couple of years ago I went back to a reunion of my old club, Lyon Olympique Universitaire. Lyon was once one of the great clubs of France. In the 1930s it was top dog. A number of New Zealanders had spent time there and even in the later years of the amateur era Lyon was still highly competitive. Along came professionalism and the club crashed. It languished in the second division for years, bereft of talent and money. All the sponsorship and support was sucked up by the Lyon Football Club, the champions of France, and it looked like the end of the road for the rugby club.

And then, miraculously, along came a couple of exceptionally rich young industrialists who pumped several million euros into it and became the owners almost overnight. These two fellows, virtual strangers to rugby and with all the brash confidence of the *nouveau riche*, decided that this was the most effective way to make a splash. And splash they did. Players were bought. A new coach was hired. A professional culture was engendered. A corporate management regime was installed. Lyon began to revive and has been slowly dragging itself back up the French competitive ladder again.

I asked them what they expected to get out of all this. Was it personal glory? Was it the satisfaction of building an enterprise that succeeded in spite of everything? Was it for tax break purposes? Neither was particularly forthcoming. Although they didn't actually say so, it became clear that the motive was essentially a business one. Being the owner of a sports club, particularly a successful one was, quite simply, good for business. And what's good for business is good for sport, and who could argue with that? This was, it seemed, a win-win situation. Certainly, from the club's perspective this was delivery from oblivion. But have the investors seen a return on their investment? Of course not.

Consider the case of the Auckland Warriors rugby league team.

Garrick Tremain

The real contest for possession.

Several years ago buyers queued up enthusiastically, seemingly desperate to throw their money away in return for owning that symbol of good old-fashioned Kiwi machismo. Prominent New Zealand businessman Sir Roger Bhatnagar couldn't resist the possibility and made a handsome bid, only to finish up furious at losing the contest to another more extravagant business acquaintance. He may in time be thankful for that because ownership of the Warriors has ever since been a constant headache, exacerbated by erratic performances on the field, social indiscretions off it, antediluvian management and perpetually inadequate sponsorship and gate takings. It is, in short, a poisoned chalice.

The cheeky suggestion in 2004 that the proud owners of the Warriors might also buy into the Super 12 by putting up a privately owned Pacific Islands team sent visible shudders down the spine of the New Zealand Rugby Union. The fact that the idea was being secretly discussed with the IRB without the knowledge of the Sanzar unions at the time simply added insult to injury and raised worrying questions about the level of trust between the IRB and Sanzar. Happily, the proposal didn't get much traction, however persuasive the Warriors' owner Eric Watson thought he could be. Rugby union, as mercantile as it had become, wasn't quite ready for the privatisation of its various franchises.

Mr Watson and his colleagues came at this issue from an interesting and very creative angle. They set their sights on the largest chink in the Sanzar armour, its inability to come to terms with the Pacific Island countries. One could hardly accuse Watson's vehicle, Cullen Investments, of cynical opportunism. Nobody in rugby union had yet come up with anything like a viable proposal in this area and the Pacific Island unions were growing increasingly desperate as the waters of insolvency rose around them. And just to add spice to the stew, the IRB was later discovered to have been egging Watson and his colleagues on from the shadows.

The promoters were actually offering to fund the Pacific franchise themselves rather than rely on the largesse of Rupert Murdoch and Herr Adidas. Precisely how they saw it yielding a return on investment what with all the travel bills on top of the usual establishment costs is a bit of a mystery. Perhaps there were tax loss attractions.

While it didn't get off the ground this offer nevertheless helped to concentrate a few minds. It served to flush out the range of options available to the Sanzar group and the NZRU in particular when it comes to dealing the Islanders into the equation. Is it just possible that in a year or two we might see a semi-privatised Super 15? The new Melbourne-based franchise, with its high level of private backing, will almost certainly spark off a new wave of demands for privatisation. There is clearly no shortage of enthusiasm even in the depths of a severe recession. Steve Tew, the Chief Executive of the NZRU, has admitted frankly that he has not been short of offers.

Tew has been commendably frank about the situation as the NZRU currently sees it. “The reality is New Zealand rugby is undercapitalised,” he said in November 2009. In an internal discussion paper the NZRU laid out what amounts to a set of conditions under which franchises would be opened up to private investors. The franchises would not be sold outright. There would, at the very least, be a Telecom-style “Kiwi share” retained, giving the NZRU at least some leverage over the new bodies. Whether this would amount to a majority share being held by the NZRU or a particular province or some other representative rugby institution remains an open question.

The issue isn’t just one of commercial viability. There are extreme sensitivities out there in rugby’s heartland. Many of the smaller provinces feel shut out of the Super rugby system even if they receive payments at the end of each season from the revenues that flow from the competition. They are deeply suspicious of many of the city businessmen who are appointed to franchise boards and they are highly critical, sometimes irrationally so, of the way the whole system is run. For them, privatisation is a red rag to a bull and their voice carries more weight in the local rugby community than that of the NZRU.

Under the current regime the NZRU employs the players, appoints the coaches, approves the franchise directors, sets the programme for the season and retains administrative control over the franchises in a variety of other ways. They are, in effect, not really franchises at all in the conventional sense of the word and they are considerably more controlled than their counterparts in South Africa and Australia. They are in reality glorified event managers. For their part, the host provinces who provide most of the services for each franchise are deeply dissatisfied with this awkward arrangement. They maintain that the conditions imposed are heavy-handed and suffocating and they want separation.

That is clearly coming. The NZRU prefers a system of bulk funding for player salaries but will introduce the devolution of player contracting to the franchises from 2011. It may well loosen the bonds in a variety of other ways but it is adamant that yielding up full control, even to New Zealand investors, is simply not a runner.

Perhaps the NZRU should take a leaf out of Roger Douglas’s book by turning its five franchises into a series of semi-independent entities, the sporting equivalent of state-owned enterprises, answerable to head office but free to run their own business in a fully commercial way and paying an acceptable dividend back to the NZRU.

The privatisation of Super rugby is under way. The train has already left the station and it's only New Zealand which has yet to move, paralysed by a fear not just of public opprobrium at what they would regard as another sell-out but the inevitable loss of income in the longer run as investors take their profits.

You would have thought there was a sufficient number of cautionary tales for those with privatisation ambitions in rugby union in the Southern hemisphere. It would seem not. The news in 2009 that the Australian Basketball League had all but imploded may not have caused many sleepless nights to those running other sports but it conveyed an unmistakable message to the sporting world in Australasia, including rugby, about the perils of private franchises. It seemed extraordinary that the professional basketball competition in Australia should be reduced to eight teams in 2009 and even more extraordinary that the competition wouldn't have a team from two of the largest cities, Sydney and Brisbane. It seems that the franchises that folded lost many of their corporate backers in the stock and money market carnage that hit the biggest cities hardest. Each was privately owned and each went straight to the bottom of the harbour tied to the fortunes of their owners.

The obvious question that hung in the air after this cataclysm was: what's up with basketball that can't soon be up with rugby? It's a fair question because there have been unmistakable signs over the years that the NZRU would rather like to partially or fully privatise the five New Zealand franchises if it thought it could get away with it. This is a no-win dilemma for the NZRU and it began very tentatively testing the temperature in late 2009 before very visibly taking no position on the issue.

On the face of it the argument in favour is a quite compelling one. It would release capital that is desperately needed to keep the game afloat below the professional tier and it would introduce new energy and new ideas to the Super rugby format. On the other hand, in the absence of some rather creative governance arrangements, it would effectively remove control over the players from the central body, something that is regarded as a major advantage in New Zealand when one considers the near-hopeless situation in Europe where private clubs almost gleefully hold the national union to ransom over the availability of players for international duty.

More significantly, privatisation would inevitably result in profits being distributed to shareholders rather than going back into the game. It is this factor that constrains the NZRU above all others. The net revenue from each of the New Zealand franchises is channelled directly to its constituent provinces. This cash flow is so important to the provinces that they have more or less given up demanding that the franchise team come and play at their stadiums because the income simply isn't enough. Take the case of the Hurricanes, based in Wellington. A few years ago at least one home match a year would be taken to New Plymouth, Napier or Palmerston North on the insistence of the provinces. Not any more. Each of the provincial unions knows that the Hurricanes lose money if they don't play every match at the Wellington stadium. As a result the provinces don't get to host Super 14 matches any more. They've stopped asking.

But the downside doesn't end there. It would inevitably lead, in the absence of an agreed salary cap, to the further escalation of full-time professional salaries, the single most intractable problem for world rugby. It would further alienate the Super rugby franchises from their support base around the provinces and the rugby public too. This is a time to make haste very slowly.

One option which does appear likely in the short term is the separation of the franchises' governance systems from those of the provinces. The initial model whereby the five host provinces, Otago, Canterbury, Wellington, Waikato and Auckland, provided management services to the franchises has the virtue of being economical but it has resulted in what is seen as an unfair advantage to those provinces. There is some truth in that, even if it is more apparent than real. Players would be enticed to the big provinces in order to secure contracts with the local franchise and the drain away from the weaker provinces would begin to cause anxiety. It is vitally important that a player can choose to play for any province he likes without the incentive of more money from a richer province, and this is the nub of the issue.

The deal agreed at the end of 2009 after protracted negotiation between the provinces, the players' association and the NZRU agreed, finally, on a realistic salary cap for provincial teams. This was perhaps the most significant step forward in the last decade: a very rare example of people giving and taking in the best interests of a desperate game. It means the equalisation of opportunity for all provinces and a stemming of the ruinous tide of payments that smaller provinces were obliged to make to secure enough talent to become competitive. It should, in theory, mean a better distribution of talent round the provinces and make for a more compelling NPC.

The provincial championship is a vital symbol of the health of domestic rugby in New Zealand. It must always be the first priority of the rugby community and it must be protected from the ravages of the market because if it fails, so too does the rugby infrastructure in the provinces — the clubs, the volunteer force and the emotional attachment of communities to their team. And without those precious commodities the game is sunk.

NZ Rugby Museum.

In more gracious days. Ian Clarke and Wilson Whineray chaired off the field as the crowd sang "Now is the Hour" after the All Blacks–Barbarians game in 1964.

Fairfax Newspapers

Springbok John Gainsford wasn't eye-gouging Colin Meads in 1965. The match was over and he was just being nice.

The grand illusion of seamlessness.

NZ Rugby Museum

The long tour. The 1905 All Blacks had 27 players and two officials.

The short tour. The 2005 All Blacks had 35 players and 14 officials.

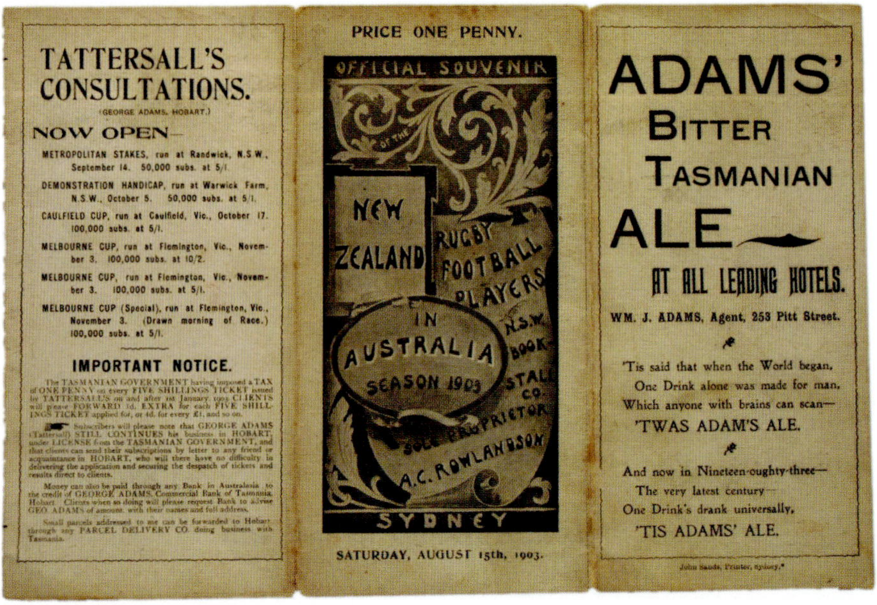

An unholy trinity: rugby, racing and beer.

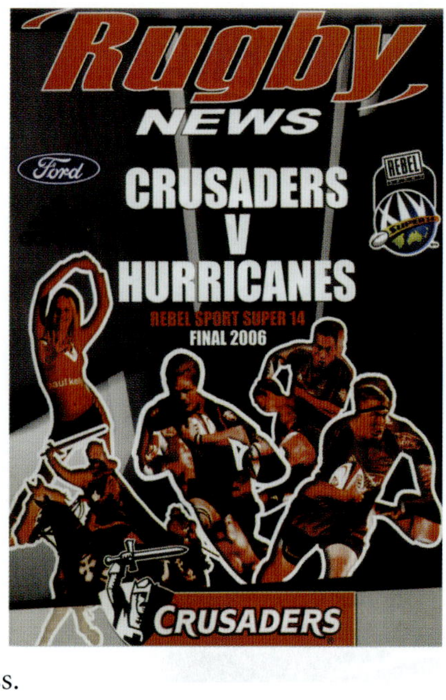

The programme. 101 years of progress.

Belfast, 1972. The IRA wanted a united Ireland. Little did they realise that rugby was doing it for them.

Peter Bush

Rugby's intolerance destroyed more than a few careers. There was none more cruel than Keith Murdoch's banishment.

NZ Rugby Museum

A little too assertive for British tastes. Above: Brownlie (1925) and below: Meads (1967) become public enemies.

NZ Rugby Museum

Peter Bush

An All Blacks enforcer at work.

The Salvation of Sanzar

AFTER ALL the fuss that has been made about the tiredness of the Tri Nations the news that Argentina is coming on board hardly seemed to raise an eyebrow. Yet this is the most significant development in the Sanzar relationship since the whole business began over a decade ago. It is the product of the so-called Woking Accord where the game's major stakeholders agreed that a transition programme for Argentina's full integration into the senior international playing calendar was a key priority.

The Tri Nations was a smart new vehicle in 1996 but a decade on it began to look like a smoking banger. The fans were sick of it, the players were tired, the TV-rights holders were desperate for refreshment of their "product" and something had to give. It was the South Africans who were most disenchanted. They threatened to heave off and take their team to the Northern hemisphere if something wasn't done to reduce the South African disadvantage by virtue of its isolation from the others.

Oregan Hoskins, the SARU president, began pushing hard for a restructuring of the Tri Nations to include Argentina and a Pacific team. Interestingly, he made this call on grounds of morality as much as anything else. As he put it in 2007, "Sanzar must look in the mirror and ask whether they have done rugby a service by their policy of being exclusive rather than inclusive." The South Africans, having fostered rugby in Argentina, had an almost familial interest in bringing the Pumas on board. He was implicitly critical of New Zealand for failing to push the case for a Pacific team, something that went down like stale cabbage with the NZRU. But he was right and when the news was released in 2009 that Argentina, but not a Pacifika team, would join it became all the more glaringly apparent that neither New Zealand nor Australia had gone in to bat for the Pacific, either in the Tri Nations or the Super 14. That is a decision that will haunt New Zealand in future.

Argentina is the perennial outlander in world rugby — hard to fit in anywhere but keen as mustard to take anybody on. Buenos Aires is one of those places where major test-playing nations visit en route to somewhere else and get suitably mauled along the way by the Pumas. All that will now change as Argentina steps up to centre stage and they are understandably ecstatic about the chance to get some really intensive international competition. There are some critics who think that Argentina isn't really up to this challenge. They are in for a rude shock because the only thing that has prevented the Pumas from becoming a front-rank rugby country has been the absence of competition.

This innovation will provide vital incentive to the majority of Argentinian players who are obliged to ply their professional trade in Europe to spend more time at home, and that can only be beneficial to the national game.

It will of course radically change the format of the Tri Nations which will have to be called something else. What's the bet Sanzar goes for "The Four Nations" as a title and while it's doing that it might have to come up with a variation of the name Sanzar itself. "Sanzargy" might do the trick. Or, if you want more music, how about "Argausanz"?

More importantly, this will mean significantly more variety, something that the Tri Nations has been desperately in need of. The proposed format will see the four teams playing on a home and away basis, meaning six matches per team and a total of 12 matches overall. This is the same as the present schedule. The competition is due to start in 2012 and will be played from mid-August (following the end of the new Super Rugby competition) for an eight or nine-week period through until early to mid-October. In a Rugby World Cup year an abbreviated format would be played through July and August.

Will it provide the revitalisation that Sanzar hopes it will? It will certainly mean infinitely more travel, more jet-lag and more cost as teams traverse the full width of the Southern hemisphere but that is the price of securing the television rights funding that the whole thing survives on. Argentina are of course overjoyed at the prospect. They are effectively getting international competition on the cheap.

Having come this far, Sanzar will no doubt come under pressure in future to consider including an Argentinian franchise in the Super 15 rather than inventing new teams in Australia or South Africa. That, however, is a rather harder nut to crack. Fifteen is already too many in the minds of most of those involved — and most spectators — and to enlarge it would mean inventing another month in the year.

Is Sanzar really here to stay? That rather depends on the sustainability of the two competitions in the fickle minds of the fans. It will depend, too, on a further erosion of the exclusivity that has bugged it for too long. The logical approach would be to reduce the number of Australian, New Zealand and South African franchises by one each to accommodate an Argentinian, a Pacific and a Japanese franchise. Logic, however, is a poor cousin of parochialism.

Lord Ranfurly's Hospital Pass

WHEN SOUTHLAND won the Ranfurly Shield towards the end of the 2009 season a collective sigh of relief went up around the provinces. At last one of the lesser lights in the national firmament had finally won it.

Deprivation is certainly a great motivator. A starving man will go to extraordinary lengths to secure a decent feed. The Ranfurly Shield, in rugby terms, is a veritable banquet. It's been a long time between meals for just about everybody except Auckland, Canterbury and Waikato. Others have been especially starved. Otago hasn't had a bite since 1957, so long ago that only the most elderly supporters can remember the day when the Shield was removed from Wellington, only to be lost, tragically, a week or two later. Since then, nothing. Other once great provinces like Hawke's Bay or Manawatu have forgotten what the Shield looks like.

It is this peculiar energy of deprivation that keeps at least some shine on the Shield. Those who have come to monopolise ownership have tended to devalue it. Aucklanders became gluttonous for far too long and grew impervious to its attractions. Canterbury is almost as blasé. It has had it, on and off, for far more time than a healthy appetite deserves. Even Waikato, which has had a more than fair share of stewardship, has become a bit casual about the "Log".

There are two very different views about the place of the Ranfurly Shield in New Zealand. One is that it should be left alone as an informal challenge-based trophy sitting alongside the national provincial championship and the other is that it needs to be given a rather more meaningful status as the ultimate national prize. One thing is certain. The Shield needs to be protected as the key symbol of the amateur game in New Zealand.

It's unfortunate that the Shield ever became entangled in the national provincial championship. The moment that happened was the moment it inevitably lost its lustre. It's clearly time for some fresh thinking. To have it sitting uncomfortably in the half light beside the national provincial championship is no longer sustainable. Frankly, it does the Shield a disservice.

It's worth noting here that the Ranfurly Shield is not dissimilar in origin to South Africa's Currie Cup. Each was presented by an altruistic Englishman for domestic competition a long time ago and until the advent of professionalism each was the premier trophy in the land. The South Africans were somewhat smarter than the New Zealanders in that they established the Currie Cup as the reward for the winner of the provincial championship and it has stayed that way ever since. Thus, it has remained at the centre of the action. Not so in New Zealand and that is a pity because if the Shield was the ultimate prize for the national championship it would have a permanent and meaningful place in the game.

All the best efforts of pundits, commentators and other traditionalists to maintain the shine on the Shield are now wearing thin. It is difficult to remember at any one time who actually holds it. When North Harbour won it in 2007 nothing much happened at all. There were few festivities. Shortly after it was gone again and hardly a tear was shed. Auckland, perhaps a bit indifferent after winning and holding it so many times, yielded it up with hardly a whimper in 2008. Nobody really cared. At least Wellington, who hadn't had it for decades, made a modest fuss about it before being given one of their now customary lessons in rugby basics by Canterbury.

There are some who maintain that the Ranfurly Shield retains a certain lustre because it is, rather than in spite of it being, outside the formal competition. They vehemently oppose any change in its status and say that the atmosphere generated by a Shield match is unlike anything else in New Zealand's domestic rugby firmament. There is some truth in that but how sustainable is it? Can a haphazard, one-off, unsystematic arrangement such as this really continue to cut the mustard? Surely the best option is to make the Shield the trophy for the national championship. This would lend valuable weight to the essentially amateur competition if and when it finally parts company with the professional dimension.

In that way the Ranfurly Shield would be able to retain its dignity as the centrepiece of the amateur game.

No doubt someone would argue that that would create a sponsorship problem. After all, you can't have a corporate buying naming rights to a competition that already has a very definite identity. This doesn't seem to have constrained sponsorship of the Currie Cup. These days it is known formally as the ABSA Currie Cup and ABSA seems perfectly happy with that. Why not, then, the Air New Zealand Ranfurly Shield? That might sound crass, but crass is second nature when it comes to commercial sponsorship and the importance of keeping the Ranfurly Shield as the lodestone of New Zealand's domestic rugby surely outweighs any other consideration.

A much more pressing problem is figuring out what to do about the provincial championship itself. For years now an at times ugly debate has raged over the future structure of the championship. It came to a head in 2008 as it became obvious that a number of provincial unions were going bust. Rapidly declining interest and a frightening escalation of costs produced more open acrimony in the rugby community than anyone had seen since 1981.

The NZRU, in classic manner, set out to please everyone and finished up pleasing no one. A public campaign to keep the 14-team competition was mounted, capitalising on all the latent anger that had built up around the country. The NZRU buckled. Fourteen teams it was. Things got worse. The NZRU consulted again and came up with a 10-team solution for 2010. The NZRU said it had the provincial unions' blessing. Obviously, it didn't because, after a hugely successful provincial championship in 2009 without the All Blacks, for the most part, involved, the pressure was again applied for something better. Finally, a measure of good sense prevailed and a compromise, two-tier competition, each of seven teams and with automatic promotion and relegation, was agreed as a part of a comprehensive deal. Rationality departed. Some distinctly low blows were inflicted.

Will it work? Or will it mean oblivion for weaker unions like Manawatu, Counties-Manukau and Northland? Will the drastically reduced salary cap be effective or will the unions waste even more precious money trying to buy talent on the black market? The championship is in a precarious position. It exists in a semi-professional twilight world. It will have some professional players but is destined to lose the All Blacks. We simply can't have it both ways but this immutable logic is lost on many of rugby's more trenchant devotees. Will we see within a few years a provincial competition that is entirely amateur? In other words, the creation of clear daylight between the amateur and the professional worlds? Logic suggests that this is the best long-term outcome, but there is little appetite for it at present because of the enormous symbolic significance of a parting of the ways between amateur and professional. Yet, something has to give. The need to spare the energies of the professionals is an irresistible force and the provincial championship is an immovable object. In the end the force isn't going to beat the object, but simply sidestep it.

Marching to the Beat of the Broadcasters

TELEVISION IS to rugby what water is to a dehydrated desert dweller. Without it the game would disappear off the world's radar screen pretty quickly. It is a frightening thought but if it weren't for the television broadcasters the whole rugby edifice would probably collapse. The professional game is now substantially — some would say dangerously — dependent on TV rights revenues for its survival. It is, effectively, a compliant handmaiden to companies like News Ltd.

So far, that relationship has been reasonably amicable and in a rising market the rights have increased in value. But that value, like oil production, is now peaking, particularly in the Southern hemisphere as other forms of entertainment begin to encroach on rugby's once private territory.

It is a fair guess that any future growth is not going to come from test matches involving the top tier nations or the likes of the Heineken Cup or Super 14 tournaments for the simple reason that we are at saturation point. Revenue growth, if there is to be any, is going to have to come from the fringes — from sevens, the lower tier tournaments, age group tournaments and women's rugby.

News Ltd, Rupert Murdoch's media juggernaut, has taken rugby as a vassal. There is nothing exceptional about that and I don't blame News Ltd or any other of the broadcasters for pursuing profit from the game. But we have to be clear about this. To an international media company rugby is just another entertainment product that will sell more subscriptions to cable TV. If it doesn't pay its way the broadcaster will drop it, cold. Sentiment or tradition have no part in this at all.

Those who sign the deals with News Ltd on behalf of the game in this country, Australia and South Africa know that all too well. They must somehow try to strike a balance between all-out commercialisation and steps to protect the essential ethos of the game from erosion. They are painfully aware that the public will not forgive them if they get it wrong.

But are they not already letting things get out of hand? There is a real danger that control of the game in New Zealand will steadily be wrested away from New Zealand hands and we will have the same dilemma that confronts us on so many other fronts where foreign ownership or control threatens to diminish the domestic options and, more crucially, undermine New Zealand's sense of sovereignty. Chris Patten, the last British governor of Hong Kong, said that sovereignty is rather like virginity. One moment it's there, fully intact, and the next moment it's gone, forever. Our sovereignty is, arguably, more important to us in rugby than in banking or insurance, the ownership of golf courses or the generation of electric power. It is the bottom line of the national personality that is at stake here and we are in danger of letting McWorld have it for a few pieces of silver. The massive deals that have been done with major sponsors were the only way of preserving a vestige of that sovereignty. But for how long?

New Zealand failed to protect the free-to-air transmission of major rugby matches in the 1990s thus leaving itself completely exposed to the exploitation of the medium by the private sector. There were some desultory efforts made to try to legislate, as other western countries have, to require a certain amount of top rugby to be broadcast free-to-air, but these were overwhelmed by the mindless dedication to market forces as the curer of all ills and the opportunity was lost.

The competitive scramble for rights by pay television companies that accompanied the sudden onset of professionalism is now but a distant memory. The era of bidding wars between media companies, except of course for the World Cup itself, is more or less over and there isn't a single professional sport in the world that can expect more, rather than less, for the same amount of rugby from their friendly broadcaster next time round. We all suspected that to be the case. Now it has been spelled out in words of one syllable in the context of rugby for the first time.

When Graham Henry made his controversial decision to opt for "conditioning" rather than competition for most of his All Blacks squad in 2007 in the run-up to the World Cup, we were given a stark indication as to who gets to call the shots. The eruption of irritation by News Ltd at not being asked if half the All Blacks squad could be stood down for the Super 14 season was palpable. News Ltd made it abundantly clear that the fact that the NZRU "forgot" to seek its broadcaster's permission to do this was, without question, the last indiscretion of this kind that it would get away with before the next TV rights bargaining round.

The implications of that were all too obvious. To News Ltd, and all the other commercial broadcasters of sport around the world, it isn't actually sport they are purveying, it is "product", and the rugby union's responsibility is to supply that product, on time and in pristine condition. The rugby union is in effect a wholesaler dealing with an aggressive, monopolist retailer. Withhold any of your best products and the wholesale price naturally goes down.

Second, and perhaps even more significantly, News Ltd has no particular taste for refining or downsizing the Super 14/15 or the Tri Nations series. Persuading News Ltd to opt for reducing either or both of these to anything less than annual competitions would be like persuading Barack Obama to invade Iran. The decision to allow Argentina into the Sanzar mix was one way of assuaging the broadcaster's relentless drive for more and fresher "product".

Much as the fans in all three Sanzar countries want to see longer tours injected into the mix, it seems unlikely that News Ltd will smile upon them as a substitute for the Super 14 or the Tri Nations. They are, at least thus far, proven money spinners and it is money spinners that broadcasters favour, not the idle whims of traditionalist fans. There is little interest in all those piddling little midweek games which hardly anybody will watch live on TV, particularly on the other side of the world in the middle of the night. News Ltd would only be persuaded that change was desirable if and when audiences for its established products started falling away.

But hasn't that already happened? Have television audiences peaked for rugby? They certainly seem to have in New Zealand. Viewer numbers have been falling for both the Super 14 and the national championship games for several years (except that in the case of the 2009 Air New Zealand Cup viewing numbers rose again slightly, an indication that there remains strong attachment to provincial rugby). In February and March the competition with cricket, particularly now that the one-dayers and Twenty20 matches dominate the evening schedules, is hotting up. Cricket appears to be winning. Much the same is happening in South Africa and Australia. Rugby audiences have reached saturation point. Other sports are intruding on their airspace.

Things are different in the UK, France and Italy. There, the reservoir of potential viewers is massively different and the inroads being made by rugby have been very pleasing — and very lucrative — for the national unions. But where is saturation point in those markets? It's out there somewhere but nobody seems to know precisely where. The only thing that is known is that the limit will eventually be reached. And it will be reached sooner rather than later if the quality of rugby as a free-flowing spectacle isn't improved.

And so we come back to the basic principles of marketing. If your product isn't selling, refresh it; repackage it; change the advertising jingle; call it green. Call it anything to get the customers interested again. This was the landscape that awaited the renegotiation of the Sanzar rights to show the Tri Nations and Super 14 from 2010. Crunch time arrived in 2009. At the previous renegotiation both tournaments were simply enlarged in order to secure marginally more money from News Ltd. In 2009, in spite of all the signals from the rugby public that enlargement wasn't wanted, the Super 14 was expanded to 15 from 2011 and Argentina was added to the Tri Nations. This begs the obvious question: what are the options next time round? Further enlargement simply won't be realistic. More is less but less is commercially unthinkable.

One area where audience growth seems to have plenty of slack yet to be taken up is in sevens. Suddenly, the abbreviated form of the game is everybody's darling. It lends itself naturally to entertainment and advertising. The games come thick and fast. The ad breaks are numerous. There is perpetual movement. The crowds are generally in party mode — none of your tense, constipated nationalism here. Half of those who turn up couldn't care less who wins. They go home without ever finding out.

In 2009, the World Sevens Cup tournament was a blockbuster, breaking all records in terms of attendance and, importantly, viewer numbers. What's going on? Who were all these new viewers? Were they traditional rugby enthusiasts or — as seems more likely — is this happening because sevens is dramatically enlarging rugby's catchment? If the latter, then we must ask: will those new viewers transfer their attention to the 15-a-side game or are we about to see sevens depart the tent and strike out on its own, with its own following?

Another question which is often asked is: how much does all this depend on the actual quality of television coverage of rugby? A great deal it would seem. Certainly, in terms of its performance over the years as a purveyor of first rate television coverage, Sky in New Zealand is as good, if not better than, any other televisor of rugby in the world. The commentary teams are, if not the most articulate, then certainly the best informed of any of the big television channels covering rugby.

John Drake, before his tragic death, was an acute observer of the subtleties of the game, especially in the darker corners inhabited by forwards. Grant Fox is certainly the most perceptive analyst of back play and Ian Jones can disentangle the most complicated of forward play mysteries for the viewer. Their insight is born of a profound understanding of what runs through players' minds during a game. Tony Johnson is one of those rare observers who can provide rich context to any commentary. He too is blessed with exceptional perception. Even Murray Mexted, if you can bring yourself to ignore the genial buffoonery, the spectacular spoonerisms, the bad puns and an ability to put his foot firmly in his mouth, is a very good reader of a game.

There is much debate about the contribution that television makes to rugby and their seemingly unhealthy mutual dependence. This was highlighted by the extraordinary decision by Sky TV to "suspend" Mexted for — apparently — his carping criticism of the NZRU's policy with regard to the national championship. Whether the hand of the NZRU could be seen upon this decision nobody would say because nobody on either side would say anything. This was exceptionally bad management and if Sky did actually suspend Mexted for airing his opinions then that is a real warning signal of media capitulation. Viewers do not take kindly to inferences of this kind. Sky can, and must, be more open in this regard if it wants to retain its integrity.

In Australia there is a more conscious attempt to entertain and their commentators do it relentlessly. Phil Kearns and his colleagues never lose an opportunity to lampoon rugby's establishment but they go easy on the players, knowing how hard it is to please the critics when you are on the field. They don't go in for humour or digs at the establishment so much in South Africa, perhaps because the long arm of the government might reach out and pluck them from their post. Listening to the South Africans one gets the impression that most of their commentators sound as if they were locked away in the 1970s and have just been let out, and apart from Joel Stransky and Naas Botha none of them seem capable of explaining why something happened as against what happened.

Theirs is the domain of every cliché in the book. The ball is "coughed up". Blood is "claret". A close game will go "down to the wire". A player exhibiting excellence is "on fire", or having a "blinder". A bit of push and shove after an altercation is "handbags". A doubtful starter is under an injury "cloud". An excessively zealous referee is "pedantic". And so it goes on. The only consolation is that they aren't as bad as rugby league commentators. Nor are they alone in the world of rugby cliché. British commentators are almost as bad. Listening to Nigel Starmer-Smith and his colleagues is like listening to one of those old 78rpm records that gets stuck in every second groove and just keeps repeating itself. It's a veritable clichérama.

When it comes to sheer, objective quality there probably isn't a more accomplished rugby commentator in the world than Grant Nisbett. His calm, insightful observations are just that much more incisive than any of his British, Australian or South African counterparts. It comes from a deep personal understanding of the game and of what players think and feel on the field. But even "Nisbo" occasionally allows himself a dignified jab at the frustrations imposed by those who run the game. He is lucky in that he is backed by perhaps the most experienced array of technical skills in the rugby broadcasting world. Most of the New Zealand directors and cameramen have played the game themselves and their ability to focus on the action is a cut above anything else, even the BBC. Anyone who doubts this should check the videos.

Precisely how the rag-bag assembly of free-to-air New Zealand broadcasters are going to find sufficient talent to even try to match that of

Sky when it comes to the 2011 World Cup is anybody's guess. TV3's abject efforts in 2007 and TVNZ's lacklustre performance the time before that showed how difficult it is to deliver real quality when you're not battle-hardened. It's rather like playing. You need to keep doing it to stay good at it. There isn't much of a case to be made for a "conditioning" lay-off.

The tragicomedy that was played out in New Zealand in 2009 over who should have the free-to-air rights to the 2011 World Cup has resulted in just about everybody having some of the action. That is a nice democratic outcome but it will result in standards falling catastrophically and hardly anyone watching the free-to-air channels when they can see the match-fit professionals of Sky do their stuff, free of the encumbrances of intrusive advertising. The ratings war has been won in advance.

But how does television hold its audiences in future? Saturation coverage produces indifference. Viewers are voting with their remotes. Sponsors of specific events are having second thoughts. Advertisers likewise. Bigger screens and digital improvements don't seem to help. People, particularly in the Southern hemisphere, are turning off. Are there qualitative innovations that might help? One of the most striking features of rugby television coverage is the relative absence of the past. Aside from Sky TV's rugby channel where old games are shown, largely to fill the space between the contemporary stuff, and the Heartland rugby series which pays occasional lip service to history, there is virtually no connection with rugby's rich heritage on television. Yesterday has gone. Today is everything.

Most other great professional sports, particularly in the United States, make great play of the link with the past. They feature former players talking about their great matches and how they compare and relate to the matches of the moment. There is a comforting sense of continuity about it all. History has a meaning. Rugby, however, with perhaps more heritage and folklore than any other team sport and with so many of its supporters hankering after the old days, has more or less abandoned its past when it comes to television. It is all about now.

The Weight of the Winner's Burden

WHAT IS it about the rugby media in other countries that makes them want to beat up on the All Blacks? For one reason or another New Zealand seems to systematically get it in the neck from the media in every other major rugby playing country. Is it simply because we win more than they do? Or is there something else going on here?

Ever since 1905 they've been hard at it. The critics in England got stuck into Dave Gallaher's team as soon as they realised that the New Zealanders were faster and cleverer than anything England could field. They were accused over over-enthusiasm, cheating and ungentlemanly conduct. Some of the reporting was the product of plain, old-fashioned snobbery which is probably forgiveable if seen in the context of the era. Some of it, however, was sheer vitriol. There was a sense of affront that a bunch of colonials could teach England a lesson in their own game.

The mud stuck and the tradition was born. In the 50s and 60s we were accused by British sports writers of being humourless and of being excessively brutal. If Welsh critic J B G Thomas had been taken seriously, many All Blacks would have been liable to arrest and summary imprisonment. It was relentless. We were considered the benchmark for unsportsmanlike ruthlessness. Dour, humourless, unfriendly and, all too often, dirty. The Brownlie brothers became the targets in the 1920s, Cyril Brownlie being the first player ever to be ordered off in a test match in 1924, and one of the least deserving of that honour. The Otago and Southland forwards of the 30s and 40s who revolutionised the creative use of the feet, both down south and in the All Blacks teams of that era, were pilloried by the foreign media over the controversial art of rucking.

Those with a particularly hard edge to their play were singled out for special attention. Kevin Skinner was the ogre of the 1950s, his fists becoming legendary in the process, and Colin Meads, ordered off in similarly questionable circumstances to those of Brownlie, became the poster boy for excessive violence in the 1960s. In the 1960s the unflattering tag "Unsmiling Giants" was attached to the All Blacks. *Punch* described the team, not without some justification, as having all the personality of a petrified forest.

In 1972–3 they howled for the scalp of Keith Murdoch, and got it, tragically. He had flattened a local drunken cretin who provoked him in Cardiff, an offence no greater than that committed by a Welsh player a couple of weeks beforehand and many others since. Murdoch became a martyr, sacrificed with extraordinary cruelty, by a rugby establishment in Britain that was intent on punishing New Zealand for a century of what they considered to be excessive behaviour. Keith Murdoch was a victim of this. Murdoch was no angel. I knew that well enough having played with him for a number of years before his banishment. If he were a modern All Black he would have been surrounded by minders, counsellors and hustled out of harm's way. Back then, he was a sitting duck.

Even now, 35 years on, the media still insists on describing him as "notorious", mistaking the treatment he received for the person himself. The guilt that rugby carries over this episode has never been assuaged and never will be. All that, however, has been lost in the desire to hunt him down. Fortunately, they never will.

At the 1991 World Cup, *Irish Independent* writer Vincent Hogan declared that the All Blacks exhibited "all the gaiety of gravediggers. New Zealand's rugger men strut and scowl and generally imply a superior presence. It is as though they are reminding you that God wears a black shirt." And so it continued. John Ashworth, Richard Loe, Mark "Cowboy" Shaw and others became notorious villains for their periodic indiscretions. There were of course similar accusations levelled at the French and the South Africans from time to time but there was never the same persistent collective finger pointing as that suffered by the All Blacks.

J B G Thomas, an otherwise great rugby writer of Wales, was almost pathologically predisposed to dump on the All Blacks whenever they came his way. So was John Reason in England. Mr Reason was rarely reasonable when it came to All Blacks ruthlessness yet he never quibbled when a British team managed occasionally to win by virtue of brute physicality. Many others have taken up the anti-All Blacks cause over the intervening years, complaining bitterly about illegal tactics, over-zealous forward play, arrogance, unapproachability and an inability to take a joke.

The foreign media, especially the British, was almost irrationally critical of the unfettered commercialism of the All Blacks in the years before professionalism until it dawned on them that English, Welsh and other teams were just as mercantile. Spiro Zavos and others have expertly catalogued the complaints about New Zealand rugby in the British and occasionally the South African press that until relatively recently were *de rigeur*. In reality it has been the politics of envy. They have never been able to accept that day in, day out our players have, quite simply, been better than theirs — tougher physically, harder minded and with more basic skills honed in the most competitive system in the world, the domestic rugby competition of New Zealand.

When professionalism arrived it all began to change. The media began to realise that maybe the All Blacks weren't so different to other international teams after all. Within a few short years the playing field was completely levelled. All international teams began to look the same even if some continued to win rather more than others. Yet the fact of All Black superiority still rankles among some in the rugby media. Stephen Jones of the British *Sunday Times*, the Jeremy Clarkson of rugby, has virtually made a career out of All Blacks baiting. Being obliged to eat his words regularly doesn't diminish his apparent distaste for New Zealand rugby one whit. On the other hand, the ex-internationals, like Gerald Davies or Stuart Barnes, who played against New Zealand, don't indulge in this puerile malevolence at all. I wonder why?

There is still the occasional throw-back. In 2003 an Australian sports writer called Ray Chesterton wrote in Sydney's *Daily Telegraph* a piece entitled "Why I loathe the All Blacks".

Mr Chesterton's words had a very 60s ring to them. It was as if he had lifted a few paragraphs from something written long ago and re-run them just for fun. I checked the date on the paper just to be sure. Consider this particular passage. "I can appreciate the ruthlessness of the All Blacks and their desperate need to win at all costs, even if it means pushing aside sportsmanship and ethics." To underscore the verisimilitude of this observation Mr Chesterton summoned up from his memory the deeds, or rather the misdeeds, of Colin Meads and Keith Murdoch.

It was as if time had stood still and that we were back in the unsmiling giant days. The means by which All Blacks imposed their superiority on their Australian counterparts clearly didn't find favour with Mr Chesterton and this has continued to pick away at him ever since. "Muggers in football boots" was his touching tribute to All Blacks in general. "Dark, visaged, menacing and morose," he notes. Just what "visaged" means remains obscure. Perhaps Mr Chesterton was watching *Star Wars* and mistook Darth Vader's visor for Colin Meads's eyebrows.

The All Blacks are, he said, "a team of fifteen men forbidden by contract to ever smile or even to celebrate some of them walking upright." He clearly hadn't passed an evening with Mils Muliaina or Doug Howlett out on the town.

But these observations were as nothing compared to Chesterton's *coup de grâce*. The All Blacks, he assured us, are "huge, hulking and menacing but lacking any evident desire to expand their game with cleverness, guile, attacking flair or exuberance." Mr Chesterton obviously wasn't around on the night that New Zealand walloped the Wallabies in Sydney that year with a matchless mix of cleverness, guile, attacking flair and exuberance compared to the Wallabies' automated "Brumbies" style. Had he by chance confused the New Zealand style with that of Australia, gone a little colour-blind and mistaken one team for the other?

He concluded, in a fit of uncharacteristic generosity. "They are a team that can never be ignored. But it doesn't mean I have to like them." Indeed it doesn't, and I imagine Mr Chesterton's affection for them has been further diminished after some of the more recent poundings that the Wallabies have suffered at the hands of the All Blacks.

There was a plaintive postscript. It said at the foot of the article that "Mr Chesterton has invited many New Zealanders to his house for dinner but never the same ones." I can well understand why. There would be no takers.

But let's not be too critical. Apart from dated curmudgeons like

Chesterton and a few sensation seeking shock-jocks around the populist fringes — something every country has to endure — the Australian sports media has been pretty generous to New Zealand rugby. Australians have recognised the All Blacks phenomenon for what it is and respected New Zealand's genetic credentials as something out of the ordinary when it comes to rugby union in much the same way as everybody else respects the freakish force that is Australian cricket. They know, too, that if it wasn't for New Zealand, rugby union in Australia would disappear as surely as the Tasmanian devil.

Some foreign critics have drawn attention to the vitriolic criticism dished out by members of the New Zealand rugby media to visiting teams. They have a point. There is a strongly complacent, if not arrogant, streak that runs just below the surface of the New Zealand media when it comes to rugby. At times it is so irrational, even offensive, that it is embarrassing to read. Where does this come from? It didn't exist a generation ago. Terry McLean, or Alex Veysey or Lindsay Knight or Bob Howitt never exhibited any of this splenetic acid. They understood what made rugby tick in other parts of the world and that was reflected in their perspectives. They were generous in their recognition of talent wherever it came from. Interestingly, this ugly aggression is largely confined to the press and radio. All of our television commentators show visiting teams a healthy respect, perhaps because almost all of them have played the game themselves at a higher level and understand it better.

The contrast between television and the other media is very striking. Unfortunately, the shock-jocks of talkback radio and the tabloid press, most of whom are devoid of any meaningful experience on the field, and some of whom are almost unbelievably stupid, give New Zealand a bad name in the wider rugby world and that in turn serves to further provoke assumptions of New Zealand arrogance. Fair-minded exceptions, like Brendan Telfer, stand out like beacons in a dark sky.

But this is not just plain old xenophobia at work. Our sports media can be almost unbelievably aggressive in criticising the rugby establishment in New Zealand. Everybody who is somebody in rugby gets the treatment one way or the other. The NZRU Board, the provincial unions, the IRB, Sanzar, the referees, the coaches, the sponsors, the broadcasters as well as the players are systematically berated for their shortcomings and stuff-ups. It was once said of newspaper critics that they tended to hide in the hills till the fighting was over, then came down and bayoneted the wounded. Our sports jocks don't do much hiding. They bayonet everyone in sight before war is even declared.

At one level this is just media sensationalism, common to all countries with a free press. As British Prime Minister Stanley Baldwin once described the tabloid press in England: "Power without responsibility — the prerogative of the harlot through the ages." The primary urge these days is not to lay out the facts but to elicit an emotional response from the reader, listener or viewer. Cheap shots, speculation, overstatement and plain fiction have become the order of the journalistic day and rugby writers are no different from their non-sporting counterparts.

But beneath the urge to sell more copy there is a more resonant recurring theme. It is deep dissatisfaction with the direction the game is taking and an objection to the commercial values that have infected it. All the latent spleen of the media has been increasingly focused on this issue and it helps to account for the extraordinary level of public disillusionment with rugby's direction.

The problem is very few among the media critics ever offer much by way of solutions. Opinions are one thing. Solutions are quite another. The blogosphere, for all its virtues, makes this immeasurably worse. There are a million opinions and hardly any facts. Only occasionally do we see reasoned, analytical arguments for change as against bald belligerence. Paul Lewis of the *Herald on Sunday*, Wynne Gray of the *New Zealand Herald* and Marc Hinton on the *Sunday Star-Times* stand out in New Zealand in this regard. They invariably take the bigger picture as their starting point. Spiro Zavos plays a similar role in Australia. Each understands the professional environment and the overlaying politics that shape the game. And each has a very good grasp of rugby's peculiar history. If only we had more of their sophisticated realism and less of the aggressive bombast that most of the media indulge in then the media might actually become part of the solution rather than remaining a significant part of the problem.

The Quicksands of Correctness

YOU WOULD have thought that the relatively banal business of conveying the ball up the field and depositing it over the opponents' goal-line wouldn't require much in the way of rules. If only. The rugby laws book is as opaque as the *Book of Kells*. It is so full of scope for ambiguity and misinterpretation that referees are on a hiding to nothing. Their problem is that all the rest of us are treated to the luxury of a televised replay of every arguable decision they make, and commentators aren't slow to point out their mistakes. The modern referees can be right and wrong at the same moment but, like traffic wardens, they dish out the ticket just to be on the safe side. They deserve better. The game deserves better. So do the players. And so do we who watch it.

This awful complexity is replicated in rugby's judicial system. There is nothing more absurd, it seems to me, than the sight of Queens Counsellors wasting their time and rugby's money at an elaborate gathering to decide the fate of a sinful rugby player. Whatever the moral intentions behind this, rugby's disciplinary system has become a pretentious farce. All too often the spectacle looks like a lift-out from *The Mikado*. A lot of pomp and not much circumstance.

Those who transgress are hauled before the "judiciary" in a manner more befitting the Spanish Inquisition than a momentary indiscretion on a footy field. Punishments are handed down with all the gravity of a Supreme Court with stern faces all round and suitably scripted admissions of remorse by the transgressors, penned delicately by legal counsel and read out to the general disbelief of anybody listening. It is ridiculous and it needs to be overhauled.

A number of years ago we had an archetypal example of judicial overkill, one that effectively set the tone for much that has followed since. It concerned none other than the All Blacks captain of the day, Taine Randell, normally the most polite and restrained of men. Randell was playing for the Highlanders in South Africa where one of his team-mates was cited for one of those offences that inevitably occur in a contact sport. This somehow escalated into a major issue in the minds of those in South Africa responsible for foul play. The player was hauled before a South African judicial panel and suspended for several weeks, much to the surprise of almost everybody who saw the incident.

Randell thought the decision taken by the South African judiciary stank but made the mistake of saying so. The full fury of rugby's clobbering machine was cranked into action. Randell was arraigned, charged with "serious misconduct", an offence which has become roughly comparable with sedition in the normal world, and an exhaustive examination of the facts began to wind itself up to full fury in New Zealand.

It is a measure of the absurd complexity of rugby's judicial system that this process couldn't be resolved in a single sitting of several hours, by a couple of rational people within the game rather than having to mobilise the legal profession, adding to the costs and the complication of it all. The Randell case was apparently far too important for that. After hours of rumination, examination of evidence, depositions of the various protagonists and extensive cross examination, the numerous participants duly departed back to their various ends of the country with orders to reassemble again several days later to finalise the matter.

It goes without saying that the lawyers' meters continued to tick inexorably while all concerned waited for Act II. Valuable human and other resources were diverted in order to enable this gigantic sledgehammer to crack a very modest nut. The facts were as plain as the nose on a hooker's face. Randell said the suspension dished out to one of his team-mates was outrageous and that the South African judiciary had got it horribly wrong. The fact that he was quite obviously right meant nothing. There wasn't any confusion because he said it again in the plainest of English when he arrived back in New Zealand. So why the melodrama?

Did it really matter if Randell voiced his feelings a little trenchantly?

Has the game really got an absolute right to muzzle all of its participants in this repressive way? Most of what the modern player says is so stupefying that nobody takes any real notice. Unless he points the finger at officialdom. Then all hell breaks loose.

If ever a case could have been made for a slap across the wrist with the proverbial wet bus ticket this was surely it. Alas, due process didn't allow for that. "Serious misconduct" required a stiff penalty. The South Africans expected nothing less and that is what Taine Randell got. It was a travesty of justice even if it was technically a breach of Randell's contract with the NZRU.

Nothing much has changed. Almost every week the same silly pantomime is repeated. Television footage shows a rolling maul of briefcase bearing lawyers accompanying suitably contrite looking players proceeding into a judicial hearing and then they show them coming out again to be breathlessly questioned by a news reporter on the ins and outs of the verdict. It is a gigantic disservice to a game that is starting to take itself excessively seriously. The QCs still line up for business and the costs to the game rise accordingly. I don't blame the lawyers for this. They are simply doing what they are contracted to do and it is exceedingly good business. But at whose expense?

It is rugby's own fault entirely for letting its judicial system become far too legalistic for its own good. Why on earth can't the union use ex-players: those who understand what it is like in the heat of the moment out there, and who are probably willing to do the job for nothing, to look at indiscretions on the field? Rugby has fallen into the same trap as other professional sports and allowed itself to be persuaded that it must have all the legal trappings if it is to be taken seriously as a sport. It is as if the game, not trusting its own capacity to be self-regulating, and fearful of being made to look unprofessional, has turned in desperation to the law and let the law get on top of it.

Playing against Wales in 2009 Dan Carter tackled a Welshman marginally high around the neck. Neither the referee nor his assistants, all of whom unquestionably saw the incident, was moved to punish Carter. The player wasn't injured. That should have been the end of the matter, but no. Carter was cited by some obscure official with that power after the match and obliged to fly from Milan to London for a hearing in the company of an eminent English QC and was given a one-match suspension. It was a complete waste of everybody's time and the game's money.

But it gets worse. The judicial arm of rugby extends well beyond what happens during the game. Take the case in 2009 when the Springboks team decided to wear little armbands saying "justice" in a test against the Lions in Johannesburg after Bakkies Botha had been given a two-week suspension for an offence which occurs a hundred times in every game but which will every now and again attract the wrath of a referee who has got out of the wrong side of his bed that morning. Bakkies Botha is a pest, a continual source of irritation to his opponents and to referees, but that didn't justify this particular dismissal. So, the Springboks decided to mount a little silent protest. It was at this point that almost everyone involved seemed to take complete leave of their senses. The sky fell. Someone in the IRB took offence at this silly protest and out came the big stick. The South Africans, including their national body, were accused of "demonstrating a clear disregard of the disciplinary process and doing so in a manner which brings, or has the potential to bring, the game into disrepute". Crikey. Is that all it really takes to "bring the game into disrepute"?

The IRB cranked up a full head of judicial steam. The South African Rugby Union was duly served notice of "disciplinary proceedings". The matter was referred to the independent judicial panel chairman who duly appointed not just one judicial officer but a whole committee assembled from various parts of the world, who duly found the South Africans guilty, imposed a monetary fine and issued a statement ringing with sanctimony, more evidence of a game that has begun to take itself much too seriously. Does a rather lame protest like this really bring the whole game of rugby into disrepute? As one commentator wryly observed, rugby's cosy relationship with the liquor industry should invoke rather more disrepute than that but never quite seems to.

This isn't to say that tough sanctions aren't ever justifed. They are entirely justified whenever drug abuse rears its ugly head. Fortunately, there are very few signs within the game of any real worries on this score, perhaps because of the vigilance of the system. When it comes to drugs a certain amount of heavy-handedness can be justified.

But that heavy-handedness seems to be applied in the wrong places.

The exotic case of the false blood used to remove English player Tom Williams from the field in a 2009 Heineken Cup match was one which deserved some measure of punishment but those involved, notably Harlequins Director of Rugby Dean Richards, had the book thrown at them. Richards, who readily confessed, should have been fined and left to get on with his career. Instead, he was effectively drummed out of the game, banned worldwide for three years and rendered unemployable thereafter. Instead, in weighed the RFU, echoed by the IRB, shouting zero tolerance. It was absurd. This was a relatively minor offence. Dodgy substitutions have become part of rugby's sub-culture. There was an almost theatrically amusing side to the use of false blood to get a goalkicker on to the field and it raised the obvious question: why can't the substitution laws be simplified.

But let us return to the relative normality of the on-field disciplinary regime. Rugby's card system is fatally flawed. Its sole virtue is that it provides a means of administering instant justice. But even in the case of a yellow card, there can be subsequent investigation and additional punishment. Two strikes for one indiscretion. Sin-binning has now become an irritating diversion. It doesn't seem to have any real impact on player behaviour, largely because most yellow card offences are unconsciously committed in the heat of the moment and many are the product of confusion over the rules. The majority of yellow cards are delivered either for high tackles, most of which are utterly harmless, or slowing play down in rucks, an area which can be relatively easily rectified by rule changes.

Why can't we have a simplified "report" system, as used in rugby league? In this way a referee doesn't need to take up unnecessary time in singling out a player, delivering the customary lecture which nobody takes any notice of, then dismissing the miscreant from the field and invariably skewing the result of the match as a result of the offender's team being reduced to 14 men. This is supremely dumb. It is scarcely justice to penalise a whole team for the indiscretion of a single individual. That is the equivalent of arresting a whole team because one member gets drunk and misbehaves at a nightclub. On the other hand, docking the pay of the player who transgresses is about as sure-fire a way of obtaining a behaviour change as you can get.

A player "on report" should preferably have his case dealt with immediately after the game by somebody appointed for that purpose by the local union. It should be based on television evidence and the advice of the referee and his two assistants if necessary and that should be the end of the matter. For the first offence a stiff fine would be appropriate. For a second offence within say a month, the player should be fined more heavily and mandatorily stood down for the next match. Such an arrangement would work, but only if the match official concerned had a sense of proportion. That is why a retired player is the ideal choice for such a duty.

Let us by all means keep the red card as the ultimate deterrent but it should be strictly reserved for gross acts of violence on the field. Should a player who is red-carded subsequently have to go through some sort of judicial process? That is debatable and it should depend on the gravity of the offence. The dangers of differential treatment are all too real. In 2009 Jimmy Cowan, the Highlanders halfback, was inexplicably red-carded for a late tackle on a Blues player and all hope the Highlanders had in that match went up the spout. So, too, did the match as a spectacle. The matter was definitely worth a penalty but the referee, to the amazement of most of those watching, dramatically produced a red card and in doing so red-carded the game.

To make matters worse Jimmy Cowan was subsequently exonerated by a judicial hearing and not given any suspension. The referee got it badly wrong, as have others all too often, partly because he was under pressure to have an immaculately clean game and partly because his so-called "assistant referees" got into the act as well. One can only lament the fact that the outcome would have been much more rational, time-saving and economical if the referee had been able to simply put Cowan on report and leave him on the field. Anyone who doubts the merits of this need only ask a spectator who has paid good money to come and see 15 versus 15 and who feels cheated when the contest is skewed in this way. It is only a matter of time before people start asking for their money back.

One way or another there needs to be a de-escalation of the judicial process. Provision for the independent citing of players afterwards should be scrapped as an utter absurdity. This silly provision has created a quasi-legal quagmire that threatens to make the game a laughing stock.

Rugby is complicated enough without wrapping it with unnecessary legal red tape.

Rugby has come a long way from its physically anarchic beginnings. There was a time when a referee would knit his brow slightly but do no more than that when witnessing a head-high tackle, a flailing fist or a thoroughly good rucking of an opponent unwise enough to get tangled up on the wrong side of the breakdown. Referees would really only react when a serious attempt to maim someone was made and most of them knew the difference between rough play and sadism.

The game certainly had its sadists. Every country had a notorious few who really did seem to enjoy causing injury to others. But these players never lasted very long, particularly at the top. They would be specifically targeted themselves and justice — the justice of the jungle if you like — would be administered. Rugby is infinitely cleaner today than it was in the 1960s and 70s. If anything, the pendulum has swung too far in the direction of player constraint. Any more and there is a real danger that it will lose its essence as a contact sport. As Tana Umaga so famously shouted at one excessively zealous referee, "We're not playing tiddly-winks here." Case dismissed.

Early in 2009 Brian Lochore offered an unusual observation during one of those bouts of public self-flagellation after a particularly offensive case of domestic violence. He suggested that rugby players of his generation were unlikely to have indulged in domestic violence because they were able to vent all their frustrations on the field. In other words, if you are to belt the opposing number 8 to your satisfaction then you are unlikely to belt your wife. This may have been wishful thinking on Sir Brian's part, and there is certainly no way of proving it, but it raises an intriguing question: are today's players unable to vent their frustrations adequately living in the virtual police state that contemporary rugby has become? Is this why so many of them appear to behave badly later in the evening? Or is that bad behaviour really no different to that of the male population at large? When an ordinary joker beats his wife the media neither notices nor cares unless it is violent enough to warrant a passing mention. An All Black does it and the sky caves in.

We have effectively removed all the opportunities to inflict damage on other players by the traditional means of punching, rucking, stomping and stiff-arm tackling. Some lament that. They feel the essential physicality of the game has been compromised. That is highly debatable. We still hear voices of nostalgia raised in favour of the right to ruck, however, and that is another matter. Southland invented it. Otago perfected it. Canterbury adopted it and so did the rest of the country. The All Blacks did it to everybody else for a century or more to howls of outrage from affronted Brits in particular. As a halfback I would often watch with morbid delight as an overly adventurous opponent silly enough to stray into our side of the ruck would come tumbling out the back of it followed by the ball.

We rather liked our reputation as a bunch of jolly ruckers. It got respect. But we overdid it from time to time and we lost respect. Every once in a while our trusty ruckers became untrustworthy stompers. The deeds of John Ashworth and others, while no doubt entirely motivated by healthy nationalism, had decidedly unhealthy impacts on unfortunate opponents — and on their opponents' supporters.

Nostalgia is nice but nostalgia for the good old days of rucking is little more than wishful thinking. Rugby's lawmakers are far too squeamish to allow use of the boot for anything other than kicking the ball. There is a steadfast refusal to draw a distinction between rucking and stomping any more and that is a pity because genuine rucking almost always resulted in the ball being freed up and continuity preserved. It is arguable that the inability to use the feet to clear the ball has been a major cause of the slowing down of recycling of the ball, the single most important key to maintaining momentum. Unfortunately, use of the hands has also been outlawed and the result is the ball gets lodged in the mass of bodies and stays there.

Ironically, many of the penalisable moments at the ruck and maul are the result of what is graphically known as the "clean-out". This recently sanctioned practice enables players on either side of the ball carrier to shoulder charge opponents out of the way at a ruck, even though they don't have the ball. It is the dopiest law yet invented, an attempt to solve a problem by creating several others.

Try as they might, the law-makers can't seem to fix the ruck and maul problem. They introduced a law whereby a player has to be able to "bear his own weight" at the breakdown in order to contest the ball on the ground. That is like asking a sprinter to guess his own speed, and needless to say results in more or less total confusion as players, half on their feet and half off, try to play to the law, and fail. Players must come into the ruck "through the gate", an imaginary portal somewhere at the back of a pile of cascading bodies. This too is asking for trouble and it too results in a constant stream of penalties.

The laws forbid any player from using his hands in a ruck yet any halfway observant spectator can see hands being used all the time to propel the ball to the back of the ruck or to adjust it so that the halfback can get at it more easily. The referees seem oblivious to this, presumably on the grounds that the ball has already been secured. This begs the obvious question: why not let players use their hands whenever they like to contest the ball? If they aren't allowed to ruck it free then it seems absurd to take away the other option as well. If the no hands law was scrapped rugby would be immeasurably improved as a contest and the recycling of the ball would be sped up. Players would no longer have to stop and think, can I or can't I? Will I or won't I? We all like watching an arm-wrestle. This would guarantee one and, if you're squeamish, it's the next best thing to rucking.

If only rugby's law-makers would make up their minds that either hands or feet need to be liberated we might see some progress. Instead we are seeing an incessant manipulation of the various laws relating to the breakdown — and there are plenty of them — to try to achieve the same outcome. Thus, new layers of complexity are added and new justifications for stopping play are added to the referee's bloated worksheet. The "experimental law variations" which came to be known as the ELVs were an interesting innovation and some of them went on to be adopted. But they weren't adopted uniformly in the Northern or Southern hemisphere and they led to discord and confusion. They showed all too clearly that a piecemeal approach to the lawbook is self-defeating.

There is no argument that rugby has benefited from the probing eye of the TV zoom lens. Television now goes where the naked eye often can't and it preserves the image, for later review, in ways that were never possible even 20 years ago. But rugby still has its darkened recesses, when bodies are on the ground and the contest for possession is at its fiercest. That is invariably the time when the only really serious offences occur. Eye gouging is the most notorious of these but there are others.

There have been calls to modify this dimension of the game by zealots who want nothing short of absolute sanitisation. Every time a serious offence occurs, as for instance when Schalk Burger, the Springbok, eye-gouged one of the 2009 British Lions, it immediately sparks off a bout of soul searching, a noisy clamour among the less informed that rugby has become brutal, dirty, unmanageable. It's the same repetitive refrain each time, entirely free of any appreciation of how far the game has already been cleaned up. Calls echo for stricter policing, more severe penalties, expulsions, life bans, executions.

Such demands should be resisted. Any more sanitisation and rugby will be relatively indistinguishable from tiddly-winks. Without the contest for possession rugby would lose its single greatest point of difference. It is this that gives rugby its most precious, random, unstructured character. American football is rough and tough but it has no real contest for the ball. Nor does rugby league. Play stops with a tackle and that's it. In rugby things are just getting started when there's a tackle.

The most ardent efforts are being made to protect players from doing damage to one another but, in one of the richest ironies of all in the modern game, the players are now so bulked up and muscle-bound that they are more of a danger to themselves than to anyone else. Most injuries are wrenches, strains and breaks caused simply because of their size and their fitness which means they arrive at collision zones more or less at terminal velocity. High tackles or late tackles, almost all of which are unintended, account for a minute fraction of the injuries sustained, yet we see penalty after penalty dished out by referees who seem to have become obsessed with removing these from the game entirely. The same goes for tackling without the arms. How many injuries does this produce? I can't remember the last one.

As for the throwing of punches, well, here we seem to have turned the law upside down. He who throws the first short jab invariably goes unpunished, but he who retaliates with a haymaker gets the book thrown at him. Excuse me? If there is a belief in natural justice then it certainly isn't being applied by the arbiters of rugby. Tempers will inevitably fray. A skilled referee like Jonathan Kaplan for instance will pause and think for a moment before deciding what, if any, punishment is most appropriate. At the moment we have excessive intrusion by the assistant referees, either piously pointing out the bleedingly obvious, or stopping the play for something the referee already saw and dismissed as too innocuous to bother about.

It is infuriating to have play interrupted by Sideline Sam who rushes on to the field to point out that a minor scuffle has occurred half a minute ago which had no impact on the game whatever but which the referee is obliged to stop proceedings for and investigate. Giving touch judges more powers is like inviting a traffic warden to issue more tickets. It is an open incentive to meddle. As these officials become ever more risk averse the number of stoppages rises accordingly as the crowd groans with frustration. Now there is talk of multiple referees. Someone as normally sensible as Wayne Smith has suggested that adopting the rugby league practice of two referees, one to watch general play, the other to police the off-side laws, is a logical next step. If there is that much consternation over offside play then why not give that job to the touch judges? Who knows, it might take their minds off other trivia.

The truth is, rugby is slowly being suffocated by the immense amount of time, effort and science that goes into defence. The so-called "picket fence" of defenders spread across the field has become the defining image of the game. Backlines are cluttered up with forwards after almost every breakdown. There is all too often an interminable delay while the ball sits at the base of the ruck until a decision is made on what to do next and players hasten to their pre-ordained positions to start afresh. This pattern is repeated until somebody decides in a panic that it's time to spread the ball wider. Unfortunately, the picket fence is usually impenetrable and the whole thing starts over again. While this is happening the referee can be heard barking instructions to any potential offender. "Roll away No 2." "Hands off, you're off your feet, No 7." "Release it, No 5."

This regulatory patter is sustained throughout the match. There are more words than whistle. Lengthy explanations are being provided even while play is continuing. Referees are also headed down the dangerous path of excessive familiarity with players by resorting to first names, as if this lends something to the collegial nature of the relationship. It doesn't. Players are increasingly disputing decisions or asking how on earth the referee could have made such a decision. There is so much information being traded that even Sean Fitzpatrick would eventually be lost for words. The most absurd element in all this dialogue is the pause called by a referee, much to the frustration of everybody watching, to deliver a lecture about the imminent consequences of further infringement of a certain kind, and a request to the opposing captains to "have a word" with the rest of his team about the consequences. It is a total pantomime. The captains can be seen muttering something which, in all probability, is more of a commentary on the referee's state of mind than any plea to his colleagues to stop offending.

Do today's referees have too complicated a job? They are thoroughly trained, expertly advised, as familiar with the rules as any human being is likely to get and they have the contributions of two assistants on the sidelines and another eagle eye upstairs to make judgements for them on whether or not a try is scored. How much more back-up does anybody need?

The answer to that is none. What they need is simplification of the rules, the complexity of which make for most refereeing errors. The lineout now has something in excess of 40 separate laws governing it alone. How many of those are vital? 10? Perhaps 20? There isn't much point in throwing more manpower into the mix when as likely as not you will finish up with four different opinions. There are now so many situations where it is more or less impossible to tell who is the offender. Around the tackle area it is a veritable lottery and one can sympathise with a referee who hasn't really a clue as to who is guilty of what but who is obliged to make a decision one way or another. The same can be said of the scrum. Very few referees have ever played in the front row. Very few of them could put hand on heart and say they know more than 50 per cent of the time why a scrum collapses. There are so many physical dynamics going on that the causes are often entirely random. There is a welter of bio-mechanical science alone in the technique of front row forward play. Prop forwards may be right when they make the unlikely claim that it takes more intelligence to play there than it does to run about like a startled rabbit in the backline. A whole new vocabulary is springing up. "Hinging" for example. I haven't a clue what that involves and I suspect that very few referees do either.

The French call the scrum the *mêlée*. The *Oxford English Dictionary* defines a *mêlée* as a "muddle". There is a connection. Most scrums are a bugger's muddle. They are confused and confusing but they don't really have to be. Collapsed scrums are a relatively recent phenomenon. They are the product of ever larger front rows trying ever harder to get an early shove on the opposition and the rest of the forward pack propelling their three stormtroopers into the collision that causes mayhem. All this "crouch-touch-pause-engage" nonsense simply heightens the anticipation of collision. The referee sounds like the caller at a barn dance. "Crouch and touch, there we go, pause, engage, do-se-do."

Surely it would be easier to adopt the rugby league-style engagement, that is, a non-confrontational engagement of the two front rows, without the massive collision between two 900-plus kilogram battering rams that causes so much worry about safety. Once the scrum is set the referee would then simply say "enter" and that would be the simultaneous signal to both packs to push and to the halfback to put the ball in. That way the contest is preserved, the aggravation is removed and the continuity is maintained. Most significantly, the likelihood of a collapse, the greatest villain of the set-piece, is all but completely removed. That is actually the way it worked until a couple of decades ago and scrums were usually over and done with quickly. This is one area where a little back-to-the-future thinking might not come amiss.

If there is a single threat to the future of the game it is the infuriating complexity of the rules. The consequences of not getting this right are all too obvious. A game that is as complicated as rugby has little or no hope of growing both in participation and spectator interest, particularly when it's competing with something as uncomplicated as football. People simply aren't going to tolerate something they can't understand, particularly when even experienced commentators can't demystify it for them.

So, let us have the bottom-up review, fully sanctioned by the IRB, with a specific mandate to simplify. Rugby's laws book is a body riddled with small tumours. It needs radical surgery, not more pills.

Nasty, Brutish and Short

LIKE MANY other professional sports, rugby has been lured into the belief that coaching represents the vital difference between success and failure. That is an illusion, and a dangerous one because it is really only at lower levels of the game that coaching has any definite effect. At international or Super 14 level the best coaches are those who are the most skilled in the art of motivation and man management. The best coaches let the players make the key decisions, invest in the players' maximum responsibility for what happens on the field and accept that their personal impact must always remain at the margins. Unfortunately, very few coaches operate that way.

The life of any international coach seems to have become akin to that of a medieval serf — nasty, brutish and short. If these were the Middle Ages a losing All Blacks coach would be stretching on the rack and the players would be outside in the stocks with rotten vegetables being thrown at them by early Sunday morning. Tolerance of failure is ever more limited all over the rugby world. The length of tenure is shortening. If a coach can last more than a couple of seasons these days he is regarded as an over-achiever. But over-achievement is in short supply for the rather simple reason that it is immeasurably harder to deliver on expectations than it ever was before. Under-achievement has become the norm because no team is unbeatable.

Coaching, believe it or not, is a relatively recent phenomenon at the international level, at least officially. For its first 100 years or so rugby tests were a coach-free zone. The very word "coach" conjured up notions of furtive backhanders in exchange for technical or tactical advice. No international team was permitted to have such a thing as a coach and for many years in the 1940s, 50s and 60s the de facto coach would be disguised as an "assistant manager".

I discovered in the late 60s that this charade was at the behest of the Rugby Football Union whose members despised the notion of professional coaching and kept the floodgates firmly bolted as long as they possibly could. In 1968 the RFU took its first, tentative step towards the recognition that coaching was finally OK, that coaches were to be brought out of the closet of unacceptability and given official recognition. Up till then, British rugby had steadfastly refused to acknowledge the growing reality that coaches had become an integral part of the game. Coaching was already something of an art in Wales but the individuals concerned were shadowy figures, never acknowledged in public — furtive little men in grubby overcoats who lurked in the shrubbery and who were let out when a club was sure nobody was watching. There were rumours that these men were actually paid for their efforts and that made it twice as bad.

There was much debate about this at the East India and Sportsmen's Club where the RFU had its headquarters. Many, perhaps most of the Old Farts of English rugby, were dead against letting coaches anywhere near the tradesmen's entrance, let alone through the front door. To let coaching gain a foothold was the equivalent of ignoring foot and mouth disease. They particularly disapproved of touring teams bringing coaches and these men often went virtually unrecognised. Fred Allen and others who coached teams from New Zealand, South Africa and Australia were an embarrassing imposition. The French of course were far more open about their coaches but then the French were, at the time, beyond the pale. So far as the RFU was concerned wogs definitely began at Calais.

There was considerable resistance to the invasion of the coaches in the English rugby media as well. Uel Titley, evoking the mood of the time in official circles, described coaches as a "scourge", an unwanted influence that somehow demeaned the amateur spirit. In his view coaches were to rugby what dogs are to lamp posts and he and others in the media made it clear that this particularly slippery slope was not one the Rugby Football Union should set foot on, however tentatively.

In 1969 things suddenly began to change. There were just enough men of vision on the union to sway the vote in favour of at least talking about the issue with officials from the various constituent clubs and counties. As is always the habit when an institution wants to make haste slowly, the RFU decided to form a committee to discuss the whys and wherefores of coaching. Perhaps because I had had direct experience of playing under formally recognised coaches in New Zealand I was invited along to offer my perspective. I was the only player to be invited and this was regarded as a singular honour by my team-mates as the RFU had never before directly consulted a player on anything at all.

I was asked, by formal letter from the RFU secretary, to present myself at the East India and Sportsmen's Club promptly at midday the following Friday. The meeting would be preceded by lunch and was expected to take up most of the afternoon. When I arrived the rest of the committee — various county chairmen and RFU officials — and of course the privileged representatives of Oxford and Cambridge universities, were in the bar warming to the task ahead.

At 1.30pm on the dot we sat down to lunch and at around 3pm the chairman, whose name I have long forgotten but whose nose which glowed brilliantly in the half-light of the dining room I will never forget, called us to order and announced, "I don't know what all the rest of you think about this coaching business but as far as I'm concerned it's a lot of bally nonsense and the sooner we're shot of it the better." With this he attacked the port bottle with renewed vigour and declared the meeting closed. So that was that on coaching.

The committee, as far as I know, never met again and it was another year or two before the RFU got serious. In 1971 the four home unions finally decided to appoint a coach for the Lions team and the RFU gave way. The fact that the coach, Carwyn James, was Welsh must have made it all that much harder but James was a genius and the Lions won and from then on coaching was almost obligatory.

The art of coaching is a mix of technical know-how, astute man management and plain good luck. It isn't a vocation for the faint-hearted. Appointing a coach is like buying a new car. The product begins to depreciate the moment you sign the cheque and coaches have two phases of life: they are either being sacked or preparing to be sacked.

The life of the coach of the All Blacks — who is invariably first on the receiving end of public intolerance — is rendered miserable by this relentless dissatisfaction. It began when the professional era began and the prospects of perpetual All Blacks victories were fatally compromised. Before that, coaches were regarded with relative respect. Brian Lochore achieved virtual sainthood by pulling the All Blacks through to win the 1987 World Cup. Even "Grizz" Wyllie who faltered in the 1991 World Cup campaign and Laurie Mains, who did the same in 1995, were given relatively benign send-offs by a thwarted rugby public. John Hart wasn't anywhere near as lucky. When his side lost to an irresistibly inspired French performance the sky fell on him.

The trouble with our approach to All Blacks coaches is that we don't like giving them enough rope to hang themselves. We like to do it for them. Each test match produces its own whirlwind of recrimination. Once upon a time a win was enough. Honour preserved. Not any more. Now, a mere win is never enough. If the opponent isn't England, South Africa or Australia, it has to be a score-fest massacre to pass muster. And a loss is of course catastrophic. It is a signal to dump the lot of them and find others who can provide instant gratification. Until of course that lot fail to deliver perfection the next time up. Then what?

New Zealand has had a number of outstanding coaches whose chief virtue has been an ability to unite their players behind a single purpose every time they step out to play. Fred Allen and his successors through the 70s and 80s relied on a simplicity of purpose, concentration on the basics and a blind faith in the absolute will of All Blacks teams to win, no matter what the physical cost. Fred's team talks were enough to scare the pants off any player, to the point where the opposition seemed almost incidental. It worked well enough in its time but as the game became more complex in the 1990s real specialist skill was essential. A single coach wasn't enough any more. Earle Kirton, a master strategist, was brought in to manage backplay alongside Laurie Mains. Brian Lochore concentrated his attention on basic forward skills, as did Grizz Wyllie while relying on backplay specialists as assistants.

John Hart was something of an exception. More of a manager than a coach, Hart was more interested in team systems and "culture". He set the tone for All Blacks coaches for almost a decade by seizing total control and paid a fearful price for that when his All Blacks team failed at the World Cup. When Hart's immaculately prepared All Blacks lost spectacularly in 1999 it was he who was pilloried yet it wasn't Hart who missed all those tackles or whose mental fortitude failed when things began to go wrong. His players lost it; not him. It was senior All Blacks like Jeff Wilson and Christian Cullen who were panicked into chaos. Somehow — wrongly — it became all Hart's fault and he was driven out of the job by the most hateful irrationality ever seen in New Zealand rugby. The reason for that was as much a rejection of Hart's corporate management style as anything that happened on the field.

From then on the theme has been a recurrent one. Basically, it has been one strike and you're out. Through the media, on the streets, in the pubs, the mob howled for blood. Wayne Smith found the pressure of this irrational negativity too much to bear and did a runner for the Northern hemisphere. It turned out to be a smart move because within a few years he was back again, stronger, wiser, and has done outstandingly well within the safety of a triumvirate.

John Mayhew, the wise and well-honed All Blacks team doctor, fired a very interesting shot on Smith's departure from the camp. It was a mistake, he said, to abandon Smith at the time the NZRU did. What he didn't say in so many words was that Smith's departure was the result of panic which was all too characteristic of that particular NZRU board and it showed how basically immature the governance of New Zealand rugby was at the time. Smith contributed to his own demise, it has to be said, by suffering a crisis of confidence in his own ability and publicly expressed doubts about whether he wanted to carry on. That situation should never have been allowed to arise. It was caused as much by an absence of solidarity around him prompted by an unseemly media frenzy in the wake of a couple of defeats. Wayne Smith was effectively driven out of office while the NZFU board hid behind the sofa.

What a contrast with the steadfast support afforded to Clive Woodward at the same time in the late 1990s, despite a rash of defeats in Europe following an embarrassingly inept England tour of Australia and New Zealand. The RFU in London had no intention of dumping Woodward in spite of a series of tabloid-led broadsides every bit as nasty as those dished up by the hired assassins of the New Zealand sports media. Clive Woodward survived all the way through till 2005, a miracle in modern sport. The mass suicide by the 2005 Lions in New Zealand was essentially the players' responsibility but it was Woodward who was finally ushered to the RFU door.

Wayne Smith's successor, John Mitchell, without reading the teacups particularly well, adopted a very uncompromising stance, yet, for all his sterner countenance, found the world bearing in on him just as frighteningly and it quickly became plain to him and everybody else that the only way he would survive in the job was by winning the World Cup. He didn't; and he didn't.

Success often masks human deficiency. It washes away the blood that is so often shed in seeking it. John Mitchell wasn't your average joker who happened to be a passably good rugby coach. He was a perfectionist and a control freak, a complicated and excessively sensitive man who didn't like having to deal with lesser beings and nuisances, rather like Winston Churchill, or Napoleon, or Joe Stalin for that matter. When he spoke publicly it was in a bizarre, management psycho-babble that nobody could follow. It was all about a "journey" but nobody was entirely sure what the stopovers were. Mitchell foolishly assumed he would be safe. He wasn't because when it comes to the World Cup the only safety is a winner's medal.

The NZRU administration frankly admitted that they got the job description wrong. They bowed, unwisely in retrospect, to pressure from John Mitchell to grant him absolute control as a result of a personality clash between Mitchell and Andrew Martin, the affable ex-military man who had become the All Blacks manager and was making a fairly good job of putting a smiling countenance on the unsmiling giants.

Martin, while he wasn't an expert at answering the more technical questions thrown up at press conferences, was a real asset that the NZRU mistakenly sent packing because he and Mr Mitchell apparently couldn't see eye to eye. In retrospect the two of them should have been put in a padded cell and told to get over it and not come out till they had. The cause was far too important for this to hijack it. Unfortunately, those differences prevailed.

The same thing happened when Mitchell surfaced again several years later as the coach of the new Australian Super 14 franchise, the Western Force. Mitchell began insisting on absolute power once again and soon got up the noses of those around him. It became so bad that, instead of just sacking him forthwith, the franchise pussyfooted its way around the issue by hiring a retired high court judge to conduct an inquiry which revealed — no doubt at crippling expense — what everybody already knew: that John Mitchell's style was just too earnest and intrusive. In a classic compromise they clipped his wings somewhat and hoped for the best.

Mitchell was particularly severe on one player — Christian Cullen — and had to face the wrath of an All Black forsaken. Mitchell was unnerved by the trenchant personality that Anton Oliver brought to any team, just as he was uncertain about the whimsical side of Andrew Mehrtens' character. He dumped them too. Christian Cullen heaved off to kiss the Blarney Stone in Ireland but must have been sorely tempted, after the World Cup débâcle, to deliver a message wrapped in a brick heaved through Mitchell's window with the words "I told you so."

John Mitchell, for all his inadequacies in terms of selection and communication, delivered up to the starting line an All Blacks team that everybody knew could and should have won the World Cup. The players blew it on the field but Mitchell was the first and arguably the only casualty. Not a single player sprang to his defence although several suggested, shyly, that defeat might have had rather more to do with their performance on the day than anything else.

The lesson, as if it really needed to be learned, was that one man cannot fulfil a job description that effectively asked for three different qualities, technical expertise, public relations panache, and managerial precision. It was a ridiculous amalgam. There isn't anything like it in the business world, well not since Tony O'Reilly stood down as President, Chairman and Chief Executive of Heinz. But then Tony wasn't your average businessman, let alone human being. It took a while before the lesson sunk in that it's better to have a coach who just coaches and lets someone else represent the public persona of the All Blacks team.

At the end of 2003 after a winter of considerable discontent, New Zealand rugby made one of the better decisions it has ever made. It appointed Graham Henry as coach of the All Blacks and the result was a big jump-shift in the appreciation of what a really good head coach can achieve, particularly when the coaching team actually like each other. The decision to endorse him and his associates all the way to Paris 2007 rested on that appreciation. It was the right thing to do.

It's a long time since we had a coach with both grace and gravitas. One has to go all the way back to Brian Lochore for that. Graham Henry has a wisdom born of many miles on life's clock, and it shows. Henry is known to have, shall we say, limited regard for those who bay for blood every time the All Blacks lose and he is not easily spooked by public criticism.

He is basically a cynic and success in the upper reaches of achievement these days demands a healthy sense of cynicism to match and at times to moderate vaulting idealism and enthusiasm. It keeps you sane and it keeps things in proportion. Henry has an acerbic wit, almost combustible in its dryness. Gone is all that talk of pathways and journeys, the management babble that John Mitchell, and before him John Hart, learned to recite like tracts of blank verse that are only partly understood. Henry is much more given to the use of plain English and that's been a huge bonus.

Henry has also succeeded in ensuring that All Blacks feet remain firmly on the ground. There is a little less strut on the part of some of those who had become inclined to believe their own publicity. The All Blacks of 2004 and, especially, 2005, showed a maturity and calmness that could only come from the kind of deep personal influence that an older man with real ability to get into the mind of his charges can exert. Henry was instrumental in bringing Tana Umaga up to full speed as a leader and to sowing a leadership seed throughout a squad that didn't seem to have much of that quality. He brought some discipline to wayward souls like Ali Williams; no mean task indeed. And he recognised the particular talents of Anton Oliver who in many respects was not dissimilar in character to himself. Henry's mantra, a simple one really, is that better people make for better rugby players and he set about making those All Blacks better people.

He didn't succeed with all of them and the evidence of that has been paraded in the newspapers and occasionally through the courts. Some people are rather more of a challenge than others and the pressure on individuals is unrelenting. There was always a hint that Tana Umaga couldn't be completely domesticated by the Henry formula. There were clashes with Jerry Collins that never quite made the public view but which didn't reflect particularly well on either man. Overall, however, Henry brought a reassuring sense of stability and pragmatism — the kind of qualities that give the Australian cricket team its competitive edge — and it worked. Henry asked for, and got, the right to pull All Blacks out of the 2007 Super 14 competition, something that raised many eyebrows and more than a few complaints, not least from News Corp who apparently hadn't been consulted. He used a rotation system that prompted some critics to declare that it undervalued the All Blacks jersey. Was he right on either or both counts? Nobody really knew.

It was almost unimaginable that an All Blacks team loaded with talent and experience, and infinitely stronger in terms of personal responsibility, should stumble again at the 2007 World Cup. But stumble they did and the finger was immediately pointed at Henry. "Rotation caused it!" thundered one all-knowing Sunday paper. "Not enough games beforehand," declared several others, equally certain that this was the reason for the failure in Cardiff. Some even suggested that the All Blacks weren't paid as much as the French and therefore didn't have enough incentive to beat them!

It is possible that the rotation policy and the early season resting played a marginal part in the defeat. The more likely reason was that fatal sense of over-abundance that can cause a great team to play beneath its full potential every once in a while. The players are so sure of their ability to beat the opposition that they forget to do the little things well enough to ram their superiority home. There is no rocket science in this. It is a well documented phenomenon in high level sport and it afflicts all teams that are red-hot favourites at some point or another. Still, it's a pity that it always seems to afflict the All Blacks at World Cup time.

The hardest coaching job in the world is that of keeping the best team's nose to the grindstone. Graham Henry knows that painfully well after 2007, and the decision to reappoint the coaching panel after that shock loss to the French was a welcome sign, at last, of real maturity of thought in the NZRU. The media shock-jocks brayed for Robbie Deans. Many of them resented Henry's subtle and sardonic manner, interpreting this as contempt for them. They may have been right but then any sane man would be driven to distraction by the growing cadre of trivialists, conspiracy theorists and addicts of sensationalism that the rugby media seems to have spawned in recent years.

Happily, the appointment panel looked at the facts and resisted the temptation. Henry, Hansen and Smith are about as accomplished a coaching team as the All Blacks will ever have and Robbie Deans's time will unquestionably come. It will come sooner rather than later if the All Blacks lose at home in 2011, even if, as the critics will of course never acknowledge, defeat or victory once the players take the field has very little to do with the coach.

The Cup that Underflows

THERE WAS a time, before the World Cup was ever thought of, when the International Rugby Board consisted of a few affable codgers meeting several times a year to exchange pleasantries washed down by a gin and tonic or two. Their vocation was to keep things as they were. They were masters of no-change management. The IRB was run as an offshoot of the Rugby Football Union in London and was more or less totally at the beck and call of the four significantly named "Home" Unions.

The decision to create a world championship, taken in the amateur era, was a good example of the Southern hemisphere finally getting its way in the face of mule-like obstinacy among the Home Unions. This was the most significant step the game had taken since the defection of the northern unions 80 years earlier. It wasn't welcomed by the Home Unions who, in the best high Tory tradition, were as appalled by the thought as they were of Britain joining the EU. The Southern hemisphere unions, through a mixture of threat, flattery and cajoling, eventually got their way. What we didn't appreciate at the time was that it put rugby on a track that was to lead inexorably to professionalism.

Sport has long been about politics and money but it seems to get particularly grubby when global tournaments are up for grabs. Rugby is no longer the exception now that we have a World Cup bidding contest that slavishly replicates what every other global sport does.

The company that rugby keeps in this context is hardly inspiring. The Olympics have become an unseemly auction. The International Olympic Committee is little more than a highly commercialised version of the UN General Assembly. The only sound to be heard above the cacophony of voices all talking past each other is the noise of mass mutual back scratching. You don't get the Olympics without scattering an awful lot of favours around capitals. The Football World Cup is much the same. It involves so much horse-trading that there may eventually have to be WTO rules devised to manage the deals. The stories that circulate about the merry men of FIFA, regularly revealed to the world by assiduous British journalists, would make your hair stand on end.

We all thought that rugby was purer in spirit, a league of gentlemen all in it for the pleasure of the game and the comradeship that originally gave the game its unique ethos. Well, all that has gone well and truly out the window now that we have the four-yearly tag wrestling contest for the right to become mine host and bag all those tourist and merchandising dollars.

Consider the competitive warfare in recent times. In 1999 England and Wales did a deal to head off the French, ruffling many feathers. In 2003 Australia and New Zealand were all set to be co-hosts until a meltdown in relations caused New Zealand to be dumped as supporting host. France finally got its way in 2007 but only after a backroom deal involving Scotland and Wales as round robin and quarter-finals hosts. New Zealand sneaked past Japan and South Africa for 2011, putting both of their noses firmly out of joint and resulting in accusations from Japan of old Commonwealth bias. For once, success was achieved without doing side deals but by appealing to sentiment, waving around virtual placards reading "A stadium of 4 million people" and "If not now, never."

The World Cup is a highly entertaining, very lucrative (at least for the IRB) and compelling competition but it doesn't actually create more global unity. Arguably, it has the opposite effect and there's been lots of back-scratching and side dealing in the run-up to the decision to grant the 2015 tournament to England and 2019 to Japan.

It has been said that co-hosting, which had become almost the norm until New Zealand got sole rights to 2011, serves to water the whole thing down. Teams find themselves hopping back and forth between countries, as do spectators. But what's wrong with that? If the distances aren't prohibitive, which effectively makes it all but impossible in the Southern hemisphere, then co-hosting should be encouraged. After all, aren't we all supposed to be in this together?

The IRB has become famous for its Shylock-like approach. The four-yearly tournament is the great money spinner for rugby. New Zealand's down-payment for the 2011 hosting rights was £46 million. That was just a down-payment. Added to that are the most astonishingly intrusive conditions which a country must meet. They bear a startling resemblance in their spirit of coercion to the IMF's lending conditions to impoverished developing countries.

Basically, the host country yields up all its commercial rights for the entire duration of the tournament. Its only source of revenue is the gate takings. The IRB's operating arm, Rugby World Cup Ltd, gets the advertising revenue in and around all stadiums. Everything that is suggestive of commercial promotion must be removed and replaced by advertising sold by the IRB for the duration. The IRB controls access to all corporate boxes and suites, which it hocks off to the highest bidder, and it enjoys an effective monopoly over all promotion and merchandising. The host country is obliged to guarantee all these intrusions in advance, something which proved exceptionally difficult for New Zealand as a subsidiary host in 2003 because what it guaranteed, in advance, was a substantial loss.

New Zealand rugby is also guaranteed to make a substantial loss in 2011 if you set aside the multiplier effect in terms of visitor spending. Were it not for fairly massive financial backing from the government, both in up-front cash and in terms of subsidising stadium development, the whole deal would be hopelessly impractical for a country of New Zealand's size and stadium capacity. Governments of course are now an essential player in the World Cup syndrome. They make their own judgements about how much that investment is likely to benefit the local economy in terms of tourism receipts and international exposure, and invest accordingly. There's nothing wrong with that in principle, even if it is hotly contested by those who maintain that governments have no business throwing taxpayer money at a professional sporting event which yields returns only to a limited range of private service industries. In other words, some will profit, most will pay for the pleasure of having the tournament.

When New Zealand was dealt out of the 2003 World Cup hosting rights there was a general feeling that that was the last opportunity; that the price of hosting would simply be beyond the capacity of a country as small as

New Zealand in future. Our view was coloured to some extent by the horrifying inequity of being a subsidiary host. And there was the lingering smell of the utterly hopelessly compromised relations between the NZRU and a government that refused to underwrite the bid, then proceeded, via the extraordinarily crude behaviour of Sports Minister Trevor Mallard, to blight our relations with the IRB and most of its members.

A couple of years later it became apparent that it might just be manageable if the NZRU and the government could actually find a way of working together. This time they were better prepared. There was real polish applied to the 2011 bid and none of the previous surly equivocation about relative cost. Fences were repaired, thanks not just to New Zealand's more decorous approach but, crucially, to new, more honest leadership at the IRB.

Nevertheless, the bill for hosting the tournament in 2011 remains a frightening one, so much so that the IRB has started a re-think of its invoicing policy. It realised that the way things were going future hosting would be confined to about four countries. So, in late 2008, the IRB announced a new tournament fee structure for Rugby World Cup 2015 and 2019 bidders in order, it said, "to give an added boost to the competitiveness of the process". The IRB Council decided that the minimum tournament fee for 2015 be reduced to £80 million from £100 million and that the minimum tournament fee for 2019 be reduced to £96 million from £120 million. The IRB also agreed to "incentivise" the host unions by building in a profit share formula for any tournament surplus it generates that exceeds the minimum guarantee. What a pity it didn't see fit to offer that to New Zealand in the midst of a major recession.

The decision was obviously prompted by the downward spiral of the world economy and much negative feedback from the nine member unions who were tendering to host one or other of these tournaments. The decision was tempered, however, by the blunt declaration that "Rugby World Cup is one of, if not the most, cost effective major sports events in the world, estimated to have the potential to generate up to £2.1 billion in economic benefits while capital expenditure costs are among the lowest for an event of this magnitude". Small comfort.

The IRB also, significantly, admitted that it had had extensive consultation with governments in the countries concerned and had reached its decision on the basis of this. In other words it had been given the message loudly and clearly that member countries simply weren't prepared to sell off their grandmothers to host the tournament. It is the "cost" in "cost effective" that has proven to be the major barrier and it is obvious that when the recession is over that threshold price will continue to go up. That in turn means only one thing. New Zealand or any other of the smaller members will never again be able to host the World Cup.

We will, instead, see the emergence of wealthy marginal rugby communities like Dubai or Hong Kong or even Shanghai entering the running as potential hosts. Is that necessarily a bad thing? Probably not. What is more important is that emerging rugby countries get more opportunity to participate.

The World Cup is having a huge impact on the growth of rugby in Africa, Asia, the Americas and Eastern Europe. The visual impact of its bash, crash body contact has attracted vicarious interest far and wide and the IRB has capitalised on an expanding television audience out at the frontiers. They watch it as a substitute for the *Transformers* or the *Terminator* here, there and everywhere. It's being played in Scandinavia where the Swedish women even do a haka. It's gaining ground in parts of China, especially in the military where the big guys from the north seem to revel in it in their time off from quelling protests or cleaning up after natural disasters. Scottish coach Frank Hadden turned up in Mongolia where the rough and tumble of rugby fits nicely with the Mongolians' rugged outdoor habits.

It's all go and much of it is driven by a desire to be involved in international competition and ultimately the World Cup. How, then, should those who regulate the World Cup respond to this? At the moment it is a relatively simple system whereby countries qualify according to their place on the international rating system or via regional elimination games. The tournament is divided into pools designed to eliminate the weakest in the round robin phase. This seems to work tolerably well, but is it the best option?

A few years ago England proposed a radical refit to the World Cup format with a two-tier competition designed to eliminate the awful mismatches that occur each time and which render the first phase of the tournament irrelevant.

England were of course at the time bidding to become hosts to the 2007 tournament and the proposal was directly responsible for England's failure to get it. The idea just didn't wash. Most of the weaker rugby nations wanted to keep the competition open. They wanted to preserve the right to play against the best no matter how humiliating. None of this upstairs-downstairs stuff for us, thanks, was the essence of the message. Anyone who saw the All Blacks play Portugal in Lyon during the 2007 World Cup would be inclined to agree. The Portuguese, on the face of it, got whipped by a century but the two Portuguese tries will be part of Portuguese folklore forever more and the fact that the two teams actually fraternised after the match caused a near sensation. We all thought this sort of thing, after all, had been going out of fashion.

The lightweights haven't since changed their minds on the merits of meeting the major powers in the round robin. Many of them are all too aware of how long it took to get through the front door of the IRB and regard a two-tiered approach as a means of shoving them back out again through the side window.

But are they not mistaken? Surely, the case for a two- or even three-tier tournament is now self-evident. The weaker nations, or the "minnows" as the television commentators patronisingly call them, seem to be hell-bent on self-destruction every time they come to the World Cup. Perhaps they are masochists who actually enjoy a public whipping because there is little to recommend this kind of ritual slaughter. Whatever their proclivities it is hard to see how any real satisfaction can be gained from a bashing by 80 points. What do they say to themselves in the dressing-room? Hey, boys, this was better than last week. Australia put 20 points less on us than New Zealand. A moral victory.

These defeats are morale mauling. And they are not really getting any lighter. Something needs to be done to equalise the opportunity afforded to teams like Tonga or Georgia to get their best players there. But nothing of this sort appears to be on the IRB agenda, prompting suspicions among the smaller countries that they simply aren't a priority in spite of the occasional puff of promising smoke from the IRB chimney pot. Thus their reluctance to let go that one chance to take the field with the Springboks or the All Blacks.

It is little short of tragic watching a team like Georgia being taken apart by teams that have arguably less natural talent and certainly less charm. The Georgians are perhaps the archetypal example of what's wrong with international rugby. Many of their players, in spite of largely unpronounceable names, are gloriously talented and their physical qualities, their big hearts and their stamina are admirable. They are likeable, open, friendly enthusiasts, made for rugby. They even like their beer which makes a welcome change from second-rate vodka, and who knows what they could achieve with rather more than the derisory share they get from the game's steadily enlarging coffers.

One thing is certain. They can't make it on their own. Georgia is a semi-destitute state. Its rugby union operates on the smell of half an oily rag. The players can't go on tour without heavy subsidisation and they live in tents while training, half expecting to be called up for military service at any moment to protect themselves against a Russian invasion. If rugby is to really grow, the international rugby community must do a lot better by such countries and there are plenty of them, most teetering on the edge of oblivion.

Isn't it time for the establishment of an international "buddy" system whereby the strong nations undertake to mentor the so-called minnows? This could be done at relatively minimal cost and would be in the best social traditions of the game. Whoever adopted Georgia could be on to a winner. And isn't this in accord with rugby's inclusive instincts?

Nothing Short of Perfection Will Do

THE WORLD CUP and New Zealand seem to have become unholy antonyms. After the first outing in 1987 when the All Blacks were so far ahead of the competition that they simply couldn't lose, the story has been one of repeated failure, causing violent outbreaks of wailing and the gnashing of national teeth. These persistent frustrations have taken a heavy toll on the game's support base in New Zealand.

It has become something of a four-yearly ritual. The All Blacks dramatically lose in the play-offs and we slump with anguish. Then, having thrown the TV set out the front window, aimed a kick at the cat, punched a hole in the bathroom wall after throwing up on Saturday night and threatened grievous bodily harm to anybody who raised the subject on Monday, the more reasonable-minded among us then turn our attention half-heartedly to who might actually win the World Cup.

The biggest worry this country has when it comes to sport is an alarming inflation of expectations. We see it at every Olympic and Commonwealth Games. Too many of the New Zealand competitors are touted as world-beaters beforehand by a society desperate for recognition of any kind on a wider stage, and when it is over and they haven't actually won there is a massive outbreak of culprit hunting.

Winning is always nice but the more you win the less you like it when you lose. And the less your fans will tolerate any slippage. There was almost a national insurrection when our team lost five tests in a row in 1998. When the All Blacks' near-record run of wins on the trot came to an inexplicable end at a drab, half-full stadium in Rustenberg in 2006 there was a sense of disbelief among the faithful. This wasn't the way it was supposed to end. The Springboks were a rabble, weren't they? The media had been telling everybody that for months. The All Blacks seemed utterly invincible. How could this reversal of the natural order have happened?

Every time we lose a rugby test the outbreak of culprit hunting is virulent. The reason for that isn't hard to understand. For longer than most people can remember the All Blacks have been expected to win. There probably hasn't been a single test match for a century or more in which New Zealand hasn't been odds-on to win it. Always an overdog and never an underdog. That is a heavy burden to carry.

The truth is that game in 2006 just got away on an All Blacks team that kept thinking that any minute the floodgates would open and they would romp away to another comfortable victory. It is a mindset that beleaguers every team that achieves a high enough measure of international dominance and it is a mindset shared by its supporters. Each of the players has it lodged firmly in the back of his mind that because he is surrounded by such talent nobody in particular has to make a supreme effort. Then nobody does and, bingo, the other team scores, scores again and begins to believe in itself. The "psychic energy" as Murray Mexted so evocatively describes it, shifts irreversibly. The unthinkable quickly becomes the reality and it is over before you do anything about it.

Although you would never get an All Blacks player in a hundred years to admit that he wasn't conscious of giving 100 per cent on the day, the truth is these reversals occur, but asking the public to bear with that law of averages is like asking a European dairy farmer to live without a subsidy.

To lose is to invoke the fury of the faithful. That has always acted as a powerful motivating force for any All Blacks team. They know that if and when they lose — and it doesn't matter to whom — the floodgates of recrimination will burst. When we plunged to humiliating defeat at the World Cup in 1999 a funereal pall hung over the country. The stockmarket wavered. Interest rates were hiked. Heads rolled all over the place: not just those of the coach and captain of the All Blacks. The ignominy was for many New Zealanders just too hard to bear.

Back climbed the All Blacks, and by 2003 they were once again at the top of the pecking order. The whole rugby world pronounced them stone-cold favourites for the World Cup once again. New Zealanders persuaded themselves that their team was unbeatable and once again the mismatch of expectation and reality played itself out. Then, four years later, as if to prove that history is condemned to repeat itself, the same appalling scenario was played agonisingly out.

The All Blacks suffer from a bad case of "choking" if critic Stephen Jones is to be believed. Do they? Are New Zealand teams somehow short of whatever vital ingredient it is that enables a team to prevail under stress? There are three schools of thought on this — the yes school, the no school and the maybes. Those who say yes simply assume that on the basis of results since 1987 it must be so. Some pin their argument on the fashionable "too many Polynesians" theory. Others say it is because of the rotation policy or because the All Blacks are "overpaid, and overpampered", forgetting that every other team at the business end of every World Cup is better paid and equally pampered. This is the territory of talkback radio and the sporting shock-jocks whose sole purpose in life is to polarise.

Those who disagree are usually more wise in the ways of rugby and of life in general. They know that the difference between international teams when the chips are down is minimal and that it is totally unrealistic to assume that one team is going to prevail at any World Cup. They understand that rugby is a game of opportunity and sometimes all the opportunities seem, inexplicably, to go to one team and not the other, and that this is what has happened to the All Blacks. They don't choke. They are just unlucky sometimes.

The maybes are less sanguine. They have a sneaking suspicion that something has been amiss in the minds of the players at crucial times. I fall into the maybe camp. There is a certain consistency in the way events have unfolded at the last three World Cup play-offs which is difficult to explain away as the result of underpreparedness or overconfidence, or plain chance. Each time this has happened there is a recurring pattern. The All Blacks have fallen behind after leading comfortably and the shock when they are overtaken seems to have frozen them into indecision and inaction; not for long and not all of them but enough to throw them sufficiently off balance to enable their opponents to drive home their often fortuitously gained advantage.

Is it the quality of leadership? Is it a want of mental toughness at vital moments? Is it the want of hard competition beforehand? Or is it the corrosive result of excessive expectations of success among players who are constantly being told they are the best in the world and they can't possibly lose. The shock of that prospect when opponents get the upper hand is just too hard to handle. Time runs out before that shock can be overcome and the natural dominance reasserted. Scottish-born New Zealand journalist Gregor Paul is convinced that this frailty of mind is the result of an inadequate apprenticeship served through the testing ranks of club and provincial football: not enough experience of taking the rough with the smooth. There is clearly some truth in this. Those who start at the top, accustomed to winning and with no emotional grounding in the school of hard knocks, are unlikely to respond well to a sudden crisis.

Can a coach inject some magic mental serum that enables a player in this situation to regain control? Nobody really knows the answer to that. The only certainty is that no All Blacks coach has yet been able to do it and it's probably asking the impossible to expect that anyone can.

Others like England or Australia or South Africa who have become eventual winners haven't had this experience. They invariably struggle unimpressively through the round robin games, sailing perilously close to the winds of defeat but then steel themselves for the three-match marathon that follows, grateful just to be there and happy to take each match as it comes, free of the burden of excessive expectations. I have always admired the dogged qualities that these teams show at World Cup time. They know instinctively that if they hang in there they have just as good a chance as the All Blacks and they have proven that to be right.

There is a palpable difference between this mindset and that of the All Blacks who generally wallop everything in sight in the intervening years and then do the same thing in the run-up to the finals, but who never quite seem to be ready for the three-game slog when the time comes. The same scenario is likely in 2011. New Zealand will be at home; domestic expectations will be sky high, regardless of how well the Tri Nations and the northern tours have gone the year before, and the consequences of defeat too awful to imagine. Perhaps it might be beneficial to lose a few games that year to dampen the fervour. It would be nice to think that the Springboks will come to the World Cup in New Zealand in 2011 as red-hot favourites. That would make for an interesting psychological challenge for both teams. But then New Zealand might need its own Nelson Mandela to elevate the minds of the All Blacks into the realms of the surreal and, if we do have such a person, he or she had better hurry up and identify themselves.

There is another dimension to this relationship between the players and the people. Excellence attracts envy. We see regular evidence of that in business, the arts and in sport. People want evidence that the high fliers are no different from them. The hunt for the feet of clay begins. The disease of the tall poppy breaks out. There is, somewhere in the New Zealand character, a perverse desire to see the top dog repeatedly humbled. In New Zealand the clobbering machine has always been an exceptionally powerful force. It has grown out of a confusion between egalitarianism and mediocrity. These days it is more often manifest as straight out envy.

That malevolent quality comes very quickly to the surface whenever an accusation or a creeping assumption that the All Blacks are getting above their station emerges. It is perhaps the greatest danger of all to the future of the game and it is a quality that has become a distinctly Kiwi characteristic. Michael King observed in his landmark *The Penguin History of New Zealand* that New Zealanders can be "good hearted, practical, commonsensical and tolerant" but they can also be introverted and destructively envious when it comes to the exhibition of excellence. Because of the game's traditional grip on the collective psyche it is rugby which becomes the sitting duck when the bullets begin to fly. Thus, we see this curious dualism in the rugby public's relationship with the All Blacks — "their" All Blacks — and it can be frightening when it gathers a collective fury. That fury is currently being compounded because of the growing perception that the All Blacks aren't playing for "us" any more but for themselves and their corporate sponsors.

This muddled demand even finds expression when it comes to singing the national anthem. It erupted in 2009 when the All Blacks played Italy. The Italians sang their hearts out. The All Blacks muttered and mumbled their way through the New Zealand anthem, clearly preoccupied with other more pressing thoughts because the heat was on them following sub-par performances in the weeks before. How dare they not sing with patriotic fervour cried the critics. Force them to sing it properly suggested a couple of our more populist newspapers. The talkback lines ran hot. Even coach Graham Henry got sucked into the debate. He coyly admitted that he had encouraged his players to sing up a bit more gustily but that this wasn't really a coach's prerogative.

Happily, it was pointed out by one or two cynics that the Springboks hardly work up a lather singing their own anthem. They might posture, hand-on-heart, in that hackneyed way that signifies loyalty to the realm, but they don't sing very much. Nor do the English. Even the French, who everybody knows have the best anthem, and a militant one at that, sing much like our lads — lips moving but not a lot of sound coming out.

It was also suggested that the All Blacks prefer to save their fervour for the haka. That has always been the case and they have their priorities right. The haka, particularly the newer version of it, is theirs. The anthem is everybody's. The haka is a very personalised form of communication. The anthem, at least the English version, is a dated hymn with hopelessly stilted lyrics which call upon God's beneficence when a test match is patently a case of God helping those who help themselves.

Jim Hubbard

There must always be a culprit. Usually it's the coach.

Do the All Blacks really owe the crowd a performance in the anthem as well as the haka and the game itself? Good question. Anton Oliver witnessed this ruckus and asked, "How obliged are the All Blacks to meet the expectations of the fans with whom they have no contractual relationship but who are ultimately the most important stakeholders? If they don't turn up to games and stop paying television subscriptions then the sponsors lose revenue and seek healthier returns elsewhere." His conclusion was that the players were there essentially to win but there was no escaping the fact that the fans want the whole package whether the players like it or not.

This issue of the contractual arrangement is at the nub of it. The players are contracted to the NZRU but the NZRU doesn't represent the public even if it tries rather hard to persuade people that it does. The rugby union is a private business which has no public shareholders and its employees, the players, are in the first instance accountable to it for performance and behaviour. There is nothing in their contracts that say they will be seen to sing the national anthem or indulge in any similar expression of loyalty to a wider cause. Of course it is a bit more subtle than that. The NZRU sees itself in an informal way as representing the aspirations of many New Zealanders, as an agent of national identity building, and naturally tries to reflect that as much as it can in the way it goes about its business. It is a very delicate path along which the NZRU is obliged to tiptoe.

Thus the dilemma facing the players when something like singing the anthem comes up. As Oliver sees it: "There are broader interests underlying the anthem debate. The All Blacks have always been the crucible of projected societal values. They've had to represent not only who we are but . . . how we like to think of ourselves. As the All Blacks have certainly changed, so too has our society. This contemporary New Zealand society is now projecting a different set of values, the difficulty being that these new expectations are clashing with historical concepts of how New Zealand used to want the All Blacks to be."

The pressure is relentless but it is understandable. The public feel that rugby is being slowly removed from their grasp and they are right. It is. The response is therefore to try to insist that the All Blacks do their bidding; in other words be all things to all people. It is a heavy burden to bear. Too heavy for some.

Is it any wonder why All Blacks in increasing numbers are seeking the solace of a "sabbatical" in an environment where most of the fans are relatively indifferent to the deeds of the numerous foreign legionnaires and the media are benign. All those worries about living up to national expectations can be laid aside in the glorious anonymity of someone else's rugby team for a handsome salary and about half the physical and emotional commitment that is demanded back home. It seems sad that it should come to this but that is the price of professionalism and that is why there is now clear daylight between the game and the people.

Perhaps this helps to explain why in 2007 the national sulk after ignominious defeat lasted only a few days whereas following the previous World Cups it lasted for months. Where before there had been anger, this time there was more of a sense of tired resignation. Now, the notion of invincibility has been replaced by the cryptic expectation that New Zealand will be world beaters but only in the intervening years between World Cups. You can now even hear that most blasphemous of statements: "Ah, well, it's only a game, isn't it?"

Why this apparent new sense of proportion? Is it simply the fact that there are so many other ways of expressing the country's nationalism that we aren't that desperate about success at rugby any more? That would certainly account for part of the reaction. But not all of it. Somehow, we who watch, comment on and love the atmosphere of rugby don't quite depend on the players who are out there for inspiration any longer for the very simple reason that they no longer depend on us. They are professionals. Their duty to us, as distinct from their paymaster, has diminished. We might not yet fully know it but we, and they, are parting company.

All this may come to a very unfortunate head in 2011. Whether we like it or not, the 2011 World Cup will make or break the long-term future of rugby in this country. This isn't just another World Cup which the All Blacks might or mightn't win. The media will see to that, and it will become a modern day Armaggedon. Every effort to downplay the horrifying reality that New Zealand simply has to win it will only make things worse. It is a scenario that is deeply scary because the fans will come to the unavoidable conclusion that if we can't win it at home we will never win it. It's Last Chance Saloon.

Dosh or Glory

THERE WAS a time when rugby administrators were called by the players, disparagingly, "alickadoos". I've never been quite sure what the word meant but it rang of distance, elevation and formality in the amateur era. The relationship between player and administrator particularly at the higher levels was distant and uncomfortable.

Today, the players call administrators "fishheads". The implication is much the same, even if the nature of the relationship has changed somewhat and there are layers of middlemen between players and management to help bridge the gap.

A generation ago the players and administrators would never see each other except in the run-up to a match or if they were on tour together. It was like ships in the night. Coaches and managers were of starkly different generations. Now it's different. Players and administrators live in each other's pockets. They meet nearly every day; they debate, they analyse, they harmonise, they socialise together. The generation gap seems to be diminishing — if you take the relatively elderly Graham Henry out of the equation — and that seems to be having positive effects in terms of mutual understanding if not always of mutual respect.

Taking notice of players' opinions is not something that rugby's aficionados have ever been particularly good at. It isn't just the IRB that's been deaf. In every major rugby-playing country the message has traditionally been exactly the same. Yours not to reason why. Yours but to do or die on the field and we'll take care of everything else. Everything else has of course included the laws, and generations of players have been trying to point out that they are rather better judges as to whether this or that rule is working than some pointy-headed theorist at rugby union headquarters. Such calls have invariably fallen on deaf ears.

Players are rarely trusted to have rational judgements about anything, let alone the intricacies of the laws of the game. Over the years experienced players have pleaded with administrators to change this law or not change that one. There is little, if any evidence that player proposals have ever been successful. Players have occasionally been asked their opinions on impending law changes but by and large it has been the back-room experts who have designed these.

In 2004, for the first time in its long and not particularly distinguished history, the IRB actually stopped and listened to the views of players. At a meeting in Auckland, the IRB cautiously opened the door to player input. But it wasn't just the laws that they were pronouncing on at that Auckland meeting. Not unexpectedly, the professional players from both the Northern and the Southern hemispheres took the opportunity to collectively declare that they were being required to play too much rugby.

Graham Henry was probably right to put the brakes on before the 2007 World Cup. He knew it wouldn't be popular and he certainly underestimated the media backlash that was to result. It highlighted the dilemma that the game faces in keeping top players fresh. Rugby isn't like soccer where the professionals can play twice a week just about all year round. The physical impact of rugby is totally different. As players get bigger, bulkier and more aggressive in the collision areas the prospect of damage steadily increases.

Interestingly, it is the Northern hemisphere players who are feeling the pinch most in terms of the sheer volume of rugby. Their season has ballooned out to 11 months and, unlike All Blacks or Springboks who are now regularly pulled out of provincial championships prior to home internationals or tours, British or French players get no such respite. At least not in theory. Their clubs see to that, maintaining selfishly that professional duty to club comes before national duty to Queen and country.

Everywhere, top players are desperate to reduce the sheer volume of matches. But hang on. Shouldn't less work imply less pay? It certainly should but you won't hear the professional players' association reps ever mentioning these two issues in the same breath. So far as the game's shop stewards are concerned it is more money for less work. They ought not to be allowed to get away with that. Only very occasionally do we see evidence that sports professionals can see anything beyond the dark interior of their wallets.

It is one of the tragic consequences of associating money with sport. As the game demands more and more of the body and soul of the individual so the capacity to relate to the outside world diminishes. The full-time athlete becomes pampered and petulant and loses interest in everything but his game and his income.

We see evidence of this every day as the sports elite, particularly in the great team games, drift further and further away from their traditional constituencies and into ever more closeted enclaves. This tendency is the very antithesis of what rugby was designed to be. An intensely socialised activity is now heading in the opposite direction. Yes, of course, coaches and managers of professional teams will tell you of all the visits made by their teams to schools, hospitals and the like; and all the help the players give to good fundraising causes, and all of that is true. But it's not really spontaneous, except when an individual player goes beyond the call of duty in a personal way. It's part of the contractual arrangement, along with publicity appearances, promotions of sponsors' products and celebrity endorsements. It's mechanical stuff. It's like the royal family's schedule of public engagements. It's visible evidence that you still have links with the great unwashed, however far you may have drifted away from them.

A few short years ago All Blacks were obliged to mortgage farms and homes or rely on club fundraisers to pursue the glory of an international career. When I went on tours in the 1960s I was granted an amateur allowance of 10 shillings a day and was expected to buy my own boots. There were no sweet deals with Adidas in those days. A small scandal broke out in the mid-1960s when it was discovered that a Christchurch rugby boot manufacturer had donated several pairs of an experimental lightweight boot to several All Blacks. Being one of the offenders I was taken aside by a rugby union councillor and advised in the gravest of terms that it might be politic if I paid for the boots. In that way I could be certain my amateur status wouldn't be compromised. I paid for the boots.

Now that the All Blacks are a global commodity the big label manufacturers are fighting over the right to have our players wear their product. There are arguments about who should wear this or that brand and which have threatened to bring the house down because some players had quite legitimately signed contracts with one boot manufacturer only to find that they were obliged to rescind these contracts because the All Blacks had opted for Adidas as a major sponsor. For a while Jeff Wilson wasn't sure what boots he had to wear. He wasn't alone.

When professionals are not training, flogging themselves in the gym or watching video analysis of their last game, they are on an endless conveyor belt from place to place, signing merchandise, posing for photographs, making television commercials and acting out the part as "brand ambassadors" for all and sundry in the passing parade of corporate partners of All Blacks Inc.

In their spare time most of them tend to sit around and watch DVDs or play video games. It is a depressing scene. When Christian Cullen was a senior All Black, he, like most others, had neither the energy nor the will to do much else. Fortunately, Christian has grown up a lot since then but many never do. An idle mind leads to an idle personality and an absence of direct involvement in the real world leads inexorably to an inability to interact with it when the playing days are over. Already we are seeing the flotsam and jetsam of the first wave of the professional rugby elite washing up on the beaches of despair.

In some desperation the NZRU appointed full-time career advisers a few years ago to each of the five professional franchises. After some initial progress persuading players to get serious about getting their minds working on something other than rugby, the results have been at best modest. Is it any real wonder? Professionalism is effectively full-time. When you are already being paid a handsome salary what's the point of trying to learn another vocation? There is no tomorrow.

Perhaps that is one of the reasons why so many of them have hunted the cash with what has increasingly looked like avaricious zeal. This is their best shot at a decent income, perhaps forever. Agents are employed to squeeze the last pip out of the union while the public watches, fascinated and somewhat appalled by it all. The price of loyalty has been severely distorted by the rampant commercialism that has gripped the game.

The brinkmanship exercised by senior All Blacks, who made it clear in 1995 that they were quite prepared to ditch the official game in favour of a private professional circus, set many people in New Zealand — and further afield — wondering what had become of the loyalty to a game so precious to the whole society's sense of self-worth. The second wave of professionals is simply following that lead. Why should they think any differently? Their objective is to extract as much as they possibly can from their paymasters without actually killing the golden goose. They are a modern day equivalent of Louis XIV's notorious finance minister, Monsieur Colbert, who maintained that extracting money in the form of taxation from the people was like plucking feathers from a goose. "The objective," he said, "is to obtain the maximum number of feathers with the minimum amount of hissing."

As costs in every country keep rising the game's administrators can be heard hissing vigorously. They must wring more and more out of the game to pay player salaries. Rugby is heading down the same dark path as most other major professional sports. The few at the top get more and more of the cake and the game around them withers.

To its immense credit the NZRU has taken the first, hesitant steps towards controlling the salary blowout. The players in this country — as elsewhere — have become particularly adept at paying lip service to preserving the traditions of the game, singing from a heavily clichéd song sheet but — as most of them demonstrated a decade ago — loyalty to tradition is paper thin when it comes to getting a better deal. Has anything changed? Not if the players' association's reaction to the salary cap offer is anything to go by. They know that the best of them can earn much more in Europe or Japan and they hold this axe to the neck of the NZRU. The signings in order to keep a core of key All Blacks in the country ahead of the 2011 World Cup have come at a huge cost, and that cost can be expected to rise in future.

Perhaps the crunch is just around the corner. The International Rugby Players' Association is preparing itself for some trench warfare as the implications for players of an income downturn begin to sink in. But this may be a blessing in disguise. Perhaps, finally, the case for salary caps for professionals within the Sanzar group will be taken seriously. Colin Cooper, the Hurricanes coach who took a close look at American football systems, is convinced that, sooner or later, serious salary caps for professionals must be introduced.

The All Blacks need not be disadvantaged by that. They will still receive reasonably competitive salaries from the NZRU. More importantly, the insidious provincial topping-up that was going on will be stopped. The All Blacks will soon no longer participate in the national championship at all and this will undoubtedly cause some critics to claim that they no longer "belong" to grassroots rugby here. But there isn't another professional sport in the world in which players are expected to turn out for club, province, professional franchise and country, and something has to give here.

Keeping All Blacks at least tenuously in touch with their club and provincial origins is a losing battle unless the NZRU is able to negotiate a contractual arrangement that will provide for the All Blacks to become domestic servants of the game while they are in New Zealand. They shouldn't be paid handsome salaries any more to simply idle their spare time away on the beaches of Fiji or sign autographs. They should be expected to work as any employee would be, to further the interests of New Zealand Rugby Incorporated out there in the heartland; something that is long overdue. Things have been moving on that front. We are about halfway towards that outcome. All Blacks and other professionals are already obliged to undertake promotional work on behalf of the game. This needs to be strengthened and more specifically codified, however, and it needs to be better understood and appreciated in the wider rugby community as a norm rather than an exception.

We are now standing on the threshold of the parting of the way between All Blacks and the amateur realm. Yet that parting could serve to strengthen the overall cohesiveness of the game rather than weaken it. A more decisive dividing line between the two dimensions of the game means greater clarity and will remove the financial bazaar that gave rise to provincial unions competing among themselves for player acquisition. It is this factor, above all others, that is driving the game in the provinces towards the financial wall. Escalating player salary packages reduce the capacity of the unions to nurture the game at lower levels.

Internationally, the landscape is much the same. Clubs in Europe call the tune. They have deep pockets and high ambitions. They are prepared to offer what seem in rugby terms stupendous sums to acquire talent in the quest for Heineken Cup glory and the personal prestige of their owners.

The players have no problem with this. Their assumption is that a rising tide will lift all boats. Their salary expectations have no bounds. They look at the paycheques of the superstars of soccer and say why not us? But anybody who looks at the facts will know that soccer is a very different beast. The depth of community support for it all over the world is truly remarkable. While there are some complaints about the mega-salaries of the game's superstars, there is an almost enthusiastic acceptance of the rags to riches mythology that underpins soccer stardom. Soccer is, truly, an everyman's game and it is the only sport that is truly global. Rugby, by comparison, occupies a relatively narrow band within the social sector in relatively few countries and it has a deep vein of attachment to amateurism which acts as a brake on salary expectations.

The relations between players, internationally, and the governing bodies are highly complicated. At one level the International Rugby Players' Association appears to be in splendid harmony with the IRB. The two bodies signed an agreement in 2007 "with the aim of working together to develop a positive and unified approach to issues of importance to players and the sport such as player welfare, while recognising the unique spirit, structure and ethos of the game of rugby union". That has a very accommodating ring to it. The RPA also enthusiastically backed the IRB's bid to get rugby into the Olympic Games in 2009. No sweat. More income for the game means more income for the elite players.

But let's be fair here. The Professional Rugby Players' Association has succeeded in establishing a programme designed specifically to address the problem of rugby monopolising the lives of the professionals. It provides "a holistic programme of support that looks to provide individual guidance and advice for all the personal and professional needs of RPA members during their playing careers, and to better prepare members for life after rugby". Does any of this make a difference? It's probably too early to tell, but it's a promising start. The RPA in England has been particularly active and is growing in importance and negotiating strength. It is a not-for-profit organisation which consults with the game's stakeholders to ensure that, in its words, it can "continue independently to deliver its essential educational, insurance and benevolent programmes to all RPA members".

So far so good. When it comes to players' income expectations as against the ability of the system to pay, however, the relationship is a little less convivial. The RPA is also a registered trade union. Behind the accommodating language on its website, its primary focus is improving the terms and conditions of its members. It is currently locked in negotiation with the RFU and Premiership Rugby over a long-term funding deal. It is a case of union and employer facing off at either ends of the table and the same thing is happening in every rugby playing country in much the same way.

Things come to a head when it comes to the World Cup. The gloves come off as international players ask for more cash incentives to win rugby's greatest prize. It begs the question: is the honour of winning the cup not enough incentive in itself any more. Answer? No.

The players' shop stewards are adamant that because it is the players who generate the cash flow of the gigantic business that the World Cup has become, it is the players who should have a significant slice of the profit. Business is business they say to the national unions. You turned the game into a commercial enterprise; you made the players professionals. Now you are going to have to pay the star performers accordingly. There would be an immutable logic to that were it not for the awkward fact that this isn't a conventional business.

The spectacle of Mr Rob Nichol, the players' chief shop steward, announcing that some All Blacks might decide to boycott the 2003 World Cup if agreement couldn't be reached had a chilling familiarity to it. Here we go again, we thought. Another unseemly stand-off as the players make another gluttonous grab for the financial spoils of the tournament. Outrage among rugby circles, particularly in the provinces, served to remind those involved that it might not be a good idea to indulge in this kind of brinkmanship.

The Australians managed to find a satisfactory settlement after months of fairly acrimonious negotiation. Each of the players was guaranteed a series of cash incentives based on performance at the World Cup. There was talk of $200,000 per player, perhaps more, if the Wallabies were to win it. Similar figures were being touted in South Africa. Doubtless the English were able to command considerably more than that. By contrast, the Welsh, who let the cat out of the bag by a threatened strike over what they might expect to get as they were about to leave for the Southern hemisphere, attracted rather less. In each of the top tier countries the ante was being progressively upped with veiled threats of the withholding of labour being used as a lever. Old trade union extremists would be very impressed by these tactics. The rest of the rugby community wasn't.

It wasn't any different here. Having botched the relationship between New Zealand's top cricketers and their ruling body, the players' representatives appeared to be about to try to do the same to rugby. Several years ago there was a confrontation between New Zealand Cricket and the players' union. NZC made a generous offer, significantly below what the players were demanding. They let the issue leak out publicly, allowed the chorus of tut-tutting about the obscene size of the offer to escalate, then eyeballed the shop steward till he blinked. The players were effectively marched out to the edge of a precipice and left with only one option: to jump into unremunerated oblivion. They backed off from what was a ridiculously unrealistic series of demands. Rugby should take a leaf out of cricket's book here.

The issue of All Blacks' incentives for World Cup success had of course arisen before. The line taken by the NZRU was that they would be amply rewarded by glory alone. But by 2003 glory had become insufficient to pay the outgoings on the Queenstown condominium. The issue was the use of what is grandly described as "intellectual property", for which read the players' names and images. The IRB, in its usual autocratic and unconsultative way, says that's all ours chaps. We run this tournament. You guys are paid by your own unions to participate. If you don't want to come then please yourselves. This is, of course, something of a simplification of it all but that's what it really boiled down to. The NZRU blinked, however, and an incentive payment was agreed. Needless to say it wasn't uplifted when the All Blacks crashed out in the semi-final. There would have been an armed insurrection in New Zealand if the All Blacks had been given a bonus for that effort.

The question whether or not the All Blacks or any of the other national teams should be entitled to a share of the receipts, in the form of prize money or through exploitation of their names and reputations, is a real one but it has to be set within the bigger picture. The IRB's vocation is to help the game grow in areas where it struggles. You might argue, as many do, that it doesn't do a particularly convincing job of that. But then most of us don't see the body of the iceberg; the large investments in rugby infrastructure in countries that can't afford a professional superstructure and payments to players.

Every dollar paid out to the upper crust of World Cup participants is a dollar less for the game in Tonga, or Romania, or Taiwan. In the end it is the players who will lose. They will lose us. Those who are doing the asking on behalf of the players should not forget that public emotions when it comes to rugby run so deeply and are so volatile that to ask for too much will be to kill the golden goose of public support.

In the run-up to the 2007 World Cup the NZRU, anxious to avoid any dissension in the unified ranks of New Zealand rugby, settled relatively quickly on an incentive package of $100,000 per player for a win. Was it worth that? Ironically, it wasn't drawn down so the argument became a bit academic.

The commercial judgement on this is that it was fair, simply because the additional revenue flows to the winning country from a World Cup victory would have made the players' share of the spoils look very modest. But is a conventional commercial model the right one, particularly when the players' association accepts, explicitly, that rugby is more than just a business and that it has other social obligations in addition to the income of the top players?

What should the All Blacks actually get if they win a World Cup? Business principles dictate that if an employee adds value to the annual bottom line or the balance sheet then a bonus is justifiable. Glory alone is no longer sufficient incentive for the contemporary All Black. He wants the dosh. His agent stiffens his resolve whenever he shows signs of sentimentality. The satisfaction of restoring New Zealand's reputation as the leading force in world rugby isn't enough. How much is enough?

What will the incentive be in 2011? It should be less, but the chances are it won't be. And if the All Blacks win, who will care? One or two administrators in the provinces perhaps, but nobody will be listening to them.

If the IRB had sufficient coherence to take this issue on globally there might be a better chance of success in holding the line but the chances of that look slim. Salary caps are notoriously complicated. There are national and international laws governing restraint of trade. There are entrenched objections from private clubs and franchisees to any interference with what they regard as an open market. Let the market decide they say, with Darwinian certainty that they are right. But if it isn't brought under control through a robust international salary agreement then the poaching of talent from the weaker to the stronger will gradually suck the life out of the game in many countries. And when you look at the facts it isn't hard to see which country will be the biggest loser from that. New Zealand.

Are we going to see the ultimate expression of player power at some time in the future: a strike? It's happened in British football, American baseball and it has come perilously close in British and French rugby. The players certainly have a fair gripe when they complain about having to play too much rugby. As the number of games an All Black has to play slowly creeps up, so the level of discontent with the system rises. Although the players are deeply anxious about this level of on-field commitment they are contractually obliged to live with it. Their situation is akin to that of adolescent Victorian chimney sweepers who worked 12 hours a day, six days a week until the law forbade it. The players' negotiators are hard at work behind the scenes trying to ease the pressure without, it seems, much success, because they don't want any erosion in salary levels. The obvious temptation is to say sorry, boys, you can't have more for less, and that argument will continue.

Every now and then, however, a prominent player breaks the icepack of silence over the issue of too much rugby. In 2006, Tana Umaga, by that time heading for the exit, openly commended the policy of standing down the elite group of All Blacks from the Super 14, something that provoked almost audible gnashing of teeth at News Ltd, because, as Umaga openly admitted, the professional rugby season was "a dam waiting to burst".

Umaga agreed wholeheartedly with the coaches who were "hanging their hats on the World Cup" that nobody would care about the standing down of players if New Zealand won it. Well, New Zealand didn't win it and there was a severe outbreak of caring all over the country. It very nearly cost Graham Henry his job as coach. Unfortunately, News Ltd also cared rather deeply, not least because it had no interest in whether New Zealand won or lost in France. In fact, it had little interest in the World Cup at all. Its contract with the Sanzar unions was for the Super 14 and the Tri Nations and it wasn't about to be diverted by tedious physiological excuses about too much footy from its product purveyors. The system is being squeezed at both ends. The sponsors and broadcasters want more for less. The players want less for more and rugby union sits, in ever more discomfort, in the middle.

The Thoroughly Modern Player

RUGBY PLAYERS don't act like they used to. There was a time before the professional circus came to town when players would have died rather than leap into each other's arms after a try was scored. Now anything goes; even, heaven forbid, kissing. Players of the 1950s and 60s visibly wince when greeted with the spectacle of a round of high-fives followed by a stacks-on-the-mill group grope after an All Black try is scored. Forget about that heads-down-I-was-just-doing-my-job routine that those of us who played in previous generations felt obligated to act out, even if, internally, our emotions were doing cartwheels.

Now it's showtime. It is the same everywhere. It's high-fives all round. The French and the Italians have no monopoly on self-expression any more. Even the English embrace each other without the slightest hint of embarrassment. Punching the air, raising the number one finger to the camera, soft-shoe shuffles, cartwheels and backward flips are almost standard fare. The latest habit is to throw the ball into the crowd after scoring a try. You aren't a real personality unless you give some personal signal or gesture after you've dotted down. For a while members of the Hurricanes team would give the Captain Hurricane salute after scoring until it began to be mocked by the media. But showtime somehow doesn't extend to the interview booth. When, after some of the wildest gesticulations on the field, the player fronts up to a microphone all the old modesty returns and there isn't an original utterance to be heard. Funny that.

These on-field antics are not something that rugby invented. They are borrowed responses, faithfully duplicated from other professional football codes. The spectacle of soccer players acting like eight-year-olds whenever someone scores a goal is one of those defining images of modern sport. It is repeated time after time in the same frenzied manner as if this goal was the one that clinched the World Cup. At one level this expression is healthy, natural exuberance; at another it is neo-conformism. Everybody must do it. It's part of the modern showbiz ritual. It's the price of homogenised sport.

Of course it's healthy to express yourself. Remember Jeff Wilson in the 1990s leaping about, shouting and gesticulating whenever anything dramatic happened? It gave some commentators the creeps. What next, they asked? Jeff, who happened to be one of the more balanced individuals in the team, maintained that it was better to let it out than bottle it up. Fair enough. But there's something slightly odd about all this emotional overflow. Surely, the more professional you become, the more utterly devoted you have to be to simply doing the job as a job rather than an enjoyable diversion, the less demonstrative you are likely to be? Somehow, the professionals are headed in the opposite direction.

There's also something slightly tacky about the new flamboyant homage to the heavens when a player scores a try. Why only then? Why not after a great tackle or an exceptional display of sportsmanship? Or is God too busy to commend these as well? Players feel that they are expected to add to the general spectacle by parading their emotions, in harmony with the crowds who are increasingly busy parading theirs. It comes naturally these days in contrast to previous generations when it would have been anathema to show such emotion. Do they enjoy all this hoopla? Some obviously do. Some obviously don't. And maybe there's nothing too much wrong with a few expressive rituals. It just seems a pity that they have to be slavishly copied from other sports.

Many things have changed in the life of today's rugby professional. Where once an amateur player was more or less the master of his own destiny and could come and go as he pleased, that luxury is no longer available to the full-time pro.

Every moment of a thoroughly modern player's life is now fully spoken for. He is an employee of a corporate entity whether that be a national rugby union or a privately owned club. He has a contract and that runs to many pages, most of it describing what he can't do rather than what he can. One of the things he can't do is publicly slag off coaches and referees and other officials of importance. That sort of thing is a breach of the terms of the collective contract and it doesn't go down at all well.

He is, of course, fully entitled to praise them; there are no apparent restrictions on that. Indeed, there is almost an obligation on the part of the player to tell the world how good the coach is and how well everyone gets along with him. Players are now so carefully scripted that their pubic utterances are acquiring a banality that is almost entertaining.

Each team will have a "spokesman" for the day or the week, someone who is thrust out in front of the daily press conferences to mutter a few anally retentive sentences about the next game being bound to be a tough one — even if everyone knows it's going to be an easy one — and how he and the other guys are looking forward to it. He will explain, with a straight face, that the outcome will depend on quality of possession, elimination of silly mistakes, on ball retention and on playing for territory. He might as well add the P G Wodehouse insight that it will be important to deposit the ball over the opposition goal-line.

After the game it's interview time. We now have full press conferences with washed-out coaches and battered players obliged to front up to the waiting hordes of media and everybody in the room knows exactly what the script is going to be. The winners will announce, modestly, that they are pleased with the result; that it was the outcome of a lot of hard work and careful preparation. If they were expected to win they will protest that they weren't taking the opposition lightly. "We knew this was going to be a tough one."

When it's the turn of the losers the same devastating insights are paraded before a breathless media. "We made too many mistakes." "They put us under pressure," or "We didn't adapt to the conditions," or "We kicked away too much possession," or "We didn't take our opportunities when they came."

Attending these press briefings is like being forced to sit through the *The Sound of Music* over and over again. The refrain is so painfully familiar, you wonder how or why everybody bothers. Is it any wonder that rugby's full-time scribes show signs of incipient madness after several years in the trade?

The players are becoming automatons. Their public utterances are so dull and clichéd that I find myself wanting to scream every time I listen. But not all players, thank goodness, are reduced to the status of incommunicative zombie. Every now and again along comes a square peg of a player who doesn't quite fit into this well rounded hole.

Anton Oliver was one such misfit. Oliver is one of those rare characters to whom honesty is everything and to whom rules, particularly those of the petty kind, need the occasional stomping. In 2004 he got into hot water for speaking out about his Highlanders franchise coach Laurie Mains. Oliver was appalled by the collapse in relations between most of the Otago players and their coach. Under the restrictive contract rules he was not permitted to do what he did — represent the players' dissatisfaction head-on with the coach — but he drew a deep breath then let fly, prompting a terse letter from the NZRU telling him he couldn't do that. But he did it nevertheless because it was the right thing to do. As a result of that initiative the poison was extracted from the wound. It may well not have been otherwise. Laurie Mains was of course livid at being undermined in this way but authoritarianism will always provoke rebellion.

Clearly, Oliver's actions and his unwillingness to be cowed by officialdom more generally cost him his place in the All Blacks and, probably, the captaincy as well. John Mitchell, who Oliver had realised was a plonker of a man-manager, conjured up reasons for not picking Oliver but they were, to put it mildly, unconvincing.

Was Oliver repentant? Of course not. And nor, significantly, was the Otago Rugby Union which stood up and backed him, such was the clarity of his argument. It was of course shown to be absolutely right as the relationships between John Mitchell and just about everybody around him went from cream to custard. This messy little episode showed all too clearly the way the game has steadily suppressed individual expression. It's as if we were back in the 1960s when All Blacks were obliged by virtue of the game's culture at the time to keep their traps shut.

Anton Oliver was a thinker. He asked questions, awkward ones, and he challenged accepted wisdoms. Where is his successor in this role in the All Blacks? Every team needs at least one restless intellect. But will we ever have another one?

This Sporting Life

AT THE end of the 1960s, when rugby union regarded professional rugby as a disreputable business played by portly thugs "oop north", and I was a student in Britain, I was made an offer by one of the rugby league clubs of £10,000 to go and play in Bradford for a couple of seasons. To do that in those days was the equivalent of joining Al-Qaeda today. All the same, ten thousand pounds to an impoverished student was too much of a fortune to treat lightly. But two long years of unregulated assault and battery in the north of England? To get some idea of what it might be like I read *This Sporting Life*, the archetypal story of the utter dreariness of rugby league in the north of England. Then I saw the movie. I turned the offer down.

By coincidence, a week later I had a call from the Club President of Nice, then one of the leading French rugby clubs. The president wanted to know if I would be willing to come and play for Nice for a month or two or three in the French Championship. Down I went to be greeted by the club's accountant, whose major preoccupation was how much all this was going to cost the club.

"You mean payment to play?" I asked him, taken aback. "Excuse me?" he countered. "You are surely not coming here just for the sunshine?" Here was a quandary. I was an amateur; sworn, if not quite literally then certainly by conscience, to never accept money for playing. Taking "boot money" was akin to robbing your granny. Swallowing very hard, I made it clear that I could not accept any payment to play. I was greeted as a genuine eccentric by the players at Nice, all of whom were looked after generously by the club. Almost every major club in the country did the same. Whenever the French Rugby Federation was asked about this by their severely Protestant Anglo-Saxon counterparts they would shrug and say we have no proof Monsieur.

Eventually, I agreed on a deal that left honour more or less intact. They would put me in a five star hotel, fly me to and from first class and arrange for me to eat at some of Nice's finest restaurants. After two weeks of feasting and an all-out attack on the local Côtes de Provence my game deteriorated to the point where Nice was glad they had not laid out a salary as well. They would have been asking for it back.

A year later I went to play a season rather more seriously for Lyon in the French national championship, but again on the basis that no money should change hands. It worked because I was the first foreign international to play in France and the rules about foreigners in the French national championship hadn't yet been written. It also worked because I was a part-time rugby player with other preoccupations. Everything was provided except money — car, apartment, champagne, restaurant meals, nightclubs — but it didn't really feel right. At the time the pressures on "shamateurism" were building up all around the rugby world and something had to give.

What impact, psychologically, does full-time footy have on those who play it today? There is mounting evidence that professionalism produces a rather one-dimensional and unimaginative individual. Peter Snell has expressed concern at the number of individuals who had given up working to concentrate full-time on their athletics career. Snell is convinced that someone who has no definable work ethic simply vegetates, whereas an athlete who continues to hold a job has a more balanced, healthy approach and is more likely to succeed.

Is this just a case of nostalgia for the good old days when everybody worked as well as played, or is there a real and perhaps dangerous new syndrome that hasn't been adequately prepared for? The truth is, some individuals can handle the peculiar lifestyle and then walk away from it unaffected and go on to prosper in some other field. Many can't and it is the many that causes the concern.

Because players are now the responsibility of their employer, everything is rule-bound. Being on the professional franchise circuit is akin to life in a British boarding school without the cold showers. Everything is rule-bound. Behaviour is prescribed. Stepping out of line is punishable, if not with the cane, then with something equally punitive. Alcohol in such circumstances becomes forbidden fruit. The more you are locked away from it the more you will abuse it when the chance comes. And, as we have seen so vividly in recent times, the propensity to go over the top when that little window of opportunity presents itself is irresistible.

As yet another prominent rugby player ends up in the court for misbehaviour of one sort or another the question is persistently asked: are our elite professionals behaving more badly than they used to? The answer to that is no, of course they aren't. It's just that they stand out rather more than they ever did and they are targeted not just by drunken wannabes late at night but by relentless journalists by day. And today there are even young gold-digging females who fancy a bit of sport with a visiting rugby player who are more than willing to hawk their kiss-and-tell memoir to the media. This is dangerous territory. The case of the England player who enjoyed the favours of one young lady in Auckland only to have her sell her story to the media, and another to cry rape after a collective encounter with several other England players on the same night, was a perfect illustration of the vulnerability of the modern international.

A generation ago much of what happened off the field — and believe me, much happened — never broke the media surface. There was a code of honour, much as there was for politicians, that kept private lives separate and off limits to the prying eyes of the newshounds.

All that went out the window with the advent of professionalism. Now, no player can realistically expect to get away with even the most trifling of indiscretions. Partly as a consequence of this, and given their public prominence, All Blacks are anointed with the laurel wreath of "role model". Too often the laurel wreath turns out to be a crown of thorns but that doesn't diminish the blinkered insistence of the public that this status be upheld. It is patently absurd to saddle a bunch of young men with virtually no real life experience and very little prospect of any in the immediate future with such a responsibility.

The same instinct prevails all over the world. Sports stars are held up as paragons then publicly crucified when they don't or won't live up to it. Charles Barkley, the great NBA basketball star of the 1990s, once declared in absolute frustration: "I am not a role model." He objected, justifiably as it turned out, to being held to a higher moral standard simply because he could score goals. "A million guys can dunk a basketball in jail," he observed once, famously. "Should they be role models?" Barkley has since gone on to demonstrate exactly why people had no business holding him up as a role model but one feels a definite sympathy with his frustration and that of countless others who have this status thrust upon them when everybody knows they can't really live up to it.

It is muddled thinking to assume that the status of role model must come naturally with the territory of being an All Black. It is unfair and unwise to put players on such pedestals. They don't have the capacity to live up to it — they never have and they never will — and they don't particularly relish the idea because they know in their hearts that status of this social kind isn't really earned or deserved. The lifestyle is idiosyncratic, the salaries are unrealistic, the work ethic is distorted and the example for youngsters unsuitable. They just aren't right for role models.

Those who run the franchises consistently claim that the professionalisation of rugby is producing more mature, balanced personalities. Are they? Compared to what? Is there hard evidence to back this? I haven't seen very much. That isn't to say that there aren't outstanding examples of balance and intelligence among the top players. Every All Blacks team has the full menu of personalities. Some, like Richie McCaw or Conrad Smith, are particularly impressive individuals who would be recognised as such even if they weren't full-time sportsmen. Others have unquestionably become more solid citizens as a result of their time in a professional rugby team. A perfect example of this is Mils Muliaina, someone who learned the hard way and rose to become if not an inspirational leader then someone who set a highly professional example to some of his less disciplined fellows. Muliaina is a living testament to the extraordinary healing powers of a team culture.

The discipline of professional football has been the making of more volatile characters like Tana Umaga, Ali Williams, Jerry Collins or Ma'a Nonu. But there are many more who hover on the brink, for whom the pressure of professionalism always threatens to become too much and whose susceptibilities to alcohol abuse or some other weakness are aggravated by the sheer relentless pressure of the experience. Rugby's equivalents of Jesse Ryder are all too common.

Almost all of rugby's contemporary players come from relatively unprivileged backgrounds. Many have had few opportunities to develop confidence in their own ability to cope under extreme pressure. There is some fascinating work being done around the fringes of professional sport to enable individuals to enhance their technical and emotional skills. Kerry Spackman, a New Zealand neuroscientist, has become internationally renowned for being able to pull professional sportspeople into the loftier zones of excellence and he has worked with numerous rugby players over the years. He has become expert at teaching the art of anticipation through the fine-tuning of muscular and other responses. He also focuses on a player's emotional "circuitry" to open the way for peak performances and to provide a wider range of mental tools to round out a sportsman's character.

Spackman noticed that many New Zealand rugby players only get this kind of special treatment at the very top level, whereas at lower levels they get virtually nothing. In other words, All Blacks get premium psychological back-up but Super 14 players get virtually none. As a result, when a Super 14 player is selected for the All Blacks he invariably comes inadequately wired for success. Thus the numerous falls from grace among those who have greatness suddenly thrust upon them.

At All Blacks level the influence of particularly skilful man-managers like Messrs Henry, Hansen and Smith has unquestionably made a difference to many in the current All Blacks squad. The very exclusive cultural milieu of the All Blacks and the drive to make more of our top players step up to higher levels of personal responsibility is one of the reasons why the All Blacks are stronger minded than they were a decade ago. The all-round quality of leadership in general in the All Blacks has visibly improved. To be convinced of this one only has to compare the 2009 squad with that of 1999 which exhibited all the leadership qualities of a New Zealand's Next Top Model contest.

The All Blacks may get premium treatment, but further down the food chain the picture isn't anywhere near as encouraging. The greater worry is all the others who at various levels below that are drifting into a lotus land in which they play a bit and spend the rest of the time sitting about waiting for the devil to make work for idle hands. As a result, the work ethic is under threat and motivation begins to slide. Is it any wonder some are driven to drink? The fact that more and more players — even those who are not earning much of a salary — are giving up work and doing nothing else but play rugby is the single most alarming trend.

The Australians got started on dealing with this earlier and by the late 1990s had a definite edge over New Zealanders when it came to clear-headedness under siege. We have had more than enough experience in this country of the absence of it to know that it is mental fortitude rather than physical extravagance that wins World Cups. Happily, the All Blacks are slowly getting there on the mental front. The gap with Australia has largely closed and the credit for that goes to those who have been able to instill a sense of personal responsibility in each individual mind.

It was inevitable that the All Blacks would have no scope for any other occupation while they play. Fair enough. Life after rugby, however, becomes somewhat more of a challenge. What they need most is help with the transition to life after test rugby and, to its credit, the NZRU has been very active in this domain. But the real proof of this apparent improvement in ability to cope will be in 10 years' time when the lights have gone down and the paycheques have stopped.

Very few professionals ever turn out for their clubs any more, unless they are told, in exceptional circumstances, to get some warming up game time. When Dan Carter and Richie McCaw turned out for their clubs after long injury lay-offs it was like Barack Obama visiting a church bazaar, such was the gulf between the international superstar and the modest amateur. It's often said that the clubs never see their Super 14 and even some of their provincial players except when they show up to the occasional social event. How long will it be before a player can simply bypass the club syndrome, instead graduating up through the ranks of various academies and age group competitions without ever having to set foot in a club match or a clubhouse at all? Fanciful? Wait and see.

Perhaps it is time to think more laterally and deploy those who are on rugby union salaries to work directly for local clubs and smaller unions; in other words to actively forge the links between the upper and lower tiers using the manpower at the game's disposal to greater effect. The better option is, of course, to do away with the twilight world of semi-professionalism altogether. This would make it abundantly clear to those involved that they need to work at something else. To get a life for the after-life of rugby.

Are there lessons to be learned from other, longer established professional sports in this context? Players in the premier basketball, football and baseball competitions in the United States are exceptionally carefully managed. They need to be. The boredom factor is a real threat. Yet they too, in their hundreds, regularly fall from grace and their administrators have great concerns about what happens when overpaid but intellectually under-endowed individuals hit the public spotlight. The endless repetition of his job reminded one NBA player of Charlie Chaplin tightening bolts in *Modern Times*. Linebackers on the gridiron who never get to touch the ball begin to wonder what on earth they are doing this for, and realise it's only for the money. It's a deeply flawed system because it warps lifestyles and ensures the overall intelligence levels of the participants steadily decline. It seems a terrible pity that rugby, once the sport that catered for, and benefited from, every level of intelligence, should now be blindly following the others along dumb-down street.

The experience of other longer established professional sports shows all too clearly what happens when money becomes the principal driver. Loyalties are compromised.

There is much academic research to back this up. As American researcher Christopher Lasch wrote in *The Corruption of Sports*: "Although players still make a point of subordinating their own achievements to those of the team, they do so in order to promote easy relations with their colleagues, not because the team as a corporate entity transcends individual interests. On the contrary, the player as a professional entertainer seeks above all to further his own interests and willingly sells his services to the highest bidder." Does this apply to rugby players as well? We like to think not but perhaps we are deluding ourselves.

There are other flies in the organisational ointment as well. The degree to which agents, managers and advisers, the reef-fish of professional sport, have invaded the lives of sportsmen and women has become a worrisome factor in just about every sport on the planet. These irritating busybodies are everywhere, assiduously clipping the ticket every time their client makes an appearance, whether it's on the field or endorsing some product or other, or simply making a celebrity appearance at some function. Sometimes the sports star has a contract with an apparel company which calls many of the shots on what the athlete does, and where, and the agent marshals him hither and fro as the middleman.

Agents are like seagulls at the rubbish dump. They circle apparently aimlessly until they spot an edible morsel. And then they swoop, fighting each other off. They sometimes have an insidious effect on their clients. They are like real estate agents. They need regulation or they run riot. The approach adopted in France perhaps shows the way forward. In 2001 the more respectable agents, a minority, formed a union and forged an agreement with the Ligue Nationale de Rugby and the French Federation. This resulted in a decision that clubs would henceforth only do business with licensed agents. The licences are reviewable every three years and since 2003 agents must pass an exam to qualify.

The extent to which agents can manipulate whole sports came to an interesting head in the United States after the Beijing Olympics in 2008. The United States Track and Field Association conducted an inquiry into why American athletes had done so (relatively) poorly in Beijing. Their findings were revealing. The sport's athletes were roundly criticised for allowing agents and shoe company representatives to make many of their career decisions, often to the detriment of their Olympic performances. It was resolved that urgent steps should be taken to free the athletes from the covetous clutches of the agents in particular, many of whom were more interested in the lucrative revenue producing opportunities of international meets at the expense of their clients' Olympic preparation.

This has a familiar ring to it. Rugby around the world has the same problem. It is fair to point out, though, that in New Zealand the game has been well served by a couple of the bigger players in the market, notably the Essentially Group and World in Motion, who have always acted in a responsible manner.

Nobody seems to be quite sure as to how or when the agent actually first appeared. We knew he was here, however, when Phil Kingsley Jones began badgering the various unions on behalf of his gullible young client, Jonah Lomu, in the 1990s. Kingsley Jones, himself a rugby devotee from way back, made every post a winning post for Lomu. He succeeded mightily in levering up the bar at a time when the NZRU were trying desperately to keep a ceiling on personal All Blacks contracts. A gigantic and, in retrospect, mistaken exception was made for Jonah, not just because he had become a perceived match-winner but because of the crowds he pulled. I recall clearly the arguments advanced by Kingsley Jones for specific recognition of that pulling power over and above all else when it came to Jonah's emoluments. NZRU directors who were around at the time still gnash their teeth in memory of being held to ransom.

This raised a very fundamental question. Should one individual be paid more than the others in a team simply on the grounds of his entertainment value? One of rugby's greatest virtues is that everyone in a particular team knows that he can't shine unless others enable him to. Even Dan Carter can look ordinary behind a forward pack that delivers backfoot ball.

It's all for one and one for all; or at least it ought to be. Rugby is probably heavier on mutual dependence than any other sport and this, until Lomu came along, was the basic principle upon which salaries were set. All that has of course gone comprehensively out the window and with it has gone part of rugby's famously egalitarian soul.

The Last Hurrah and the Mid-term Break

HOW LONG is too long at the top? There is always a measure of sadness when a great athlete's career at the top begins to tilt downward and he can't quite find the right moment to get out. Some players, no matter what the sport, invoke intense emotions when their time to move over finally comes. Jonah Lomu was one. Sean Fitzpatrick was another. Some don't want to go and have to be dropped in order for the harsh realisation that it is really and finally over to set in. Others go out with dignity before they are pushed. Brian Lochore went out with dignity in 1970 then got pulled back, fatally, in 1971 because there wasn't anyone else good enough.

The pattern in the professional era is now somewhat different. These days there is a semi-retirement option available, in the Northern hemisphere, but the secret is to know how and when to activate that option without tarnishing a hard-earned reputation.

As the traffic to the Northern hemisphere accelerates there have been numerous cases of diminished reputations and intense unhappiness as a result. Take two extreme examples — those of Tana Umaga and Christian Cullen, both genuine superstars of the game as All Blacks but both of whose reputations dived once they took the easy road to riches in Europe.

Tana Umaga couldn't quite bring himself to shout his last hurrah to big-time rugby. He wanted out but he still wanted in. Like so many before him he found the habit a hard one to kick. Having done his OE at Toulon, cashed several handsome cheques along the way and downed some of the best Provencal wines, he returned for another Super 14 season in 2007 and in a few ill-tempered and error-ridden appearances for the

Hurricanes demonstrated vividly the virtue of getting out while you're ahead.

He needed to go out at the top because in so many ways he had become symbolic of the ethos of the thoroughly modern All Black. It isn't just the imagery of dreadlocks, blockbusting energy, deft off-loading, the immensely engaging, gap-toothed smile or the utter dedication to the collective effort around him. It was all that and much more.

Umaga is an example of the power of sport to bring out the latent qualities in an individual who might otherwise have ended up at the wrong end of the social stick. A Pacific Island Kiwi from the extremes of modesty in Wainuiomata, he grew so profoundly as a player and as a personality that he came to dominate the All Blacks landscape so much that it became almost unthinkable for him not to be there.

He started, like so many young Polynesian players, without a clue as to what it takes to be a successful international sportsman. He learned the hard way. In and out of the Wellington team in the early 90s after a flirtation with league, he looked like your typical, on again-off again winger. But then Alama Ieremia got hold of him. Ieremia was not your average local boy. He was Samoan-born, of chiefly origin, very devout and the natural leader among Wellington's Samoan players. He helped Umaga to realise that, with more application and more self-discipline, he could do just about anything he liked in rugby.

And he did just that. When they gave him his chance on the wing for the All Blacks he grabbed it and, with Jonah Lomu and Christian Cullen, constituted as potent a back three attacking force as has probably ever walked a rugby field. Opponents were never quite sure whether they were going to get a ramrod fend in the face or be left embarrassingly stranded by a sidestep that might go left or right. When it became apparent that the All Blacks needed Tana at centre he did the job. Then, when necessity called again, he moved in a place, once again to do for the All Blacks what others couldn't in midfield — provide stability. He became the captain because he was mentally stronger than all the others.

But when the body began to respond more slowly to the demands of all that international pressure, Tana's game began to deteriorate. We could all see it but nobody really wanted to admit it, and even at 50 per cent of his potency he was still good enough. The crunch came in 2006 when he announced his retirement from international rugby. He later bailed out to Toulon, first as a player, then as a coach. It didn't work. It wasn't all his fault that it didn't work. The owner of the club who had decided to buy success at any price simply didn't understand rugby, or Umaga, well enough and the whole thing ended in tears as Toulon limped along in the French championship and Tana carried the can.

Christian Cullen, perhaps the best running fullback the game has ever seen, managed eight years and that is considerably higher than the norm these days. Most professional players who are obliged to put their bodies and their emotions on the line from February to November don't last that long. Even the great Philippe Sella admitted that he couldn't possibly have lasted his 13 years of internationals or achieved his world record 111 caps in the hot house of professionalism. George Gregan managed it by a miraculous combination of wiry durability and an ability to keep out of trouble.

The hardest part of all is to find the right time to quit or to take the now well worn path to prosperity and a lower tempo in the Northern hemisphere. Christian Cullen suffered agonies in New Zealand over this question before taking the initiative personally and signing off. Was it too soon? Some of us, many of us, thought so. We felt he was playing well enough to be retained in an All Blacks World Cup squad in 2003 in which he could well have finished up once again as the leading, perhaps the only, specialist fullback. Cullen's story is an archetype. He arrived on the international stage in a whirlwind of try-scoring feats that had us gasping for superlatives. His debut against Scotland was so breathtaking that the Scots simply gave up trying to catch him by the end of the game. He dished out the same treatment to all comers.

He humiliated defences, running round them or threading his way through them by a combination of electrifying speed, a dazzling sidestep and an ability to wriggle out of tackles. It was all done instinctively. There really was no way of coaching Christian. There was no real need to. If anyone made a break in midfield there he would be, ghosting up alongside with that uncanny timing and finishing yet another try with a nonchalant trot round behind the posts, defenders far in arrears.

It seemed at the time almost churlish to turn one's back on a phenomenon like Cullen when we were scratching for talent at fullback.

But the ravages of eight years of full-time professionalism had taken a huge toll. After a knee reconstruction the blistering pace wasn't there any more and Cullen began to get caught from behind. His defence wasn't quite as robust and his certainty under the high ball likewise. He fought back but coach John Mitchell wasn't convinced. And so Cullen limped off to Ireland for many pieces of silver and got steadily worse. It somehow just didn't seem right. Had he retired in glory at the end of 2002 his reputation as one of the best ever would have remained intact. He didn't and it isn't.

Where's the moral in these two cautionary tales? I guess it is that no matter how great a reputation may be it can easily be compromised when money alone is the driver. The problem with taking highly paid contracts in Europe after a stellar career at home is that expectations are always unrealistic. The club paying the big bills wants someone at the height of his powers but what it gets is never that. The landscape is littered with examples of this. Even those who have succumbed to the lure of the pound or the euro in mid-career like Chris Jack, Doug Howlett or Aaron Mauger play well enough but do they add the kind of value that their paymasters expect? Answer: no. Perhaps the only exceptions to this rule have been Carl Hayman and Greg Somerville, but then props are more honest.

The anticlimax of playing anything less than test matches is inevitable. The Heineken Cup might be big but there is a gulf between that and a test match. This reality is slowly sinking in at both ends which is probably a very good thing. The huge inducements will inevitably become more modest, aided by a severe recession, and the truth as to how hard it is to make this sort of thing work will sink more meaningfully into the minds of ageing Southern hemisphere gold-diggers.

That is evident in the number of inducements to mid-career All Blacks, Springboks and Wallabies. The so-called "sabbatical" has become the new morality play. The national rugby unions concerned are slowly giving way under the pressure from star players who want time off to underperform in Europe by way of refresher and escape from the relentless attention of media critics in the home country. Is it so odd that so many of them seem to get injured early in the experience? Probably not. Daniel Carter's groundbreaking experience at Perpignan could hardly be said to have benefited anybody, let alone the All Blacks. Was this the first pillar to fall in a slow collapse of the basic principle that All Blacks only get selected if they play in New Zealand. That principle is already on the skids in South Africa. Percy Montgomery was the first to be brought back from Europe to play for the Springboks and he isn't going to be the last. There is much wringing of hands among the national unions at what this implies for the future. Can the line be held on the basis of the "occasional" exception? I doubt it. There is mortal fear, not just in New Zealand, that once the floodgates open the assembly of an international team will be like a clan gathering on a remote Scottish island where they come from all around the world to briefly partake of each other's company.

The NZRU knows that if it lets the floodgates open the consequences could be disastrous. It therefore manages the issue round the fringes. It has worked hard to induce some of the All Black mid-term breakers back. It offered Carl Hayman a handsome package in 2009 only to be told by his English club that it could "buy" Hayman back for a startling fee. The offer was declined.The qualification rule, as it stands, is that any player wishing to make himself available for the All Blacks must play in either the Super 14 or the NPC to be eligible. It is only a matter of time before this sensible rule must be set aside.

When Tana Umaga retired from test rugby in 2006 he didn't cite age as the primary reason for getting out. He talked, instead, of the way that professional sport simply blots everything else out, including family, and it was this, the continual absence from home and the virtual impossibility of indulging in any other serious activity, that prompted his withdrawal.

This raises interesting questions about the longevity of modern professional players. The key issue these days is not age but burnout. The professional year is now virtually a 12-month one. The little holiday around Christmas for our elite rugby players is brutally short, and grew shorter as the Super 12 gave way to the Super 14, and the number of test matches in a normal season continues to balloon out.

In the Northern hemisphere the pattern is the same. Full-time rugby means exactly that. The club competitions have got bigger. The European club championship has got bigger. The Five Nations is now the Six Nations. The mid-year tours to the south have become an onerous farce. The end-of-year northern tours by Australia, Argentina, New Zealand,

South Africa and the Pacific countries keep coming at them, wave upon wave. Wall-to-wall footy.

All this means that fewer players will be able to last the distance into their thirties. By the age of 25, you're a veteran. At 30, you're in danger of becoming a zombie. Aaron Mauger underlined this when at 25 he announced that he couldn't maintain this lifestyle without a break so he arranged a couple of seasons in Europe, free of the oppressions of New Zealand and hoped to come back refreshed for another sortie. Selfish? Maybe. Sensible? Probably.

Yet at the same time players in the limelight come to depend on all the attention they get. There is nothing new in that. All Blacks down the ages have been idolised, hounded and harassed and come to accept it as the norm with a kind of "shucks, I'm just an ordinary joker" response. They might hate it but, like junkies, they find it exceptionally hard to live without it. Thus the temptation to get as much of it as you can while the body can take it.

More Brawn, Less Brain

WHERE HAVE all the students gone? A troll around the ranks of the professional elite these days will be lucky to find one and there are many who feel that rugby has paid a high price by sacrificing the university dimension of the game. For its first 100 years rugby was the chosen game of British and Commonwealth universities. It was the universities that took the game to the world. Now the rugby world has turned its back on the universities and is paying a price for that.

The homogenisation of the playing ranks has some very severe downsides. It is a fair guess that in 10 years' time there will not be any students or ex-students in the All Blacks any more. It just won't be physically or mentally possible to do all the work and sit all the exams as well as stay astride the professional treadmill. All Black Conrad Smith managed to gain a law degree before becoming a professional player and Anthony Boric is an Auckland University engineering graduate, but that prospect for any other aspiring student, given the intensity of the escalator system these days, is now very remote. Perhaps these two players will go down in history as the last tertiary-qualified All Blacks. That is a scary thought.

It's not quite as acute in Australia where a number of professionals are still studying part-time at university but those numbers are diminishing, as they are in South Africa and Britain. Everywhere the pattern is the same. Talent is identified at school and channelled straight into the academy and age-group system. There's no time for much else and those who are destined for a pro career are snapped up almost immediately before they have even begun to turn their minds to some form of qualification or gainful vocation. We are rapidly moving to a state in which there may be nobody with any real life experience at all — let alone a tertiary qualification — outside the hermetic cocoon of rugby in this country. That is an even more scary thought.

Oxbridge has always had a special place in world rugby. It is where the university game was born and reached its highest level of importance. By the late 19th century the two universities were the star attraction of British rugby. Their teams were stacked with internationals and both clubs had special representation on the Rugby Football Union. To gain a blue at either university was almost as much value as a degree when it came to finding a job "in the City". The great merchant banks, insurance companies and finance houses fell over themselves to hire Oxford or Cambridge rugby products, with or without degrees, in the certain knowledge that these men, however unerudite they might be, were the stuff that made the world go round; or at least the empire go round; and what could be more important than that?

I arrived in Oxford in 1968, a time when it was becoming clear that neither university had the physical resources to foot it with the heavyweights of British rugby any longer. The centre of gravity had shifted to the north of the country. The Home Counties were in relative decline, locked in a curious time-warp, wanting desperately to preserve rugby's upper middle-class power base in London and denying the obvious reality that the game was steadily democratising around them.

Oxford and Cambridge still had their exclusive seats at the table — and remember, in those days the RFU was running world rugby, not just the game in Britain. In effect, the Oxford delegate probably had more say in the governance of the game than the New Zealand or South African national rugby unions, not least because he was right there on the spot at the cocktail parties where decisions were taken, then later ratified by the RFU.

I became aware of all this when, together with Oxford's official representative, a retired don, I attended an RFU Annual General Meeting in London in 1969 as the Oxford captain. This was akin to having an audience with the Pope and I was advised to be on my very best behaviour. Mr Pickwick himself wouldn't have felt out of place. Queen Victoria would have been proud of the demeanour and the proceedings which were distinctly light on the realities of the game but heavy on decorum.

Photosport

Blood bin? What blood bin? Alan Whetton bleeds on against Scotland, 1990.

There was a time when lineouts were a free-for-all. Today, they are an exercise in mathematical precision with twice as many rules.

NZ Rugby Museum

Photosport

Photosport

Set it again, Sam. Yet another scrum collapse.

Photosport

The dreadlocked dreadnought. Enough was never enough for Tana Umaga.

Christian Cullen on the burst. With that much talent who needs a coach?

NZ Rugby Museum

All Blacks haka, Brisbane 1932. An exercise in restrained animation. At least they got their timing right.

Photosport

Above: The All Blacks' provocative new haka, "Kapa o Pango", is unveiled in 2005. After all the fuss we've hardly seen it since. Below: Ali Williams well worked up during the All Blacks' "indoors" haka in Cardiff, 2006.

Photosport

Photosport

Above: “Please, sir, I think I may have the answer.” Graduates Conrad Smith and Anton Oliver.”

Right: Writing on the wall, 1995.

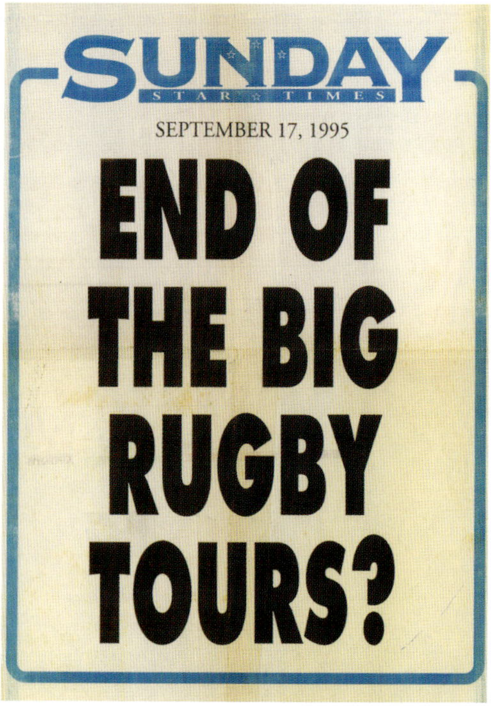

SUNDAY
STAR ☆ TIMES

SEPTEMBER 17, 1995

END OF THE BIG RUGBY TOURS?

Nevertheless, it was obvious that the universities were very much at the centre of the power broking on the world game. That centrality persisted right through into the 1990s, but when the game went professional the universities quickly shifted to the margins.

Rugby at Oxford and Cambridge has steadily declined in importance and in quality since then. The varsity match retains a certain faded glamour even if it must now be officially known as "The Nomura Varsity Match" in deference to the Japanese purchaser of the naming rights. Both universities languish in the lower orders of the club competition, unable to foot it with the full-timers of Leicester or Northampton, clubs that it would once, effortlessly, have walloped. And now that the game has been restructured into amateur and professionals both Oxford and Cambridge have ended up playing second-rate club teams outside the ring road that separates the amateur from the professional game. And there's no way back in. You just can't be a full-time student and a full-time footy player at the same time. It's one or the other.

The same sorry situation applies in New Zealand, Australia and South Africa. The university teams are slowly sinking towards the lower tiers in their respective club competitions. While a few, like Stellenbosch, Sydney University or Otago University, remain reasonably competitive and still throw up the occasional Springbok, Wallaby or All Black, that is very much the exception and by and large single university teams do not play against professional clubs any more.

Gone are the days when a combined national university team would go head to head with a touring international side. There's no room in the schedule or any enthusiasm for it among those who decide the itineraries any more. As a consequence, in Australia, South Africa and in New Zealand, the bottom has dropped out of university rugby. Only in Japan, where the universities' competition is effectively the second tier of the game, below the professional corporate-based clubs, is the game holding its own, but even there the best players are systematically poached by the professional teams and crowds are steadily diminishing.

It illustrates vividly the hopeless incompatibility of a professional rugby existence and serious academic study. It also signals the parting of the ways between tertiary education and professional rugby, one of the more ominous side-effects of full-time rugby. Despite desultory efforts by rugby administrators to encourage players to take up some form of part-time study with a view to having a qualification when the game is over and the paycheques stop, the results, overall, have been a dismal failure. If you need further proof of this ask yourself this question: how many students, let alone graduates, do any of the world's professional sports teams have these days? A more important question is what are the consequences of that for applied intelligence on the field?

This is not about intellectual elitism. It is about the value of trained minds applying themselves in a creative environment in which decision-making and clarity of thought are prime requirements. Enormous effort is invested by professional rugby institutions to get players with little or no experience of higher education to think clearly and to take responsibility. Although Graham Henry would never say so publicly he would be delighted to be able to call on more graduates in his All Blacks squads. So would most other international coaches. Unfortunately, they are never again going to have that luxury.

But there's another related threat. It means that rugby, certainly at the elite level, will lose one of its most precious qualities, its appeal to the middle classes, the decision-makers. It will drift down-market in social terms. It will become no different to league with young, uneducated players in it essentially for the dosh, uninterested in and unappreciative of its history, its mystique and its inclusiveness. How far down that track are we? I'd say about three-quarters of the way; and I know of no way back unless they make rugby an authorised tertiary subject and do away with the exams.

The same phenomenon is occurring all over the world in tertiary educational institutions. As the *New York Times* lamented in 2009 as recession began to bite ever more deeply, "The gap will widen between the haves with television and sponsorship deals and the have-nots that rely mostly on alumni and their universities for funding." It could not be put more succinctly when it comes to university rugby.

Is there any hope of salvation? If, as the IRB has been hinting, the longer tours are brought back, would it be possible to reinstate the national university team as a fixture? That is probably just wishful thinking. University rugby, if not completely comatose by then, may be just too weak to respond.

Is Brown the New Black?

A DEDICATED spectator at an inter-school rugby match was overheard saying to a parent from the opposing team, "We will win because our Samoans are better than your Samoans." All over New Zealand, and increasingly abroad, the pattern is repeating itself. More and more school and age group teams are reliant on youthful Polynesian vigour to make the difference. Hulking youngsters dominate the landscape at almost every game. Fifteen-year-old dreadnoughts weighing 100-plus kilos, and playing at centre, have become the norm.

It is an arresting sight, not least for the modestly proportioned Pakeha lads who get run over every Saturday morning and wonder how many more times they must be offered up as a human sacrifice. As a parental spectator in Auckland 20 years ago I often found myself wincing on the sideline as the puny foot-soldiers of mainly Pakeha teams were comprehensively flattened by the heavy artillery of their mainly Polynesian opponents.

A few years ago some rugby unions began to get serious about weight limits for schoolboy rugby rather than age groups. That was a necessary step and a logical response to the reality that Samoan and Tongan boys quite obviously mature physically much earlier than those of European origin. There is, too, emerging evidence of ethnic differences in levels of physical coordination and balance that tend to favour the Polynesian youngsters.

But never mind all the physiological stuff. There will always be arguments about that and there are dedicated schools of politically correct thought that insist that we are all the same. We aren't, and it couldn't be more obvious when an ethnically mixed bunch of early teenagers take the field. In spite of the rules, many local unions are constantly beset by coaches and parents complaining that the weight limits are honoured only in the breach. It has been said that some secondary schools that are overwhelmingly Polynesian in complexion have difficulty these days finding enough youngsters who are light enough to qualify for the under-50kg weight group without raiding the local primary school ranks. I can believe it.

There are regular reports of some talented but physically intimidated young Pakeha players growing dispirited by these disparities in size and athletic firepower and giving the game away. My own son, a talented player, gave up before the end of secondary school because he simply became tired of being tossed around like a rag doll by Polynesian boys the same age but twice his size. All around the country the same pattern is being repeated. That is a pity but as rugby becomes more and more specialised, and as the average size and aerobic capacity of players continues to rise, we will begin to see a much more obviously stratified system in which those who can compete physically will play seriously, and those who can't will simply drift away.

The 21st century will be an age in which some sports will be dominated by young Polynesians. The transformation is well under way and it is unstoppable. Bryan Williams was one of the first of Pacific Island descent to play for the All Blacks; in 1970. He was a novelty at the time even if he didn't act like, sound like or particularly look like a Polynesian. Since then the trickle has turned to a flood.

To offer the thought that this is actually good for New Zealand society is to state the obvious. Our new society is no longer monochromatic and few doors still remain shut to Polynesian people. The ethnic imagery and dynamism that the modern All Blacks project is about as powerful as it can get. The glamour of it all is irresistibly attractive. It does not go unnoticed in other parts of the world. Robin Williams, the actor, watched a video of the All Blacks in action and his preconceived, identikit vision of New Zealand society as a bland, white backwater was shattered. He was so impressed he immediately ordered tickets for the World Cup.

This new, vibrant multicultural image is a metaphor for a society whose hard shell is finally being broken. The upper reaches of sport provide a huge new employment avenue for youngsters from the wrong side of the tracks who would otherwise have little chance of breaking through. Sport is where race relations works best.

The inevitable question is where does all this lead? Will the day come when some of our national teams no longer feature a single white face? More importantly, will it matter? Some New Zealanders openly fear the loss of European identity that a browning of the All Blacks, the Tall Blacks or the Silver Ferns implies. If those who complain watched any premier league soccer match in Britain or NBA basketball match in the United States they would soon realise which way the wind is blowing. Fortunately, the numbers of ethnic curmudgeons are in decline.

This factor of unity in diversity is a powerful one. Philippe Legrain, a British economist, has spent a lot of time analysing the reasons why diverse societies seem to be more productive than more uniform ones. The author of *Immigrants: Your Country Needs Them* draws attention to the phenomenal success rate of football teams like Manchester United or Barcelona which are veritable racial polyglot melting-pots. Those teams, he says, owe their success to their diversity as well as their collective footballing prowess.

We all know that sport provides an ideal medium not just for better race relations but for the building of respect for, and within, distinctive ethnic communities. The profile of the New Zealand Samoan community has been enormously enhanced by the phenomenal successes of so many young Samoans on the sports fields. The Samoan dimension is just as significant a part of the All Blacks make-up as the farmers, the students, or the South Islanders once were and we are growing accustomed to it.

Better still, Pakeha New Zealanders are coming to see Samoans in a new light. They see the courtly, disciplined manner of so many of the new stars and are impressed. They notice that their own kids' idols are no longer white. And New Zealand rugby has unquestionably profited from that infusion of Polynesian talent. The loss of international superiority based on the forbidding power of white farmers in the All Blacks forward pack has to some extent been compensated for by the astonishing dynamism of Polynesian players like Olo Brown, Jerome Kaino, Rodney So'oialo, Keven Mealamu or Jerry Collins. We can't get enough of all that fast-twitching muscularity.

There has been some unease at the way Polynesian players have begun to dominate the domestic game in New Zealand. There have been accusations, the sort that were regularly levelled at Maori players a generation earlier, that the Samoans, Tongans and Fijians weren't reliable enough; that they lacked mental fortitude and wilted under pressure; that their defence was suspect; that they lacked sufficient calm and calculation to overcome seemingly smarter opponents. It was said that the All Blacks were weakened by the infusion of Polynesian players because of this and it was said often and seriously.

It is of course something that is impossible to prove one way or the other but it must be said that, simply because of that explosive energy, Polynesian players sometimes make themselves more vulnerable to missed tackles and because of all that instinctive brilliance they sometimes just go their own way on attack, compromising a team's tactical plan. Pita Alatini offered some interesting insights on this front a few years ago when he said, with commendable candour, that the predominance of Polynesian players in a team induced a more relaxed atmosphere which in turn led to more inconsistent results. "We'd be up for one game and down for the next," he explained.

Other Maori and Polynesian players have said much the same thing. When there is a loss of confidence among one or two Polynesian players it can rapidly infect the others, dragging the team performance down. It is often said that Pacific Islanders are not thinkers on the field and that too many of them in a team means a dumbing down of tactical acumen. It isn't a very persuasive argument, particularly at the top level. Frank Bunce gave the lie to it a decade ago in the All Blacks for starters. So did Pita Alatini, Alama Ieremia and, of course, Tana Umaga. But it is, clearly, a factor in some teams because, on balance, Maori and Pacific Islanders tend to be more instinctive than measured in their approach and every team at the top level needs someone who can plot and plan, adjust and adapt. There will always be a place for a Grant Fox or a Conrad Smith and it is this accommodation of variety that gives rugby its strength of character.

Sometimes it takes a fresh eye to see what we have failed to see, though we have been looking at something for a long time. In 2008 I sat beside an American visitor at the Westpac stadium in Wellington to watch the feature match of that year's Super 14, the Crusaders against the Hurricanes.

The American confessed before the match started that he had never seen a live rugby match before, although he had heard from colleagues at his university back home who had played a bit that it was an advanced form of hand-to-hand warfare minus the incendiary devices. My companion found it rather hard to believe that there might be another game derived from the same origins as American football that could possibly be even more violent and have even less by way of protective clothing.

He was not disappointed. He was appalled. It was a classic crash, bang, wallop encounter, played at breakneck speed with massive collisions, frequent injuries and various individuals, notably Dan Carter, invalided off. I tried to explain to him that rugby is never as bad as first sight suggests; that there is actually more order than chaos even if it doesn't seem so, and that it is a game in which tactics are usually the source of the final outcome.

It was at this point that his perception began to get the upper hand. "Funny you should say that, " he observed. "I noticed that the smart guys in red beat the dumb guys in yellow." He had noticed, he said, that one team, the Hurricanes, was predominantly Polynesian in complexion while the other, the Crusaders, was overwhelmingly white. "The two things are obviously connected," he observed.

Now, as it happened, my American visitor tended, as many Americans endearingly do, to speak in a voice which can be heard some distance away and I became conscious that his pithy observations about race and tactical nous were being listened to by other people around us. I assured him that we don't tend to draw such distinctions in this country. In fact, I told him in lowered tones, we don't much like talking about these kind of differences in New Zealand.

"Hell," he replied. "We talk about little else in the US. That's why you'll never see a black quarterback. The thinking guys in any football team are all white. This ain't prejudice. We have the stats to prove it." One thing was plain. He may not have known much about rugby but he could see a glaring difference in organisation between the guys in yellow and the guys in red, and he was right in that respect. The difference was remarkable. The Hurricanes were systematically exposed by a Crusaders team that kept thinking, kept calm and, with clinical precision, reduced their opponents to a squad of Keystone Cops.

The question is why? Both teams had about the same number of

All Blacks so it wasn't a question of experience. Nor was it talent. If anything the Hurricanes had more natural ball-running ability. Was it a one-off? No, because the Crusaders so often have a habit of making everybody they play look dumb.

When John Mitchell became coach of the All Blacks he quite clearly had reservations about some of the more explosive Polynesian talents. He seemed particularly anxious to eliminate the instinctive and potentially wayward element from his All Blacks team in 2003. He opted for an almost Polynesian-free starting line-up and I drew attention to this in a newspaper column as an interesting phenomenon, stating that it was probably no accident that the selections had cut this way, and that Mitchell appeared to be opting for reliability over instinctive brilliance. This was immediately interpreted by some enthusiasts as an accusation of racism levelled at Mitchell. All hell broke loose. "Mitchell accused of racism!" shouted one newspaper, gloriously missing the point, and Mitchell himself was, understandably, not amused.

It got worse. I happened also to be at the time an occasional commentator for Sky TV and the producer of the rugby programmes panicked and issued a craven apology for the remarks, presumably on my behalf, when the matter was nothing to do with Sky.

It showed just how sensitive the issue of race still was and how easily the notion of prejudice will instantly replace objectivity. And how quickly we duck for cover. Alas, we still have some distance to travel down the road to that objectivity today. Any suggestion, from any quarter, that Polynesian players might in some way be different from Europeans has audiences darting for the exit and a chorus of moronic voices shouting "discrimination!" Will there ever be a time when we can look at this comfortably and objectively and see that difference for what it is; and rejoice in it?

It is our point of difference. It is what makes the All Blacks such an intriguing outfit to sports followers all over the world. But it is also the single most important reason why we win more than other countries. If there is a better combination than a bunch of hardened, pragmatic Pakeha tight forwards surrounded by a Polynesian loose forward combination, marshalled by a dictatorial Pakeha halfback or first-five and a backline of lightning fast, sidestepping Polynesians then I don't know what it is. We have the best of both worlds and it is an advantage we should be rather more grateful for.

Of Poachers and Gamekeepers

EVERY TIME I visit one of the three Pacific Islands rugby powers I find myself marvelling at the resilience of the game there in spite of just about every disadvantage imaginable. Fiji, Tonga and Samoa are the most remarkable rugby countries on earth. The collective catalogue of negatives — isolation, minute size, relative poverty, an absence of administrative experience, virtually no local income generating capacity and the rest of the world pinching their best talent — would have defeated even the most ardent of rugby spirits anywhere else in the world, but not here. All three of them regularly deliver up a reminder to the major powers that size and numbers don't always win.

Until recently rugby in the Pacific was still in that semi-divine state in which it is played for the sheer joy of it. Yes, there's some money here and there which complicates things but by and large Pacific rugby has been a model of how the game ought to be. Tragically, all that is fraying at the edges as the long arm of professionalism reaches out and takes the game by the throat in the islands.

It was a long time in the coming but the International Rugby Board finally acknowledged a year or two ago that it had an urgent case for treatment on its hands. The public recognition by the IRB that Pacific Islands rugby was at death's doorstep was an uncharacteristic admission of failure but it showed a welcome willingness to bite the bullet and do something to save the game in the islands.

If ever a country needed urgent rescue it is Tonga. There, in that most conformist of societies, an outbreak of non-conformism threatens to swamp the game. It all began when an opportunistic entrepreneur thought he would set up a rival organisation to the Tonga Rugby Union. This body announced to the world, and the IRB in particular, that it was open for business as the new owner of the game in Tonga. Needless to say the old owner took a dim view of this and there followed a succession of skirmishes which ended up in court. Like Tongan politics, everything happened under the surface and the IRB became unsure who precisely was in charge in Tonga. The driving force behind the attempted *coup d'état* was of course money. The new body offered a variety of inducements to players to join its competition with the lure of big money in a professional future the actual shape of which remained mysteriously vague. Sione Taumoepeau, the chairman of the official Tonga Rugby Union, became increasingly frustrated at the inability of the TRU to impose itself, not least because of its haphazard approach to its legal obligations which the rebel organisation exploited cleverly.

Graham Mourie was despatched by the IRB to Tonga to try and unravel the situation but couldn't even get the two warring factions in the same room. The stand-off continues. At stake is the subsidy that the IRB pays to the emerging national unions to grow the game. Tonga remains on the brink of forfeiting IRB support if it can't get its act together. It needs help if it is to be brought back from the brink of extinction. The Tongan government realised that if this fracas wasn't settled, Tonga was not going to be allowed in to the World Cup in 2011, so it stepped in and took over. It had no choice when the IRB issued an abrupt ultimatum.

This raises an awkward question. How deeply into the affairs of a national union must the governors of the international game immerse themselves? There was considerable resentment in Tonga — and elsewhere — when the IRB introduced its high performance programme to the Pacific. There were complaints that the model was one that didn't fit with the Tongan way of doing things. If the Tongans are to be believed it took several years before the IRB began to listen and enable the Tongan union to do it their way. Whether "their" way will yield better results is probably debatable but this revealed the tension that exists between donor and recipient.

What this episode also revealed was the absence of any genuine pan-Pacific cooperation. The IRB will never be able to solve the essentially cultural problems that arise when it comes to coping with the corrosive impact of professionalism. What is desperately needed is a South Pacific Forum-type agreement involving Australia, New Zealand and the Pacific unions with the larger countries acting as the delivery agents of assistance in a long-term programme designed to build the game sustainably in the region as a whole. Up till now Australia and New Zealand have been acting like regional robber barons rather than partners. This just isn't good enough when rugby, symptomatic of whole societies in the Pacific, is in a state of growing crisis.

There are two interconnected issues at the centre of the Pacific problem. The first is the unavailability of Pacific Islanders to play for their country. This has been driven by professional franchises elsewhere offering the best players deals to which they simply can't say no. When the well being of a large extended family is on the line nobody can blame those players for going where the wallets are fattest. Pacific players are the remittance men of the 21st century.

There has been a huge acceleration in the poaching of talent from Tonga, Samoa and Fiji. Scouts from all over the world converged on the islands in search of another Jonah Lomu. Hundreds of muscular youngsters were offered contracts on the cheap. It began an era of talent trafficking which has never slowed down. The Pacific countries have been shorn of much of their emerging talent and their unions have been angry and resentful at the cynical way this has been pursued by clubs, schools and universities in bigger rugby-playing environments.

Critics in the Northern hemisphere have tended to point the finger at New Zealand in this respect and there is no doubt that New Zealand, because of its intimate relations with the Pacific Islands, has been the leading offender, but others must share the blame as well. The Pacific is awash with talent scouts from just about every rugby-playing country in the world, all touting contracts, and the price is steadily rising. And, after all, Northern hemisphere criticism about New Zealand living off Polynesian talent has a hollow ring when you consider the vast numbers of players from abroad that England and France are hoovering up.

What can be done to protect Pacific talent? Is it fair that their best players can be enticed so easily, and for so little in material terms, away from their home and, all too often, their eventual eligibility to play for their country?

This traffic is seemingly unstoppable. It is the market at its most pernicious at work and in all free markets the weaker are at the mercy of the stronger. The IRB is not powerless, however, to arrest the latest trend whereby those absentee players cannot be released for national duty because of club obligations in Britain or France. It is outrageous that big, private rugby clubs can shelter behind laws which were never intended for this purpose. European restraint of trade laws are not insurmountable and if the efforts currently under way to provide exclusions in the sporting context are successful, the player availability ball game could change dramatically.

This outrageous development needs to be stopped and stopped quickly. Anybody who is selected for his country, and is available, should be released from club obligations and the only way this can be guaranteed is by the IRB resolving to enforce it and where necessary providing compensation. What better way of subsidising Island rugby than ensuring that their best players take the field in international competition?

But that is only part of the solution. The Pacific Island countries need to be bolstered by more genuine international competition and competition that yields genuine cash flow. One thing we do know and that is they can't make ends meet on the basis of gate takings from home internationals in the Islands. In Apia or Nuku'alofa the grounds are so decrepit that half the crowd simply climb the fence and watch it for free. The Chinese have stepped in, recognising how much kudos there is to be gained by providing rugby stadiums, and are busily granting Samoa and Tonga rather better facilities than they ever had before. This, however, is only a palliative in terms of the need for real revenue generation.

One option is to provide the opportunity to play "home" games at venues like Auckland or Wellington where there is an assured "home" audience for any team representing Samoa, Tonga or Fiji and at which the Island union would take the lion's share of the gate. Imagine the turnout to a game featuring Pacific Island countries at the Wellington Stadium or Eden Park? Think of the revenue raising possibilities for these impoverished Island unions. Think of the benefits in terms of PR for New Zealand rugby.

We in New Zealand have been hounding the Northern hemisphere unions for years over revenue sharing. Why shouldn't Fiji, Tonga or Samoa be entitled to a similar deal from us on a regular basis? Their case is a rather more compelling one.

To its credit the IRB hasn't been idle after all those years of neglect. The Pacific Rugby Cup tournament which features two regional teams from each of Fiji, Tonga and Samoa, introduced in 2006, is a useful step towards providing worthy competition between club rugby and the genuine international stuff. Whether the experimental Pacific Nations Cup, the second-tier tournament involving countries from around the Pacific basin, serves as the best vehicle to raise competitive levels remains to be seen.

There should also be opportunities for big one-off fundraisers, not just as a disruptive tack-on but as part of the official international programme in both the Northern and the Southern hemispheres. The Pacific countries are going to need access to places like Dubai, Hong Kong, Los Angeles or Shanghai in exactly the same way that the All Blacks and Wallabies are.

Another more ambitious option would be the creation of a genuine professional franchise operating out of the Pacific, a team that could compete in a constantly evolving Sanzar competition and perhaps go on periodic tours of the Northern hemisphere on a revenue sharing basis to cover the heavy costs of running any team out of the Pacific. That would require solid sponsorship backing and the strong support of both Australia and New Zealand. Neither is currently on the horizon.

Would it work? The Pacifika concept isn't new. Various options have been tinkered with in recent times but none has had serious backing from those whose support really counts, apart of course from the abortive attempt by a private sector group, led by Eric Watson and clandestinely encouraged by the IRB, to establish a Super 12 franchise. Then there is resistance within the Island communities themselves to the inherent loss of national identity. Xenophobia is a constant enemy. It is one thing to declare what a good idea it would be to unite Fiji, Samoa and Tonga into a force that can take on anybody in the world. It is quite another to get them to agree on subsuming their identity. When it comes to collective strategic thinking they just don't get it.

The truth is, however, that, alone, none of them will ever be better than second tier nations and until there is a rigorous eligibility rule applied internationally, their talent will continue to be pillaged by the rest of the world. One can only imagine what drawing power a combined Pacifika team would have on the world stage. With access to sponsorship, the very best in coaching and other expertise, the Islanders would shake the game to its core. They would bring in valuable business to their home countries and add immeasurably to unity within the Pacific Forum community, something that is in rather short supply at the moment.

The great fly in the Forum ointment is Fiji's inability to settle the internal differences that have led to a succession of disruptive coups and which have pushed Fiji rugby out to the margins of international acceptability. Sitiveni Rabuka, a not so bright, rugby-playing soldier, started it all in 1987. Rabuka showed depths of aggression that he had never shown on the rugby field. His successor in the art of constitutional crash-tackling, Frank Bainimarama, has proceeded down exactly the same career path. A military strongman who came to power through the barrel of a gun, Bainimarama is nuts about rugby.

But all Fijians are nuts about rugby. They play it on the beaches, among the coconut palms and in the streets. They have always been the rugby world's great entertainers. They are quick, mercurial and totally unpredictable. The Fijians' game plan is to have no game plan. Until recently their approach was joyous; their spirit of adventure unquenchable.

If there is one great gift Fiji has bestowed upon the rugby world it is the thoroughly modern winger. To the rugby world, Fijian wingers became fashion accessories. Like Gucci sunglasses they were rather flashy, instantly recognisable but neither entirely necessary or very durable. And, like sunglasses, they tended to get lost very easily. Now, things are very different. The Fijians are no longer optional accessories. They have become a domestic essential: the sporting equivalent of an electric toothbrush, something that gets the job done faster, more comprehensively. Something that penetrates every little gap.

Every team now seems to have to have at least one Fijian speedster. The whole world is waking up to the virtues of the Fijian winger. Everyone wants one. Talent scouts from a dozen different countries can be seen trolling around the grounds of Fiji in search of the next wonder boy winger. Offers are being made here, there and everywhere and they are generally irresistible to a kid whose job prospects at home are at best modest and at worst catastrophic.

The Fijian game was built around dexterity, magic footwork, a sudden eye for a gap and the Hail Mary pass. The Fijian sevens team prospered on the back of this inventiveness but the 15-a-side game has languished as more and more positional specialisation became necessary. The physical attributes of Fijians just didn't seem to fit the mould. Except of course on the wing. It was as if a process of genetic engineering had been taking place in some darkened Lautoka laboratory. It has become the norm to think in terms of what your Fijians can do for you rather than what you can do for the Fijians. Having ransacked Fiji for a decade or more you would have thought that the rest of us owe them something in return.

In the Pacific Islands the professional era is just dawning. There are opportunities to have sport, particularly rugby, spearhead a whole new area of productive activity and employment. There is both an opportunity and a responsibility here for Australia and New Zealand. So far the record of real assistance has been hopelessly unimaginative and inadequate.

This is the time to get serious about backing the game as an enterprise in countries like Fiji where it can do so much to heal political wounds. The approach by the Labour government to the situation in Fiji after the 2000 coup was sanctimonious and stilted. New Zealand stood on ceremony, taking a very literal line on sanctions and finished up making no progress whatever by closing the shutters.

If there is a single activity which can act as a circuit-breaker it is rugby. It is by far the most potent form of soft diplomacy available in the Pacific and could yield surprising results. Commodore Bainimarama has shown copiously that he will go to great lengths to keep Fiji up there when it comes to rugby. As it demonstrated in South Africa, rugby can become a potent weapon for reconciliation. But only if the will to harness it exists.

If ever there was a time to establish a Pacific Forum-backed consortium dedicated to developing the game in a genuinely regional context, uniting the complementary resources of New Zealand, Australia along with Fiji, Tonga, Samoa and perhaps others, adopting a regional approach to competitions, exchanges of administrative and coaching expertise and regulating the flow of playing talent around the region — then that time has come. There is clearly interest in the idea in Australia. Prime Minister Kevin Rudd has promised assistance via the Australian aid programme. John O'Neill the ARU boss is also keen. Now that rugby is a business, and one capable of generating employment and foreign exchange, it is time we started using it to do exactly that.

Tatou Tatou

FOR A very long time there was one obvious difference between New Zealand and all the other major rugby nations. We weren't all white like them. There was always a sprinkling of Maori players in the All Blacks who were regarded with fascination wherever we went. We did a haka, inexpertly it must be said, before each match. It was the faintest nod in the direction of a biculturalism yet to be taken seriously, let alone coherently articulated.

The British or the French or the South Africans or even the Australians were never quite sure what to make of this "otherness". They clearly weren't particularly comfortable with the notion of a New Zealand team as some sort of rainbow outfit, a mix and match of races and cultures. So they did what the British have always done when something awkward or potentially embarrassing rears its head: they ignored it.

There was never any overt reference to the All Blacks being other than good, loyal colonial boys. Kith and kin. And that was in the 1960s when the ties of empire were suddenly about to loosen and New Zealand was about to be finally persuaded that it was on its own in the world.

Waka Nathan, the greatest Maori player of the age — and one who looked every inch a Polynesian warrior — was the subject of unending curiosity and social awkwardness wherever he went, just as George Nepia had been a generation earlier. In the 1960s the press in Britain adventurously labelled Nathan the "Black Panther" and there was some tut-tutting in more sensitive circles about the appropriateness of this but his exotic ethnicity was never raised in his presence. Waka was vaguely aware of this but much too concerned about playing well to pay it much attention. He was not, in any case, very anxious to be singled out as an oddity and he was one of those individuals who was relatively comfortable in his own bicultural skin.

Sometimes this awkwardness produced hilarious results. One night at a very fashionable little bar adjacent to the All Blacks' hotel in Mayfair, Waka and I were approached by an elderly gentleman who was clearly intrigued to see a very brown and a very white man drinking together in such a place. He tentatively introduced himself but couldn't quite bring himself to ask the obvious question. I decided to force the pace. "Allow me to introduce you to the 'Black Panther'," I said. Waka flinched, but the gentleman, without a moment's hesitation, looked me in the eye and replied, "Aha, and I take it you, sir, are the Pink Panther."

Times have changed. Nobody with 20:20 vision can avoid the reality that our team is no longer overwhelmingly white. Far from it. But nor is England's for that matter. Nor France's; nor even Australia's. And of course the South Africans continue stumbling towards a better reflection of their new identity as a rainbow nation on the rugby field. Multi-racialism is transforming the imagery just as powerfully as money and professionalism. If you aren't white, sport is the quickest way through the glass ceiling.

Integration is the contemporary catch-cry. Against this background it might seem odd that the only country in the world which openly encourages ethnically exclusive sports teams is New Zealand. People have often asked, how can a country like New Zealand which is so conscious of its image of relative racial harmony, persist with a racially selected team: the Maori XV? The answer to that is quite simple really. It's precisely because, rather than in spite of, the relative racial harmony, it can be sustained as a valid form of expression for Maori identity without undue wailing and gnashing of prejudicial teeth.

The objections voiced in South Africa in 2009 to the possibility of a "racially selected" Maori team visiting the Rainbow Republic illustrated this complexity. At one level it was almost comical to watch earnest South African officials wrestle with the prospect of a racially exclusive team violating strict rules in the republic that forbid any team based on race from taking any field. Their anxiety was understandable. Having made so many sacrifices to eliminate discrimination there they were faced with an ironic dilemma. Had they been aware of the history and place of Maori rugby in New Zealand that anxiety might have been alleviated.

Maori rugby has been a distinctive element in the New Zealand game for more than a century. It began quite innocently. Maori communities would field their own teams in their own competitions largely because there was nobody else around to play against at the time. As Maori gradually filtered into towns and cities they also began to play for Pakeha teams as racial prissiness began to dissipate. But Maori, being Maori, remained determined to maintain their distinctive identity in spite of immense pressure to assimilate. They continued to insist on the right to field all-Maori teams and, by and large, they got their way.

They got off to a flying start because of a private initiative which gave rise to perhaps the most bizarre rugby tour ever undertaken: that by the New Zealand "Natives" to Britain in 1888. At the time the imperial spirit was in full flower. It was, of course, in the midst of the Enlightenment, the period when the "noble savage" was given due deference by the colonial powers, so long as he didn't get in the way of progress. This lesser being from the ends of the earth could, with proper instruction and leadership, rise from his rude beginnings to become a civilised man, if not quite as civilised as his white mentor.

Illustrated London News, 1888

The natives get even in 1888.

Sir George Grey who, more than any other individual in the colonial administration of New Zealand, epitomised the confused attitudes toward indigenous people, and who was a senior politician at the time, thought that the idea of a Maori rugby team strutting its stuff in Britain was a particularly good one. It might, after all, help divert them from continually pestering the government — and Queen Victoria herself — over the recent loss of much of their land, thanks largely to Governor Grey himself.

This odd team — all but four of whom were Maori — demonstrated how completely rugby had spread from colonist to indigene and how symbolic rugby had already become as a form of colonial glue.

The *Daily Telegraph* observed loftily on 28 August 1888 that: "The spectacle of the noble Maori, coming from different parts of the earth to play an English game, is a phenomenon that is of the very essence of peace. It is one of our proud boasts that wherever we go, whatever lands we conquer, we find a great national instinct of playing games. Plant a dozen Englishmen anywhere . . . and in a wonderfully short time . . . the level sward is turned into a cricket field in summer and a football arena in winter." Britain was about to find out just how adaptable the Maori could be.

Goodness only knows what the Maori thought they would get by way of a reception in Old Blighty. The English weren't too sure what they were in for either. All they really knew was that these Polynesian people had only recently, or so everybody hoped, eschewed the practice of cannibalism. But, as the *Daily Telegraph* made abundantly clear, colonisation must be doing something right if a bunch of erstwhile cannibals can be persuaded to play proper games, properly. Maybe the colonisation of New Zealand had been worth it after all.

It must have been immensely satisfying to the average *Daily Telegraph* reader to know that a dozen Englishmen planted on New Zealand soil could quickly induce a willingness among the uncivilised to play up and play the game. Imperialism was obviously working. From all reports the team members dressed immaculately, as gentlemen, and were very quick to pick up the social graces of upper middle-class British society.

The Maori team also dressed up to play. Although there is no record of the colours they played in it is unlikely they chose black. The team's badge, worn on their jerseys, was a creative mish-mash of symbols, perhaps illustrative of the confusion over their national identity. It consisted of a set of goalposts, a ball and a small thicket of fern leaves. Under this was written the elevating phrase, "Play up New Zealand".

And play up they did, in more than the classical sense of the expression. The team swept around Britain and Ireland, playing at least three times a week against anyone who cared to face them, completing an astonishing total of 107 matches. In between they partied till they dropped, striking a blow for enlightened multiracialism wherever they went. There were, it seems, plenty of broken hearts among maidens from every station in British society when the time finally came to return. Some didn't return at all, such was the attraction of the bright lights of Victorian London.

The Natives team might not have been quite the model tourists, no matter how apparently noble their Maori character may have been. Owen L Owen, in his epic *History of the Rugby Football Union*, which is as good an antidote to insomnia as has ever been written, was far from impressed with the unruly natives. "Many people objected to the extreme vigour of the Native forwards on occasion and their tendency to protest violently against decisions by the referee . . ."

Several of the Maori actually walked off the field in the game against England in exasperation at the referee's mystifying decisions. The last of these, the incident that prompted the walk-out, was a moment of high farce. T R Ellison, writing about it later, described it thus: "I tackled Mr Stoddart (the star English player) but he escaped, leaving a portion of his knickers in my possession."

The aforesaid portion was apparently not extensive enough to inhibit Mr Stoddart from his purpose. "He dashed along and the crowd roared; then suddenly discovering what was the matter, he stopped, threw down the ball and in an instant we had the vulgar gaze shut off by forming the usual ring round him, stopping play, of course, for the purpose. While we were thus engaged Evershed, one of the English forwards . . . seized the ball and flew for the goal-line. We of course disputed the try and while the discussion was proceeding Mr Evershed boldly picked up the ball from the corner and carried it between the posts and claimed a try there, which the referee very happily granted."

Evershed was obviously a cad. The only surprise is that any of the

Maori stayed on the field at all after that. One commentator at the time suggested that it was a case, neither the first nor the last, of courtly natives being taken for a ride by unscrupulous Englishmen. He might have likened it to the signing of the Treaty of Waitangi. The Natives succeeded in making their mark, however. They went on to beat Ireland with what the press described as "swashbuckling" style in spite of spending the previous night out on Dublin town. *Punch* became quite intrigued by this exotic company of dusky footballers. It said that they had "flabbergasted Surrey and scrumplicated Kent and it is a rum age when a New Zealand team could lick us at goal and scrummage". *Punch* had no idea just how prophetic that remark was going to be.

Maori were of course not the only non-Europeans to play rugby in the late 19th century. Cape coloureds began playing it in South Africa not long afterwards and spent the next 100 years trying to get the South African rugby bosses to recognise them, without success.

The game spread to other African colonies — Uganda, Tanzania, Kenya and of course Rhodesia but the European world turned its back on all these enthusiastic efforts, to its shame. New Zealand became part of that shame almost from the outset. We tend to date the beginning of the disquiet over contact with South Africa at around 1960. In fact, there were many instances of duplicity, double standards and downright prejudice much earlier as settler New Zealand rationalised its own relations with Maori against those of our enlightened white South African imperial cousins, and the South Africans invariably came off best.

Outrageous as it seems now, we meekly complied with South Africa's standard demand that no Maori should ever be allowed to tour South Africa with the All Blacks. Stars like George Nepia, Lui Paewai, Bill Gray and a host of others over the years were quietly shouldered aside when it came to tours to the republic. Rugby was inclusive but not that inclusive.

South Africans, during the era of apartheid, were utterly flummoxed by the Maori team. Here they were, in their own country, being lambasted by the whole world for insisting that rugby — and everything else for that matter — be segregated, and yet nobody seemed to raise more than an eyebrow at New Zealand openly encouraging the Maori to keep their separate identity via rugby. There was of course a rather significant difference, usually lost on those who believed in apartheid. Maori were eligible for all other teams as well whereas under apartheid black or coloured players were kept in their tiny corner. Nor were Maori players ever obliged to play for Maori teams. That was a matter of personal choice. It still is and so it should remain.

Other rugby-playing countries have never been entirely sure how to deal with the Maori phenomenon either. At times there have been suggestions, accusations even, that a team representing one racial group was inappropriate. There was periodical tut-tutting at the IRB until they realised that the "separatism" of Maori rugby was actually a positive, rather than a negative phenomenon.

Maori rugby became a fascinating sub-plot of the game in New Zealand. Maori teams played against every touring team and went on their own tours of other countries, particularly the Pacific Islands where their matches, and their after-match antics, became legendary. They were hugely entertaining. Most of the time. Some of the time, due largely to an inability to prepare together, they would fall apart in the face of really high class opposition. But they kept the flag flying and it has been a proud one.

The issue of qualification for the Maori team has always been a highly intriguing one. I don't know if the likes of Christian Cullen, who miraculously discovered that he possessed a whiff of Maori identity some years ago and duly appeared for the Maori team having been spurned by the All Blacks, could ever recite his whakapapa but it didn't seem to matter to anybody that he appeared to be giving new meaning to the expression born-again Maori.

Even as much as a rumour of Maori blood seems to be enough to satisfy the Maori selectors, as witness the Maori squad of recent years. In another generation the entire population will be eligible for the Maori XV, if not perhaps for a fishing quota.

Tragically, because they are now locked away to prepare for six relentless months of other professional obligations, none of the annually selected All Blacks squad is available for the Maori team any more. Playing for the Maori team is very much a second-best choice. Third-best if the concept of the Junior All Blacks is also taken into account.

As other professional demands encroach, the NZRU commitment to keeping Maori rugby alive has begun to falter. Where will the Maori fit in the new, jam-packed international season? Not out front, you can be sure of that. Yes, there has been some effort to include them in the Pacific Nations tournament but that is an on again, off again commitment.

From time to time it has been suggested that the Maori team should play independently of the All Blacks in the World Cup. After the first World Cup Albie Pryor, the great Auckland Maori player, someone whose main preoccupation was kickstarting Maori cultural pride through sport, laid out the case for a Maori team at the tournament. He was dumped on so hard that he retreated from the game altogether. The NZRU, still picking the shrapnel from its flesh wounds of 1981, was in no mood to experiment.

A few years later Matt Te Pou, the coach of the Maori team, floated a similar suggestion and received a message from the NZRU that he would be boiled in oil if he said such a thing again. Matt offered what in political circles is known as a clarification. In other words he denied he had ever said it.

Since then there has been a deafening silence on this issue and it is unlikely ever to be seriously mooted again. Too many hurdles would need to be jumped. There would have to be a separate Maori Rugby Union. Maori players would have to choose between the Maori team and the All Blacks and would it be appropriate for an All Blacks team, denuded of Maori, to perform a haka?

Maori rugby is typical of many Maori institutions: a little separatism is permitted but it is rarely enough to preserve, let alone promote, Maori interests or identity and it will never be acceptable to the majority to go any further. Are Maori aspirations adequately served by the present arrangements? No they aren't, and rugby's relentless homogenisation can take the credit for that.

The Cultural Calling Card

IN A country riven by a black-white divide, symbolism has always been important. In 1970 the All Blacks were told that the haka should not be performed in South Africa as it would be "misinterpreted" by both the black and white sections of the crowd. To my intense disgust our team management agreed to this arrangement without consulting the players and we were prevented from performing it. Several of us tried to provoke a rebellion but had to abandon it in the greater cause of team unity. It was a mistake, typical of the unassertive approach that New Zealand for so long took to its relationship with the South African establishment.

When rugby relations were restored in 1992 in a special one-off test match at Ellis Park there was never any question that the All Blacks would do a haka. They did it with particular relish and the point was not lost on anybody. Was it my imagination or did I detect a little extra edge of ferocity to it that day? It was as if New Zealand was declaring: "Here is our multiracialism; now where is yours?" Today the haka, no matter what form it is delivered in, is accepted in most countries without demur as an expression of New Zealand's national diversity. They understand.

Some don't, however. Particularly the British. Criticising the haka has become something of a call to arms for British rugby writers who derive a vicarious pleasure in mocking anything that smacks of "native". At any international played in Britain the press box echoes with, "Oh no, here we go again," whenever the All Blacks line up to do their haka. Many observers consider themselves to be thoroughly haka-ed out. They may have a point.

In 2008, *Guardian* columnist Frank Keating called for an end to a "once diverting wheeze [that] has long passed its sell-by date". In case readers hadn't got his drift, he also called the haka a "native rumba", a "danse macabre" and an "over-rehearsed, over-choreographed production number with a nasty malignant edge to it". Keating recalled the occasion when, as a schoolboy, he witnessed "15 rather sheepish white men line up and enact an amiably harmless mime-charade for about 15 seconds". His memory was entirely accurate. For too long New Zealanders paid little more than lip service to Maori custom. The performance of the haka was little short of a cultural disgrace. It didn't much matter how badly it was performed. Pakeha didn't care and Maori had trouble having their voices of concern heard.

The haka was an amiable nod in the direction of a culture that was on the way out. It was indeed a "diverting wheeze". I know this because for a decade in the 1960s I was complicit in this sad patronage. It wasn't until the late 1980s that the haka began to have any genuine cultural meaning. Its evolution mirrors perfectly the cultural renaissance of the Maori in New Zealand. Maori have become infinitely more sensitive to the use of the haka by non-Maori. Most of this has centred round "Ka Mate", the haka devised by Ngati Toa warrior chief Te Rauparaha in the 1830s. There was a terrible stink when the Fiat car company had a bunch of go-go girls doing a very inexpert version of "Ka Mate". The Spice Girls tried it and were equally castigated. The actual owners of "Ka Mate", the Ngati Toa tribe, tried to have it legally proscribed as an item of intellectual property. In their treaty settlement with the government in 2009 this "ownership" was acknowledged but it was also agreed that the right to perform it should not be denied to others.

Many New Zealanders are acutely aware of this background when they watch or perform the haka. It has real, emotional resonance when the All Blacks do it for the simple reason that they, perhaps more than any other feature of the modern New Zealand cultural landscape, most emphatically embody the country's contemporary multiracialism.

Many of the All Blacks' opponents are also now more aware of this. They know instinctively that this is something that matters to New Zealanders. This is where Frank Keating loses the plot. He is a generation out of date.

Anyone who has any understanding of its origins knows that the haka is not an insult or a deliberately provocative act. It is not a war dance. It is a challenge, but a complex one; a challenge to those who perform it as much as those who must stand and face it. And, after all, the Welsh have their mass choir whose collective power is real and palpable. Australians counter the haka with loud and usually tuneless blasts of "Waltzing Matilda". The English drown it out with raucous renditions of "Swing Low, Sweet Chariot". Everyone, it seems, has his antidote.

But Keating has a point when it comes to the so-called malignant edge. There are times when the aggression gets the better of the performer. Then the margin between personal exhortation and war dance disappears. This came to a head when a new haka created by Derek Lardelli exclusively for the All Blacks was unveiled. It created a sensation. With its unmistakable allusions to Samoan and Tongan challenges as well as Maori, the new haka ended with a drawing of the forearm across the throat; or at least that's what it looked like to many of those who first saw it. And they didn't like it. Suggestions of throat-slitting somehow took the performance into the realms of direct provocation. Frank Keating was right. It was malignant. And the way it was delivered was a step up in the aggression stakes. It was one-upmanship at a time of extreme nerves and emotional vulnerability at the beginning of a match. It just wasn't right.

Illustrated London News

A genteel haka — through the eyes of a British beholder.

Loud were the protests. At first they were ignored by the All Blacks' management. Then, clearly chastened by the criticism, they toned the last bit down and the objections became more muted. But it won't go away and the reactions of opposing teams may well be the deciding factor in its future.

A few years ago, a headstrong Welsh Rugby Union tried to diminish the impact of the haka by scheduling it between the two national anthems at a test match in Cardiff. The All Blacks performed the haka in their dressing-room. It is said that it was one of the more vehement performances never witnessed by a crowd. Spectators, many of whom were seeing the All Blacks perform live for the first and last time, were robbed of the chance to view one of rugby's great spectacles. They didn't approve. The Welsh team was duly annihilated and, it seemed, honours were about even on the day.

In 2008 Wales tried another ploy. The Welsh players lined up to face the haka and, after it was over, they eyeballed the All Blacks for several electrifying minutes. The players on both sides stood rigidly still. The world stood still. The referee pleaded with either side to break the impasse. They ignored him. His law book didn't cover this so he did nothing. It was a little moment of pure theatre. The Welsh response was as calculated as the New Zealanders' challenge. Not only did they test the All Blacks during the game, they challenged them before it in a manner that was entirely in keeping with the spirit of the haka.

Fair enough, but where does it all go from here? Clearly, a five-minute stare-down isn't something that can become standard practice. Equally clearly, the All Blacks aren't going to be persuaded to sanitise the haka to the point where it starts to return to its original "wheeze". Something has to give and it ain't going to be the haka. Some things are simply non-negotiable. Will the British or the Australians ever get over their resentment? Probably not.

There needs to be some measure of formal understanding — a protocol or two — as to the place of the haka. That is not beyond the wit of the IRB. If rugby is what it proclaims to be, a modern form of entertainment, then surely the haka becomes indispensable! And by all means let the English have their Morris dancing as well. There's no business like show business.

Uncomfortable Bedfellows

HAS RUGBY been decoupled from its history? Does tradition have any enduring relevance when money becomes the master? On the face of it business is business and sport is sport and the ethics of each do not blend at all comfortably. But rugby now finds itself competing in various marketplaces for investment and support and its security as a, if not *the*, cornerstone of New Zealand's cultural identity is at risk. The competitors are catching up.

One of the great curiosities of New Zealand life is the reluctance of sport and "culture", in the sense interpreted by those who are the guardians of the highbrow, to lie comfortably in the same bed. The implications of this for rugby have never been seriously explored but it is becoming increasingly obvious that as the arts grow in strength, confidence and popularity the zero sum impact on rugby could be severe.

The truth is the cultural elite still tend to thumb their noses at sport and certainly don't expect sport to stick its nose around their door. We're not completely alone in this. The same awkwardness presents itself in many other countries. Sport goes this way and "serious" culture goes that. Governments, never entirely sure what to do about either, and always on the lookout for ways of saving money, tend to make as little commitment as possible. Except when the moment for a photo opportunity comes around.

Culture and sport have traditionally been two different streams with little in the way of confluence; each catering for a particular clientele and each with a faint distaste for the other. The intellectual v the physical; the aesthetic v the prosaic; the chardonnay v the Lion Red. There has always been a tendency among the intellectual elite to belittle the place of physical pursuits. As H L Mencken, the extremely sedentary American columnist, put it: "Exercise is bunk. If you're healthy you don't need it, and if you're sick you shouldn't do it." Mencken died of heart and kidney failure.

Throughout our history there appears to have been little of the natural attraction of these apparent opposites. But are sport and culture really that much at odds? Aren't they more like Siamese twins, often uncomfortable in each other's enforced proximity but unavoidably bound together and often sharing the same vital organs. There is not much difference in essence between modern dance and gymnastics. Yet one is art, the other sport. In organisational and funding terms they fall into different worlds.

Why then this peculiar standoffishness? The working assumption has always been that culture in the classical sense has been the preserve of the higher educated, what are now fondly known as the chattering classes; those who read *The Listener*, hang out at the opera, who prefer to watch serious British drama rather than local reality shows on television, who listen to the Concert Programme but never to Radio Sport, and who will gently sip pinot gris rather than belt down a Tui straight from the bottle.

On the other hand, it has always been assumed that sport — the opiate of the masses — is for those who prefer doing to thinking, action to contemplation. Rugby has of course been the quintessence of the former, yet it, too, has its reflective and creative side rarely acknowledged by any except those who can see poetry in a back movement, drama in a sudden breakout try and a strange beauty in the composite use of mind and body. It is as much about expression as a performance of *King Lear* or *La Traviata*.

The history of this cleavage is fascinating and it tells us much about contemporary attitudes towards rugby. In New Zealand in the 19th century the few who were interested in the arts — and they were indeed few at that time — looked only to Europe for inspiration while the many who became interested in organised outdoor sport looked only to their own backyard; to getting on with it here and creating something that they could claim was distinctively local, even if all the sports were imports.

By the end of the 19th century sport in general and rugby in particular had established itself as perhaps *the* defining point for the new society. It might have been a borrowed suit but it fitted our nationalism very nicely. As the newspaper *Zealandia*, the mouthpiece of the opiated masses, pronounced in 1899 with ill-disguised relief in contemplating the massive popularity of rugby: "There is now no danger of New Zealand rearing a nation of milksops, effeminate fops and luxurious dandies . . ."

The die was cast. Those who favoured the more aesthetic pursuits were steadily marginalised and became increasingly more contemptuous of the muddied oafishness of sport. And it's never really been any different. It's partly a question of money. While the arts perennially teetered along on the edge of insolvency, sport, and rugby union in particular, became positively prosperous by comparison. Rugby paid its way. The arts needed patronage.

Once professionalism came along the difference was further exacerbated. So much so that it became apparent that the government would need to intervene to subsidise a number of arts activities of national importance if they were to survive. This raised some intriguing questions. Is professional sport the same as professional theatre? Or a professional orchestra, or ballet? Is giving money to rugby the same as giving money to a dealer gallery?

Financial support for the arts is now second nature, even if there are rumblings in drier economic circles about the iniquities of "picking winners". Helen Clark's enthusiasm for public sector investment in the arts kick-started a whole new era of relative equality with sport. Our artists, performers, musicians and even our comedians are now competing on a world stage with a confidence that has really only become apparent in the last decade or two.

Where did that confidence come from? Spiro Zavos attributes this broad-based success essentially to the trail-blazing achievements of the All Blacks. "Having a rugby team able to compete around the world with every other nation, a team that was arguably the rugby team of the twentieth century in terms of its achievements, has given New Zealanders the confidence to take on the rest of the world in every other form of endeavour . . . New Zealand writers, songwriters, military people, scientists, academics, economists, mountaineers, journalists, businessmen, Olympic athletes, actors, film-makers, inventors, diplomats, artists, farmers, IT experts and those in many other fields of endeavor have played above their weight round the world. It is not fanciful to assert that this exuberant, expansive and clever attitude to life . . . has been motivated by the success of the All Blacks, in doing the same thing on the rugby grounds of the world . . ."

Lonsdale

Marketing the rump of the New Zealand economy.

This might seem to be drawing a rather long bow but it's not entirely fanciful. Riding on the coat-tails of the All Blacks may have some cultural spin-off after all. There has been much national navel-gazing in recent years about how New Zealand can boost its creative capital in a world in which ideas will dominate the future of profits. In a curious way the extraordinary creativity of the All Blacks over the last decade has carried a very distinctive torch for others to follow.

It is time that those who run the arts in New Zealand began to understand the power of this creativity and to use it more imaginatively to showcase our national imagination alongside our singers, musicians, writers and artists. Just imagine what a flutter a monster inflatable rugby ball like the one that was used in Paris during the 2007 World Cup would create at the Venice Biennale. Rather more, I dare say, than the various obscure contraptions we have sent to Venice the last two or three times.

Rugby has been a powerful determinant of the perceptions of other people about New Zealand. From the moment I stepped off the plane at Heathrow on my very first international tour in the 1960s it quickly became apparent to me that, to most people outside New Zealand, the All Blacks were New Zealand and New Zealand was the All Blacks. One and the same, indivisible.

It seemed to be the only frame of reference that many people abroad had of New Zealand, apart from the vague impression of a pleasant, quiet and unruffled sort of place; a bit sheepish, unswerving in loyalty to Her Majesty and everything piously closed down at the weekend. The All Blacks provided a substance that otherwise seemed to be missing. People who otherwise thought of New Zealand as a cultural Hicksville had that impression modified by the All Blacks. Here was something that demanded respect. It was a nationalism that arrived early, and stayed at the front of people's consciousness. For much of the 20th century, New Zealand artists, writers and others concerned about creating a local voice, an idiom that was distinctive from that of Europe, took the best part of that century to achieve it. The All Blacks achieved it almost immediately and the aura has never diminished.

Being on an All Blacks tour was a bit like being a stunt man in a circus act. It was assumed by those who came to watch the All Blacks play that what you saw was all there was. In some respects that was true. Our sense of identity was constructed around our apparent invincibility as a team and of course a loss on the field represented a savage kick in the private parts of that identity. We therefore went to great pains to avoid such a threat.

But beneath the veneer of sporting swagger, we were a collection of uncertain and unassertive beings. Until, of course, we hit the field of play. The changing-shed was our phone box in Metropolis. We went in as Clark Kent and came out as Superman.

Our personality was woven into the black jersey. Our nationalism was one provoked by the immediate circumstances; by an intense pride in consistently winning and an equally intense fear of defeat; of letting down all the folks back home who looked to us to keep their sense of self intact. To lose to any British side, particularly England, was a form of colonial capitulation and the thought of having to tug our forelocks to the lesser athletes of the old country was a deadly motivator. Wherever we went, whether in Britain, or France, South Africa, Australia or just about anywhere else, as New Zealanders we were seen as different from the locals, but only by the factor of rugby.

This mindset materialised as early as 1905. The great "Originals" team that toured Britain and France, led by David Gallaher, went away assuming that they were British and came back realising that they weren't;

they were something different. The New Zealand identity, which has always been said to have been discovered at ANZAC Cove in 1915, was actually discovered a decade earlier, via the playing fields of England. As Lloyd Jones put it in his brilliantly wistful reconstruction of that defining All Black tour:

"People flocked to see us
as they did
the African pygmies
sword-swallowing Moroccans
the bloated Japanese carp
and Annette Kellerman
at the London Hippodrome.
We were up there
With Asia and the floating icebergs
A thing of wonder

We who had come to discover
Found ourselves discovered
And in the process discovered
Ourselves —"

Ever since, the issue for New Zealanders has been the same. To be beaten was, in a way, to yield up that part of our identity that made us different from the British. That is why we were just that much more motivated than any other team; and still are. We were busy asserting our point of difference. Whenever the All Blacks faced a British team, that hard core of new world assertiveness lent the team a little more impetus. This mental determination may not quite have the same deadly edge that it once did but it is still there nevertheless. We still hate losing to anyone, anywhere, anytime.

It is often said that New Zealand enjoys an unfair advantage because of its long-standing adoption of the colour black as its national sporting uniform. Black carries an unmistakable connotation of brooding power. There is a hint of evil, of ruthlessness, of unforgiving aggression. It is the ideal colour for sporting intimidation.

To be dressed in black on a rugby field is always worth points on the board. There isn't the slightest question that it has always helped give the All Blacks an edge over opponents even if it is nothing more than the power of imagery at work. I can remember the adrenalin shot of confidence I got each time I was handed the black jersey. People seem to look bigger in black. I felt bigger. I can remember the gasps of anticipation as the All Blacks ran out onto a foreign field and the immediate psychological advantage that this conveyed. That phenomenon has never changed. The imagery is never lost on a single spectator at a test match. Hopefully, it never will be. Every now and again the All Blacks are obliged to play in another colour so as not to clash with the colours of their opponents. Some say we should flatly refuse to do this as it seems to send our team into a clueless funk. Whoever decided that they should turn out in those awful grey outfits in the fateful 2007 World Cup quarter-final should have been fired on the spot.

Black works. It has worked even more forcibly as New Zealand teams have got darker in complexion. It has also worked well for other New Zealand sporting campaigns. In the 1990s when Team New Zealand was challenging for the America's Cup the choice of black for the boat gave the challenge a sense of expectation that no other colour could summon. American commentators became aware of this, almost subliminally, and the mystique that shrouded the big black boat was a factor behind the ruthlessly executed victory.

New Zealanders know instinctively that they can take on the world and win but only rugby enables them to say that no matter whatever else happens they are perennially the world's best at something. New Zealand might be small, isolated, lonely and not very confident but it bows to nobody when it comes to rugby. That is why the nagging question — can we sustain that pre-eminence in the face of full-blown professionalism — becomes such an important one. Are we producing dramatic, game-breaking ideas or inspirational leaders? Do we have clear and uncluttered goals? And, above all, do we still have an adequate sense of community backing?

Another question that has to be constantly asked in the New Zealand context is how do we maximise the positive energy that sporting success can inject into a society in constant need of collective reassurance? If it is to be achieved in any sport in New Zealand that sport will be rugby, the only institution with anything approaching the level of resources, or the track record necessary to keep it internationally competitive. But there's a problem. Professionalism polarises public opinion. The more professionalised the sport gets the more public opinion divides as to its legitimacy. Resentment builds up around the exclusivity and earning power of a professional sports team even if, on the face of it, there is devoted support for the brand. This issue is an intensely complicated one and the research is really only in its infancy.

When it comes to hosting a World Cup, however, there is no contest. Everything else gets shoved into the shade. So far as the government is concerned it is an investment on the basis of a calculated return to a wider economy. Those in the arts industries legitimately ask why similar investments don't come their way. Why, for instance, are governments so reluctant to underwrite the New Zealand Festival of the Arts, some would say every bit as significant a showcase of this country as a rugby World Cup? If there is an answer it is that one way or another rugby generates more obvious fervour, more overt nationalism, vastly more income from the liberal spending of 60,000 visitors, and of course enhanced prospects for the re-election of the government. If we win.

The 2011 World Cup promises to gobble up every penny a reluctant government is now obliged to push its way. There are obligations afoot that became inescapable when Helen Clark in a forbiddingly feminist way persuaded the IRB to let us have it. This will severely constrain discretionary expenditure in the broader cultural field for years, particularly in the midst of a severe recession. And what will that do to the relations between the arts and sport? It could polarise them in a way that will make the reconciliation — and thus the wider acceptability of rugby as a valid form of cultural expression — more problematic.

There will, of course, be plenty of Maori inputs to the programme and that is as it should be. There will, too, be some astute arts enterprises who will leverage off the World Cup on their own initiative but it's the largely Pakeha arts community that needs to be woven in. Here is about as good an opportunity as we will ever get, with the world's cameras focused on New Zealand, to show others and ourselves that rugby can actually live in harmony with the arts; that New Zealand culture is much more than just rugby.

When it comes to the use of public money to promote sport a single question confronts any government. Should we be consciously picking winners or should we be spreading the resources across the mass participation programmes? There are many who believe that any taxpayer money devoted to sport should be spent on mass participation. Professional sport, they say, is a business that the government has no place in. It is the preserve of the private sector. It's the business of business, not the taxpayer.

This is the same argument that has been applied to the economy as a whole since the market reforms of the 1980s and by and large it continues to hold sway, even if governments are now routinely having to buy or bail out large private enterprises as a means of keeping national economies afloat.

The sports funding tide has turned somewhat in New Zealand, prompted by the obvious examples of other countries that place great store on sporting success and who patently do pick winners, and fund them accordingly. Australia, New Zealand's muscular neighbour, is about as vivid an example of investment in sporting success as any society on earth. Do they think it's worth half a million dollars to produce every gold medal at the Olympics? You don't hear too many complaints because that's the return on investment that Australian athletes usually deliver. It's comforting to know that Australians are still curiously dependent on sporting success. The Australian public demands nothing less — perhaps because of a lingering uncertainty as to what Australia represents in a broader cultural context, a dilemma not dissimilar to that of New Zealand — and they are happy to pay for it.

Should rugby be the beneficiary of precious public money? After all, if you're picking winners then rugby's your obvious choice, even if it is professional. Holding one's breath on this would be ill advised, however. Rugby may be the most likely international winner but it gets precious little from government. There has been a long-standing assumption — not least in the Wellington bureaucracy — that New Zealand rugby is rich enough to make its own way. But is it? It certainly wasn't able to provide the funds to create a stadium capable of holding 60,000 people for the 2011 World Cup finals. Much of that had to come from the public purse. In the end it was the community who had to stump up much of the

$100 million plus needed to satisfy the IRB that New Zealand could meet its World Cup obligations. It is the ratepayers of Wellington, Hamilton, Napier, Dunedin and Christchurch who are paying for bigger and better stadiums. And it is the taxpayers who will have to pick up the residual bill after the World Cup has come and gone. The cost per head of the 2011 tournament will be infinitely higher than any other host country has had to bear in the past.

That obligation has raised a certain tension between the game's administrators and the country's beleaguered taxpayers. In the minds of many, the game is seemingly awash in dollars. To then put its hand out for a government grant to help pay off the IRB and to build a big enough stadium to host the finals is more than a bit rich for many taxpayers. Precisely how strongly this sentiment will impact on support for the game after 2011 is anybody's guess. Who will be complaining if New Zealand finally wins? Hardly anybody. But what if we lose? New Zealanders will have paid, by their standards, spectacularly high prices to watch the key matches on top of the vast public investment in the tournament and they won't be in the mood for another brutal humiliation. This, they will conclude, is not a good return on investment.

There are issues of relativity in all this. By comparison with the Northern hemisphere rugby superpowers the game in New Zealand is slowly becoming a ragged cousin and the traffic is all one-way now that pure professionalism begins to bite. It is hard to avoid the conclusion that it is actually going to be all about purchasing power from here on. We just don't have enough of that to compete with France or England, or South Africa or even Australia for that matter.

There may come a time when rugby goes cap in hand to the government for a bail-out. Then the test of loyalty to our cultural flagship will really be on the line.

Climbing the Stairway to Heaven

THE STAIRWAY to stardom is a long one and it starts at school. A generation ago a schoolboy player with ambition would not expect any premium attention until he left and joined a club. Not any more. The long arm of professionalism has reached down the throat of the school system and seized control of the process.

In what he described as the death of the apprenticeship, journalist Gregor Paul traced the alarming capture of the pathway by the academies and age-group systems. Instead of earning their stripes through club rugby, the best of the juniors are purloined onto the escalator and have virtually nothing to do with club rugby — and the searching apprenticeship that represents — at all. This suits the elite but it has tragic results for the clubs.

The New Zealand pathway system has been regarded as the most successful in the world but that lead is diminishing rapidly. In England in particular the system is little short of breathtaking. Through the Advanced Apprenticeship in Sporting Excellence scheme the most promising players combine their senior school experience with an intense rugby training programme. The schools in the AASE programme work in association with the big club academies. Players are identified at age 12 or 13 and the best of them are fast-tracked through the programme. Although it is never explicitly stated, all of these kids are expected to abandon any pretensions of a career outside rugby. They enter a hermetically sealed environment and they stay there if they are offered a professional contract. It is frightening stuff and the schools have become fanatically competitive in search of the right talent, not least because they benefit from the subsidy of externally funded scholarships. Slowly but surely the few top schools are monopolising the talent. The many who can't, or won't, play this game quietly withdraw from the race and rugby declines in popularity. This is a pattern that is being repeated in Wales and elsewhere in the United Kingdom and it hardly bodes well for the future of the game as a mass participation sport.

New Zealand schools have for many years gone out and head-hunted talented players for the First XV. John Graham, the former All Blacks captain who later became Headmaster of Auckland Grammar, did this in a subtle, almost undetectable way but always seemed to come up with a steady stream of exceptional players, not always it seemed from within the school's arbitrarily imposed catchment "zone" in Auckland. He knew all too well the attractive power of an all-conquering First XV. Other schools did likewise. It became an epidemic. Schools were openly poaching the best from each other. A recent truce was called, but it seems that that hasn't lasted long with a resumption of hostilities, and it can turn nasty. In 2008, College Sport, the organisation that manages secondary school competitions, had to arbitrate in 15 cases of alleged poaching. There is now a complicated rule-book on transfers from one school to another. Where will it end?

St Bede's College in Christchurch offers scholarships to kids from as far afield as Japan and Wales. The premise is that they'll get a good Catholic education as well as bolstering the ranks of the school's footy teams. Lads from the three rugby countries in the Pacific with real rugby talent don't need much of a scholastic record to pass muster at just about any New Zealand secondary school these days. The same could be said of Australia, and in South Africa talented black schoolboy players are like a talisman of the school's progressiveness.

Whatever else may have changed in the contemporary school system the core belief that a good First XV delivers prestige has not. The gladiatorial nature of rugby means that the elite will always attract patriotic attention. Take the case of Warwick School (for boys) in England. Once a bulwark of hearty amateurism, the game being the thing rather than the winning, Warwick has catapulted itself well and truly into the 21st century and is now one of the top rugby schools in the country.

Rugby is struggling to hang on to boys' hearts and minds everywhere. Schools, almost without exception, are facing declining participation rates in organised sport. Teachers no longer turn out after school to coach. They want to be paid overtime to do that. Or they just don't care any more.

Rugby isn't alone in that. Various surveys place the attrition rate for American sporting youth at anywhere between 40 and 50 per cent by the time they start their second year of high school. A hefty number of those who quit say — significantly — that it is because too much emphasis is placed on winning. Youngsters realise fairly early on that there is not much glory in coming second and the increasingly large time commitment just doesn't seem to cut the mustard if you don't win consistently. It isn't fun any longer, they say, and they are damn right. There are many more attractions in life beyond the dreary gym and training field routines.

Boys seem to be struggling with the old-fashioned notion that it's good enough to play sport for the enjoyment value, rather than being duped into judging their entire experience on the strength of the result. They are naturally competitive. They'll try to win without anyone needing to repeatedly badger them about the ignominy of coming second, but they are turning off high performance sport in droves.

A University of Michigan study seemed to confirm this. In the biggest survey of its type, young athletes were asked to rank their motives for participation. They provided a clear-cut response. The runaway priority, regardless of gender, was to have fun. The next was a combination of factors: the interplay of skill development, physical development and social interaction. However, the motive "to win" was rated only the eighth highest priority for school-sponsored sport, and wasn't even listed by non-school sports participants. Translated? An overemphasis on the result was a turn-off. Unfortunately, the range of opportunities to enjoy the experience of just playing it for the hell of it is steadily diminishing in the United States.

Interestingly, this is actually serving to promote rugby union in America because of its reputation as a fun game in which the fun continues into the after-match festivities.

In New Zealand, the other end of the spectrum, the tendency is not to play at all because of the stigma associated with failure in the game.

Perhaps the most alarming trend is away from lower level participation at secondary schools. Many youngsters come to a simple conclusion. If I can't make the top team it just isn't worth it at all. So, the game increasingly consists of the top tier and the rest who just give up and watch, the same result that American football has produced in American schools. The NZRU has turned itself inside out and upside down looking for ways of breaking the turn-off cycle at secondary schools and the post-school period but it seems it is fighting a lost cause.

Part of the trouble is the sheer commitment involved. Top schoolboy rugby players live in a different world — the world of the semi-professional player. No matter where in the world it is the same — Buenos Aires or Bloemfontein, Cardiff or Christchurch. They arrive at school before dawn, pull on their rugby boots, train themselves to a standstill, shower, head to class and then to the gym. They push man-sized weights, adhering to a strict regime set by their fitness trainer. On their nutritionist's advice they stuff themselves with protein and carbohydrates and sometimes more sinister stuff. Then it's on to the video analysis, using the same tools the All Blacks use to study techniques and tactics.

Boys are now built like men, train like men and the best of them are faced with commercial decisions that men face even if they don't think like men. And sometimes they don't act like men. They lose it. The ugly riot that erupted in 2009 at the end of a tense match between Auckland Grammar School and Kelston Boys' High was a frightening illustration of the effect that all this pent-up ambition and aggression can have on immature minds. The two sides flew at each other for no justifiable reason the moment the final whistle sounded. This was the product of minds that had been so totally wired to winning that their sense of proportion deserted them completely. It is that loss of proportion that is the worrying factor.

There was talk at the time of racial insults from the sideline but this couldn't adequately account for the ferocity of the fracas that followed. Needless to say both schools denied responsibility, as did the game's administrators. The boys who were judged to have been primarily responsible were given severe sentences and justice was seen to be done. But was it? Of course their behaviour was unacceptable but nobody paused to consider that it might actually have been the environment in which these youngsters now find themselves as much to blame as the boys themselves.

Once again rugby's nanny state intervened and over-reacted, effectively driving a number of youngsters out of the game and onto the streets.

Many secondary schools players just like those who momentarily lost their marbles in Auckland are hounded by talent scouts and offered attractive little "packages" with the promise that if they perform they will become decidedly bigger packages. There is a lot at stake. More and more talented young rugby players are focused only on the pot of gold at the end of the scholastic rainbow rather than an actual job. They know that with a little luck they will be picked up by the system and with a lot of luck they will go all the way to a professional career.

Of course if they don't get a bigger offer on leaving school they rapidly lose interest and in pretty short order are lost from the ranks of the playing. It's a lose-lose outcome.

Whichever way you look at it the conclusion is undeniable; the better the best get the more likely the rest are to bail out. What does this mean for the future? The best are, of course, going to continue to get bigger and better and the gulf between them and the rest will widen to the point where, as in America, the numbers participating at the lower levels dwindle away. That means one thing: schoolboy rugby numbers seem fated to decline. Can this cycle be broken? If it isn't, then it's good morning America and goodnight nurse for rugby.

The Magic of Seven

THERE ARE some killjoys in rugby who maintain that sevens is just an irritating nuisance; a watered down diversion which plucks away at the hem of the real game and which threatens to devalue it as a genuine contact sport. Happily, those few who find sevens a nuisance are rapidly disappearing as this truncated form of the game goes steadily more global and leads the charge in terms of entertainment value. Sevens is to rugby what Twenty20 is to cricket, the showtime end of the game. Soon it will be in the Olympics with all the attendant hoopla that this provides.

But it's more than just the froth on the top. Sevens is now seriously challenging the traditional game for attention, sponsorship and airtime. It also appears to be leading the charge when it comes to innovation and inclusion. The cleavage between sevens and 15-a-side is perhaps sharpest in South Africa. The sevens squad has changed dramatically in the space of three or four years. Now it is demonstrably black whereas the Springboks are still predominantly white. What's going on here? Can it be that sevens has become the leading edge in the emancipation of South African rugby?

Sevens has been around for a long time and it got left behind when the game suddenly went professional. Now it is catching up.

It all began in Scotland more than a century ago. Ned Haig, an innovative Melrose butcher, was, history has it, the inventor of the truncated form of the game. Perhaps he just got tired of failing to muster a full 15 for the weekend's match and did some trimming. Whatever, Haig the butcher got more ambitious. He suggested that Melrose should host a sports tournament to help bolster club funds based around an abbreviated form of the game and on 28 April 1883 sevens rugby was born. It is now enjoyed the world over.

It took a long time, however, for sevens to gain any real credibility. Apart from Scotland and parts of England it was no more than an eccentric diversion, played by those who preferred the intense tactical dancing about looking for an opening or an overlap to the direct confrontational stuff. It helped fill an autumnal gap in the rugby season and it was very friendly in character. Serious rugby players, apart from a few border Scots, tended to laugh it off as a wimpish cop-out and the game was virtually non-existent in New Zealand, Australia or South Africa. I played serious rugby for most of the 1960s around the world and the only time I encountered sevens was in Scotland.

How things have changed. Sevens rugby is slowly but surely shifting out from under the heavy shadow of the traditional game. Hong Kong took the early initiative and very soon its annual tournament became a popular way of having a lot of fun in an exotic setting with a modestly competitive flavour. It gradually got bigger and bigger. Television became seriously interested. Hong Kong began to see a wider tourism opportunity and began to market the sevens weekend all over the world. Chris Patten, the last British governor of Hong Kong, saw the sevens weekend as a useful means of maintaining Hong Kong's international status once the colony returned to China.

As the Hong Kong tournament got bigger the competition stiffened and people began to take it seriously. So much so that Hong Kong established itself as an essential part of the international rugby programme. When the IRB finally got its hands on it there was no question as to its future. Rugby suddenly realised that here was another device with which to grow the bigger game rather than just remaining an irritating diversion. In 2009 the Hong Kong tournament broke all attendance records. The international circuit that has been established is going to be a major crowd-puller in the future. This is Hong Kong with bells on; a tournament that each of the major rugby nations is taking more and more seriously as they realise the phenomenal drawing power of this rapid-fire exhibition of open field running and tactical acumen.

Anyone who watches the international tournament at the Wellington Stadium will have realised that sevens has finally made the big-time in this country. It is here to stay. Like a cricket one-dayer, it is tailor-made for entertainment. It is not so much a series of mini matches as a rolling event; rugby's equivalent of the Big Day Out, with almost as much debris to clean up afterwards. Sevens has become one of Wellington City's premier events. It is as good an example of the immense drawing power of well packaged, well promoted, full-on party-time with rugby added. The fact that the first Wellington tournament in 2000 was the first time that a New Zealand sevens team had actually taken the field in this country came as something of a surprise to many who were present.

Sevens might have become the fun end of rugby but it has had a lot of difficulty attracting heavyweight attention from the rest of the rugby world. New Zealand might have been at the forefront of international participation but the game can hardly be said to have been a favourite around the table at NZRU headquarters. Even now, it costs the union bucketfuls of money to administer. The same can be said of England, or France or Australia or South Africa.

In spite of its obvious attractions there remains considerable reticence among those who act as the guardians of the traditional game to letting sevens in through the side door. Questions are regularly asked as to whether it will eventually siphon off support for 15-a-side. The answer to that is hard to predict. On the one hand sevens should enhance the core attractiveness of rugby by its sheer exuberance. It can be relied upon to deliver entertainment. In theory at least sevens should grow the bigger game by getting newer countries on rugby's escalator. On the other hand its very lightness might actually undermine tolerance of the more complex aspects of the traditional game. In other words, 15-a-side might be upstaged by this new, consumer friendly version and suffer from a shift of attention.

Whatever the answer to that, and we simply don't know yet, it is obvious that for a country like Fiji, which has such difficulty coping in international company at 15-a-side, is deriving enormous benefits from its status as one of the world's leading sevens nations. Several Fijian players, most notably the phenomenal Waisale Serevi, became so totally tuned to the sevens format that they were no longer able to play 15-a-side effectively at international level.

That is an interesting development. It proves what many had expected — that the skills and tactical mindsets are diverging; that the two games are going their own way and will eventually be so different that players will be forced to opt for one medium or the other. But does it really matter? If the Fijians, with their ability to produce utter magic on the sevens field, can profit from increasing specialisation at the expense of their performance in the conventional game, then so be it. The question is, who else will be tempted to head off in that direction?

When New Zealand won the sevens tournament at the Kuala Lumpur Commonwealth Games it seemed that a high-water mark had been reached. The New Zealand squad was packed with talent that was also starring in the 15-a-side stuff. With Christian Cullen, Jonah Lomu and others, including Eric Rush who had become a remarkable sevens tactician, the New Zealand team was unstoppable. It was a mixture of blinding speed and an almost grotesque assembly of physical power. The opposition was swept aside almost contemptuously.

Now, both Fiji and New Zealand have discovered that it has become steadily more difficult to preserve any margin of superiority as the others, particularly Samoa, England and South Africa, have crept up behind and regularly pounced. It's partly a question of the availability of talent. Coach Gordon Tietjens has had to deal with ever fewer top class professionals as he prepares his squad for each coming campaign. The demands of Super 14 have seen to that as the franchises' hearts harden earlier each year. Thus the increasing resort to experimentation with teenage wonders.

The age of the big-time ring-ins is obviously over. The professional market is drying up. Slowly, inexorably, the sevens squad is becoming a team that does little else besides play sevens and a little NPC, if they are lucky, on the side. There simply aren't enough months in the year any more to fit sevens rugby in alongside all the rest of it and expect top players to indulge in both. The professionals are complaining about too much 15-a-side rugby and very few are queuing up to join the sevens squad now for the simple reason that to do so is to sacrifice a career in the senior game.

It is noticeable that all of our main opponents — England, South Africa and Australia in particular — are themselves picking more and more sevens specialists for much the same reasons. Many of those overseas specialists are only semi-professional; some of them are amateurs just like their New Zealand counterparts.

Fiji doesn't have quite the same problem. It has a ramshackle professional dimension and its players can quite comfortably oscillate between sevens and 15s in a single season. And, in any case, the way the Fijians play there isn't an awful lot of difference between the two. Fiji is the first and only country where the game has taken over from 15-a-side and become nationally iconic. Even a *coup d'état* would have gone unnoticed in 2006 when it was announced in the streets that Fiji had won the World Rugby Sevens title. After months of bad news — about crime numbers up, tourism numbers down, sugar in the doldrums and the military threatening to take over again — here at last was something that Fijians could cheer about. And cheer they did. So hard that the government declared a national holiday in honour of the triumphant Fiji team.

Waisale Serevi, the Fiji mastermind, declared that this had been God's doing on his arrival back in Suva. "We just ran with the ball in accordance with God's tactics." Unfortunately, it has been rather thin gruel for the Fiji sevens team ever since. Even God's tactics can't seem to help.

God seems to have intervened to get sevens into the Olympics, however. This will start in 2016 and promises to generate interest in and sponsorship money for the game. Analysts estimate that rugby sevens will easily double its current sponsorship income of $US15–20 million when it becomes an Olympic game. How much, if any, of that will come from the 15-a-side sponsorship pool? Sponsors aren't stupid. An audience of a billion-plus is an irresistible attraction.

When you think about it, rugby satisfies all the criteria set out in the Olympic Charter for inclusion in the programme of the Olympic Games as well as any sport and rather better than most. Rugby stands for, even if it doesn't always practise, the original ideals of Olympism, thanks to its long-standing ethos of fair play and friendship. Sevens is now an official sport at the inter-American games. It is being heavily promoted in the West Indies and Africa where teams like Kenya are slowly but surely closing the gap on the established heavyweights. Rugby sevens will reach out to a new and younger audience. It does not need new, purpose-built stadiums, and it will extend the number of potential medal-winning nations. Countries like Fiji or Samoa will have genuine chances of winning gold medals, something they simply can't do otherwise in a world in which medals cost megabucks.

But there are other attractions as well. In many countries, rugby will enjoy increased funding and access to facilities from National Olympic Committees as an Olympic sport and various other state-provided forms of support.

Having trundled along clinging to the coat-tails of the bigger game, sevens may turn out to be the saving grace of rugby. It isn't hard to imagine a future in which sevens steps up alongside 15-a-side, with its own international administration and a year-round programme culminating at the Olympics every four years. Who knows, perhaps it could someday even replace 15-a-side rugby as the dominant form of the game. If entertainment continues to become the determining factor, that prospect is wholly credible.

Sibling Rivalry

APART FROM the fact that it is repetitive, inherently obsessed with machismo and very badly run, I think rugby league is a great game. Those who practise it have taken to calling it the greatest game in the world and the rest of us assume that this is said tongue-in-cheek because if there is a world's greatest game it certainly isn't rugby league.

This less genteel cousin of rugby union always appears to be in a state of crisis. In New Zealand, when they aren't being arraigned for some form of anti-social activity, the players seem to be in a semi-permanent state of shock, waiting for the imminent collapse of the ramshackle administrative edifice around them or the prospect of having their team sold off to some ill-advised speculator with a good deal more money than sense. Such speculators, learning the hard way, usually finish up with a good deal more sense than money.

The game's administrators seem to be in a perpetual state of war, mainly against each other. Like Sicilian families, the various factions have these deep set grudges against each other. People who should know better have, to their cost, plunged into the administration of the game only to be disgorged a little later covered in sprig marks. To the surprise of many people even David Lange indulged in a running flirtation with league in this country for some years, ascending dangerously close to the presidency before being politically kneecapped and leaving it all in high dudgeon. Helen Clark, who, probably for politically correct reasons at the time while she was Prime Minister, announced that she was an admirer of the game, obviously had second thoughts about going down a similar road. Even for the Labour Party, consorting seriously with rugby league is a risky business.

Why on earth are there two codes, almost identical to the casual observer, when logic dictates that there should only be one? Thereby hangs a tale, a rather tragic one really and, because both were born in Britain, it was all about class.

The 1890s saw a clash of cultures within rugby, between working men's clubs of northern England and the southern clubs of gentlemen. Two very different worlds. A dispute revolving around the nature of payments within the game arose. Needless to say the lads in the north wanted to keep the gate money to meet the weekend expenses of players who usually had to work weekends, and the toffs in the south, who naturally called all the shots, wouldn't hear of it. The lads up north promptly called their bluff and went their own way. It all became official with the formation of the Northern Rugby League. A similar schism opened up in other rugby-playing nations.

The sibling rivalry has been as long-running as it has been silly. It's now a century since the "All Golds" and their Australian counterparts severed the link with rugby union and went north. It seems amazing that in all that time it hasn't been possible for the two codes to find any real accommodation in an ever more crowded sporting landscape. It's even more amazing that in all that time there hasn't been a single serious attempt to find common ground.

Rugby union was reserved for the gentlemen and league was for the players. Other sports like cricket and tennis managed to heal the amateur versus professional divide but rugby never did, and perhaps it never will in spite of some obvious convergence in recent years in terms of rules and tactics.

The class divide in Australia was considerably more stark than in New Zealand. Union was the preserve of the private schoolboy and the city executive while league was the game of the suburbs, generally the poorer suburbs of South Sydney and Brisbane — and the "battlers" from Balmain.

In Australia, rugby union was regarded with ill-disguised contempt by the *nouveaux riches* of rugby league during the second half of the 20th century as the wealth of a professional game enjoying enormous public popularity in the poorer suburbs ensured that just about any really talented player that rugby union threw up would be instantly gobbled up by league's pokey-driven purchasing machine. The dollars fluttered about like confetti. League, like a cockney betting shop millionaire, was suddenly able to thumb its nose at union, a shabby curate by comparison. It took grim pleasure in stripping the other game of talent.

For its part, Australian rugby union would sniffily dismiss this tawdry commercialism and soldier on like an impoverished aristocrat rattling round in a mansion on which he couldn't pay the rates. It meant that rugby union in Australia was constantly on the back foot, bleeding talent to league and having an awful time trying to remain competitive with the other great rugby union countries, particularly New Zealand. Now, the traffic is beginning to run the other way. The ARU has taken to buying in talent from the league clubs, much to the chagrin of the ARL. Both compete for the same sponsorship dollar and the same TV exposure. Now it's war on a level playing field. Both codes have a powerful grip in Sydney and Brisbane and both are competing for attention in Victoria and Western Australia.

In Britain, the transformation from hard-core community expression to a gaudy branch office of show business in the gritty environment of northern England, its heartland, is one of sport's great anachronisms. Anyone who read David Storey's searing 1960 novel *This Sporting Life*, set in a drab northern city, couldn't help but be moved by the sheer poignancy of it all, and the grubby way in which crass professionalism intruded into the local values system. Who would have imagined that in another generation we would be seeing something similar happening in New Zealand rugby clubs as quasi-professionalism tears away at the spirit of the club.

Storey made several interesting points in the late 1990s as rugby league sank to its knees in Britain. He bemoaned the absurd adoption of American-style fripperies, not least the host of stupidly macho new names like "Bulls", "Broncos" or "Gladiators" that the traditional big city clubs were obliged to adopt. He is not alone in that. But perhaps more significantly he said that the rhythm of the game — tackle, play-the-ball, tackle — was that of a miner chipping away at rocks and that rugby league was in fact an extension of the mechanical, repetitive process of the coalmining industry. The society's ethos and the game were very much in harmony and the invasion of commercialism undermined the very social validity on which the game rested. Whether or not this is an extreme view remains to be seen. Rugby league seems to have weathered the initial storm of new age professionalism in Britain, evolving as the communities around it evolve, but whether it has the resilience to survive ever escalating financial demands within its limited catchment area remains to be seen.

People who are unfamiliar with either game wonder how on earth the rugby world can have been sufficiently obtuse not to have negotiated a merger before now. Is it too late? Have the two games become so saturated in their own cultural authenticity that they are simply no longer capable, like Hutu and Tutsi, or Catholic and Protestant, of finding a mutual accommodation?

There are constant arguments about the respective merits of the two games. League is faster, simpler, more continuous and more exacting when it comes to man-on-man confrontations. But what it lacks is variety. Storey's characterisation of the miner chipping away at the coal seam is remarkably accurate. League moves in repetitive phases up and down the field, rather like American football. Rugby union has infinitely more variety, more uncertainty, more asymmetry, more mess and more disruption. What it gains in breadth it loses in length because the amount of down-time in a rugby union game is significantly greater than it is in league.

Some say the inventors of league pulled a masterstroke when they abandoned lineouts and simplified scrums. The scrum has become rugby union's Achilles heel. Every year it seems the scrum laws are tinkered with but the difference in terms of continuity is minimal. Yet nobody yet wants a league scrum. Historically, the scrum has been one of rugby union's great sub-plots. Front-rowers were like the stokers in a ship's engine-room, grinding away at their particular task more or less oblivious to all the other activity going on up on deck. Much of the game's folklore has been built around the arcane nature of the scrum. There is something almost Pythonesque about it, 16 men crouched, clutching each other like comfort blankets, locked in what looks like a group grope, then giving a great heave before, as often as not, collapsing in a disorderly heap and having to start over again. It is surely ironic that the most traditionally homophobic of games should have the most seemingly homoerotic of activities.

For all but the most pedantic of followers, however, the scrum is a gigantic turn-off as it repeatedly collapses, or skews, or buckles upward or otherwise wastes valuable playing time. Is it any wonder league took the initiative early on and turned the scrum into something resembling a short prayer session. It was a smart move because it eliminated all opportunity for jiggery-pokery. The modern league scrum is like a moa. It has lost its primary purpose — the contest for possession — just as the moa lost the means to fulfil its primary purpose of flying — its wings. You have to admit, however, it's a very efficient way of restarting the game. Yet, somehow, you just can't escape the fact that rugby without a decent scrum has about as much substance as a George Bush press conference.

And what about the numbers game? Is 13 better than 15? Here, too, it is easy to pick a fight without ever winning it. Fewer numbers might mean more space but they also serve to remove just that little bit more of the complexity of the game. In other words, league has set out deliberately to eliminate what it sees as unnecessary congestion and concentrate on the basics. Played well, by the Kangaroos in Australia in particular, it can be a sublime spectacle. Played badly, it's like David Storey's coalminer with a bent pick. But then rugby union, played badly, as any league fan will remind you, has as much movement as a Galapagos tortoise colony.

Rugby league's so-called World Cup is a hopelessly inadequate vehicle for international enlargement. The mismatches between Australia and all the rest are a gigantic turn-off and there is no sign that that lopsided situation will ever change given the impoverished or chaotic state of league everywhere outside Australia and the north of England. There seems slim hope of the Kiwis ever being able to compete on a regular basis with Australia at league. For every surprise victory there are six abject defeats. Unless this gross imbalance is rectified, league will never really be able to compete with union for the hearts and minds of New Zealanders. Somehow the script remains depressingly familiar. The Kiwis, bristling with testosterone, go at it with flamboyant ferocity for half an hour. But the big hits and high drama are then followed by a clinical dismemberment as the Kiwis are ruthlessly exposed by the harder minds and superior basic skills and tactical sophistication of the Kangaroos.

So, when you think about it, there is every reason for and hardly any reasons against an eventual merger. In the long run there simply won't be enough room for both to expand. In recent years the two codes have drawn closer in terms of what actually happens on the field and, interestingly, all the movement has been by rugby union towards league rather than the other way round. Tackling techniques, defensive lines, regulation of foul play, kicking out on the full are a few of the borrowings from league. If this continues then, logically, we will see the two codes converge to the point where, like a couple co-habiting for a couple of years, there doesn't seem much point in remaining single.

How far off is that? A decade? Two? Who would bet against it in the long run as the demand for non-stop entertainment intensifies and as the competition for sponsorship dollars and access to television rights income gets ever hotter. Will we see, eventually, a 10 or 12-a-side game emerge from both codes, leveraging off the obvious entertainment success of rugby sevens? Imagine them, as one: the "greatest game in the world" and the "game they play in heaven". Result — heaven on earth. The only certainty is that if, and when, the trigger is pulled on integration it won't be pulled by the administrators of either game. It will be pulled by those who really call the shots, the media managers.

But to expand the imagination even further, is it too fanciful to imagine, one day, a unified, hybridised, rebel game emerging to ambush rugby the way the one-day format ambushed cricket, prompted by media interests? Neither code can be complacent about the future. Nothing is sacrosanct when profit is the driver.

Being There

THERE WAS a time when going to a rugby match was an expedition. If it was a big match the odds were that you queued on a frosty night outside the single ticket sales outlet and waited all night for the sweet pleasure of buying your seat. Well, it may not have been anything so luxurious as an actual seat. It was probably only the right to stand on a windswept terrace with every possibility of not being able to see a thing.

Before rugby went professional nobody thought much about the stadium. It was the public facility that opened up every weekend and closed down again after players, spectators and the usual assortment of drunks dribbled out. Now, the stadium is part of the commercial equation. It does deals with local unions or franchises. It is caught up in the desperate grab for profitability. It must provide all the trappings that the ever more capricious punter demands. It charges as much as it thinks the market will bear and often that isn't enough to pay the spiralling bills.

The first great generation of stadiums of the rugby world was built in the late 19th and early 20th century. Wooden grandstands on either side and sloping terraces at either end. If you lived in South Africa things were organised on your behalf. If you were black you stood at one end. If you were white you sat in the middle. At Twickenham, that last fortress of the Forsytes, much the same pattern was repeated, if not with the assurance of a law to back it up. Royalty and any members of the aristocracy would be found in the royal box right in the middle. If you were upper middle-class you sat in the upper reaches of the main stands facing the halfway mark. If you were lower middle-class you occupied the far reaches of the main stands and if you happened to be working class you stood at the ends on the terraces. All around the rugby world this basic theme was replicated, even in New Zealand where the members of the NZFU and their invited guests naturally always got the best seats in the modest grandstands, but beyond that it was a free-for-all contest. The earliest in got the best position. You could even bring your banana box and rise above the muddied throng for a premium view.

The stadiums were grubby, hard to get into and out of, hopelessly underequipped with toilets and generally exposed to whatever weather was thrown at them, which meant, in places like Wellington's Athletic Park, the best of both the northerly and the infamous southerly. All you could hope for by way of sustenance was a warm pie and whatever quantity of booze you could bring with you. You invariably got cold and you often got wet, but you loved it because it was an occasion like no other — a once a year event. If it was the Springboks or the Lions or the French or the Wallabies it was a must-do thing. History was being written and your little chapter of it you could write yourself.

Spectators hung from trees nearby. Locals built their own grandstands in adjoining properties and charged admission. The more parsimonious of Dunedin's patrons assembled along the railway line above Carisbrook in the "Scotsman's Grandstand". There would be an intensive series of curtain-raiser matches to keep people amused during their long vigil waiting for the main event. Crowds of 60,000-plus were the norm in Christchurch and Auckland for a test match. Most of us stood to watch and most of us walked home.

All that is but a distant memory. The places we now frequent to watch rugby are radically different. You buy your ticket online. It is almost invariably for a specific seat, probably under cover. If you are in Cardiff, or Melbourne, or now even in Dunedin you won't have to worry about the weather. It's all indoors. You stock up on food and drink at the ground. Everything from sushi to shish kebab will be available. You can fuel up again at halftime and you can get more money from the ATM inside the stadium to consume even more. There will be on-field entertainment before the game starts. Forget those tedious curtain-raisers. Now we have provocative cheerleaders and, of course, consistent with 21st century distraction, we have wall-to-wall music to save you the trouble of thinking or talking to your neighbour.

It seems such a shame that the ignoble art of streaking seems to have been more or less completely suppressed by all that security at every stadium. Streakers were once part of the fun. They are now regarded as a threat to the carefully choreographed continuity of the event, a disruption that the authorities take a very dim view of. Hulking security guards, whose main ambition in life is to crash-tackle a female streaker, lurk hopefully in the shadows all round the ground. Will we ever again see anything like the moment a few decades ago that most mature patrons of Twickenham will remember forever? The day a topless young lady stopped the show by prancing out into the middle. For a minute or so nothing happened. Eighty thousand witnesses remained spellbound by her audacity and, it must be admitted, by her extremely generous personal endowments. The Duke of Gloucester, who happened to be present, was seen to reach surreptitiously for his opera glasses. Finally, a thoroughly abashed policeman engaged her as delicately as possible given the circumstances and attempted, with a single helmet, the impossible task of covering her more controversial features. She was an instant star: coverage in every newspaper and a modelling contract in the mail.

Stadiums are complicated establishments. They cost a bomb to build and a leg and an arm to maintain. If there is a myth there is money to be made by buying football teams, the myth that there is money to be made by running rugby stadiums is a preposterous one. To own a stadium is a more comprehensive way of losing money than owning the team that plays in it.

Sports stadiums all over the world are either in crisis or about to be, yet they are still being built with what seems cavalier abandon. Perhaps the most extravagant example is the new Dallas Cowboys stadium in Arlington, Texas. Owner Jerry Jones persuaded the city of Arlington to stump up $350 million to subsidise a project amounting to $1.2 billion. Build it and they will come, said Jerry. They built it but not enough people are coming. They can't get naming rights sponsors, they can't sell memberships and most of the corporate lounges are destined to remain empty. It is a Greek tragedy in the making and the ratepayers of Arlington will be picking up the pieces.

Of the dozens of international class rugby stadiums round the world there isn't a single one that genuinely pays its own way. Most are at least part-owned by local authorities who are obliged to pump subsidies into them to keep them solvent. Some are owned by non-profit trusts, but most of these, too, are obliged to go cap in hand to local or central government or sponsors, or all three, for support in one form or another.

In some cases, notably in France, the premier stadium — the Stade de France — is actually owned by the government and operated by a management company on its behalf, bolstered by a handsome subsidy without which it would have closed down a week after opening. Stadium Australia was built for the Olympics in 2000 as a grand statement about Australian sporting prowess and more than half a billion dollars of private money went into it. Partly because there is another perfectly serviceable stadium in Sydney, the Sydney Football Stadium, the great, cavernous, and usually half empty Stadium Australia is a deathly white elephant. The lease that its operators have is due to expire in 2031 at which time ownership will revert to the state government. Watch out Sydneysiders, a lot of bills are coming your way in 20 years' time.

In Durban, the Natal Rugby Union, which leases the ABSA stadium complex, is under intense pressure from the city and the South African government to move the Sharks franchise across the road to the new Moses Mabhida Stadium, built for the 2010 Football World Cup, immediately after the tournament. They don't want to do so because they will move from a barely break-even arrangement to a certain loss.

It is a painful fact of life that stadiums lose money. As an investment they are a dog and it's hardly surprising that you would have to search very thoroughly to find a single rugby ground anywhere that is privately owned.

All this became a meaningful backdrop in New Zealand after it was awarded the hosting rights of the 2011 World Cup. The main rugby stadiums round the country went immediately into competitive mode in order to parade their credentials before Rugby World Cup Ltd and those credentials made for interesting reading. Auckland was always going to be the frontrunner if for no other reason than its far greater population base and tourism infrastructure.

The IRB made it plain that a capacity of 60,000 seated was the minimum threshold for whoever hosts the final and it was also emphasised that both semi-finals must be played in the same or a similarly equipped stadium. That caused shockwaves through the rugby fraternity. Only

Eden Park had, at the time, any hope of crossing that threshold but it became clear that it would cost someone an arm and half a leg to get it right in time. It was at that moment that rationality seemed to depart the scene. Somebody said it would be a good idea to build a bold new stadium on Auckland's shabby waterfront.

For reasons which will never be entirely understood the government suddenly jumped at this option, assuming, erroneously, that much of the money for this could be raised from Aucklanders. There followed an unseemly squabble until the regional council stepped in and said it wouldn't support the idea and certainly wouldn't go about winkling the money from ratepayers to pay for it. The NZRU was left lying vulnerably on the bottom of this very loose ruck hoping that they wouldn't finally be saddled with a bill they had no hope of meeting. It was they, after all, together with the government, who had promised the IRB that they would have a stadium holding 60,000.

In the end, rationality more or less returned. All the various parties swallowed hard and accepted that the only option was to tart up Eden Park. Needless to say the Eden Park Trust Board wasn't offering to pay for this and so it was largely left to the government, with a token contribution from the NZRU, to meet the cost.

This whole episode revealed a new truth about the national willingness to pay up large for a game which appears to be swimming in money. A consistent refrain began to echo around the country: why should we have to pay to provide a professional activity — a business in other words — with its own infrastructure? The government and the NZRU kept banging on about the enormous benefits to the economy that RWC 2011 promised to New Zealand. Hundreds of millions were at stake. Huge tourism returns, incremental investment in New Zealand, were the raucous promise. Whether the public have been persuaded by this is difficult to say. One question does, however, remain hanging in the air: would there have been a similar reaction if rugby was still an amateur game? Arguably not.

I claimed earlier that rugby stadiums invariably lose money. That isn't strictly true. Westpac Stadium in Wellington does actually pay its way but only because at the outset the regional and city councils between them pumped in $35 million in loans which are in effect grants because they will probably never be repaid. Westpac Stadium is governed by a non-profit trust and is a genuinely public facility and a very cost-effective operation. It manages to make a small profit each year because of the remarkable range of sports and other activities it can cater for. Almost every day of the year there is something happening, even if it's only a corporate lunch. It can cater for 35,000, a figure which, before it was built, was derided as far too small. In reality the capacity is generous because the only time it is now actually filled is for a major concert or for the occasional rugby test.

AMI Stadium in Christchurch is running desperately to keep up. It, too, has undergone a major revamp timed to enable it to cater for a crowd of more than 40,000, although more of these are in uncovered seats. It, too, is a publicly owned facility managed by a company comprising city council and business representatives. Dunedin's circumstances are rather more precarious with the transition away from Carisbrook and into a new covered stadium being something of a leap in the dark, a leap that many in Dunedin felt decidedly uncomfortable about making. Here, too, there were well-voiced objections from ratepayers bemoaning the fact that they should have to pay for rugby's pleasure, ignoring the fact that the new stadium is designed to be multi-purpose, but painfully aware of the huge challenge of actually being able to fill it often enough to pay the bills.

Each of the major stadiums in New Zealand is fearful about the future. All are desperately keen to widen the range of activities beyond rugby, knowing that future income from rugby is more likely to diminish than to increase. The number of games being played is now at a maximum. There isn't room for any more, particularly when cricket, league, soccer and a variety of other events have to be fitted in too. A stadium can switch from rugby to cricket and back again in a matter of hours through use of the drop-in cricket wicket but the wider field takes a fearful pounding. Even in the most sophisticated arenas large clumps of turf are chewed up and flop about as players churn their way around the field. It's almost like the good old days except that, then, the turf simply turned to mud. New techniques involving synthetic additions, like implanted hairpieces, are beginning to appear.

Oddly, Astroturf, which has become almost the norm in other field sports, still seems to be resisted by rugby, perhaps because it somehow lacks a sense of authenticity. Perhaps it's because so many of our stadiums are multi-purpose with cricket as a key sport and cricket and Astroturf are uncomfortable bedfellows. Astroturf certainly hasn't caused any obvious inhibitions in American football. Way back in the 1960s Joe Namath, the great, anti-establishment American quarterback, was famously asked if he preferred grass or Astroturf. Joe may have replied that he wasn't sure because he hadn't smoked Astroturf but his preference for the latter was well known.

But forget about the grass. There are other more daunting challenges. Rugby crowds are declining. Memberships and season tickets are not being renewed and, most worrying of all, there seems to be a gathering trend away from corporate box renewal. In other words, the substantial income from better endowed patrons, the vast majority of whom have been attracted by rugby, is declining. This poses severe challenges for every stadium, particularly those, like Wellington, which are approaching the end of the first phase of their very lucrative membership subscriptions and corporate box ownership. Initial indications are that many corporates or other private interests are thinking twice about renewing. What then?

Twickenham, Cardiff Arms Park, Murrayfield, Loftus Versfeld, Boet Erasmus, Ellis Park, Eden Park, Lancaster Park and, perhaps the most evocative of them all — Carisbrook. How important is the name of a stadium? How often can it be changed before that name is so devalued that people cease to associate a stadium with its history?

Now, they associate almost every major stadium in the world with the sponsor who happens to currently have the naming rights. But doesn't this make a mockery of the identity and historical integrity of a stadium? This is an intriguing question and one that is being posed ever more frequently as the owners or improvers of stadiums scratch around for ways of raising the necessary cash to pay for them. Everything is effectively up for sale. Stadium memberships, corporate boxes, sometimes even whole grandstands go to the highest bidder.

Naming rights over the stadium itself have become a central element in that process. Where community money is limited, corporate participation becomes the factor that determines whether or not a stadium is commercially viable. Some stadiums elsewhere in the world have so far been able to resist the urge to have a corporate name substitute for the old, well recognised and much loved venue. But not many. Ellis Park in Johannesburg, one of the three or four most famous stadiums in the rugby world is now — wait for it — Coca-Cola Park. But then Johannesburg always was a rather crass sort of place.

Even in Pretoria, however, where conservatism might be expected to be a bit more enduring, they have also succumbed. Loftus Versfeld was a fabled place, the very name conjuring up images of rampant Springbok hordes pulverising unfortunate touring teams. The stadium was officially named Loftus Minolta, not exactly a name to stir the juices, except perhaps among avid photographers. Minolta didn't stay long. It then became Securicor Loftus for a while and then, in 2005, the renaming process went full circle when South Africa's major telecommunications group, Telcom, took over sponsorship from Securicor, renamed the stadium back to the original Loftus Versfeld in a remarkably selfless nod to tradition. Vodacom didn't show the same selflessness in Bloemfontein where the Free State Stadium is now known as Vodacom Park. The same thing has happened in Durban. Kings Park became ABSA Stadium after the Natal Rugby Union swallowed very hard and kissed goodbye to their famous name. Only Newlands in Cape Town seems to have resisted the charms of the naming righters. But its time will undoubtedly also come.

A change of name for Twickenham, once a doughty old last fortress of the Forsytes, with soaring wooden grandstands immediately identifiable all round the rugby world, but now a very flash Harry of a stadium, is unthinkable. The very word Twickenham is a synonym for "Headquarters". They couldn't possibly flog that off, could they? Don't count on that. Everything, it seems, now has its price. Cardiff Arms Park might have morphed into the Millennium Stadium and has resisted the urge to sell its name to the devil. But for how long?

We aren't so lucky here in New Zealand. Mammon is steadily devouring the identity of all our major stadiums. Thus, the transmogrification of Lancaster Park to Jade Stadium to AMI stadium in Christchurch where the sale of naming rights has been vital in the survival of the old cabbage patch as the city's primary venue. Many people in Christchurch were less than impressed by the airy abandonment of the name Lancaster Park, which symbolised so rich a store of recollections. They were even less impressed when Jade decided it couldn't afford the rights any more and bailed out in favour of the AMI Insurance group. AMI has even less of a romantic ring to it than Jade but there's nothing that resentful Cantabrians can do about that. The stadium doesn't belong to them. It might be a publicly owned facility but somebody stole the right to name it.

Naming rights were also a key feature in Wellington where the Westpac Bank put up more than $15 million to have its name on the new stadium that finally replaced that dear old, tattered, windswept Athletic Park. Westpac has renewed its contract to have its name on the stadium wall, not without a lot of haggling over visibility of the company logo just about everywhere, and for less money. Westpac didn't take kindly to just about everyone calling the stadium the "cake tin" instead of its formal name. Believe it or not this has become a real problem. The Stadium Trust constantly has to point out to transgressors in the media the error of their ways and some of the responses are not exactly cooperative. Nicknames and naming rights are uncomfortable bedfellows. But nicknames are hard to shift and the cake tin label is bound to stick. Perhaps, when Westpac loses interest, a company like baker Ernest Adams could really make a virtue out of sponsoring something that really does look like a cake tin.

Then there's the big upgrade in Auckland. Want to take a bet on Eden Park keeping its name? That would not be money well spent unless, of course, the purchaser's name happened to be Eden. Given the funding gap of $20–30 million that everybody is ducking away from, it seems inevitable that a corporate will buy the right to have its name up there in lights just as Jade Corporation then AMI did in Christchurch.

It has happened in New Plymouth and Palmerston North. The same thing is happening in Dunedin. Carisbrook is a very beguiling moniker. It is redolent with history, known all round the rugby world as a graveyard for the ambitions of visiting teams, and there is a fierce resistance to the loss of that. But Carisbrook is a mid-20th century stadium trying to survive in the unyielding climate of the 21st. It is tired, ragged and utterly inadequate for modern test matches. Commercially, it has indeed become a house of terminal pain.

After all the commercial gymnastics to try to raise the cash for a new, covered stadium for the north end of the city, the green light was finally flashed in spite of spirited resistance from many of those who will be paying for it for the next 40 years. There was never going to be any chance that the name Carisbrook would be retained. No naming rights buyer would be sufficiently magnanimous to forego self-identification and all the profile benefits that accompany that, and just pay to remain anonymous. The market doesn't work that way. Dunedin's smart new venue has the romantic moniker "Forsyth Barr Stadium" in recognition of the exceptional generosity of Eion Edgar and his colleagues in the company, and nobody would seriously begrudge them appropriate recognition through the naming rights. But it just seems so sad that the great evocative name "Carisbrook", which carries such meaning for so many rugby enthusiasts all over the country — and well beyond — will be so blithely discarded.

Have you noticed that the way rugby stadiums are built these days mirrors the evolution of society itself? Over the last generation we have become more stratified, more defined by purchasing power and ever more beholden to the private sector. So are the spectators at modern rugby matches. There are those who occupy the private, exclusive zone of the corporate box and the upper lounges of the grandstands where liveried waiters serve food and booze to those who can afford the pleasure. Below these are the covered grandstand seats where the moderately well-to-do find themselves. The best of these are sold as memberships of the stadium community or season tickets. Beyond the covered stands are the uncovered zones where the faithful get a lesser view and get wet when it rains, and where most of the unruly behaviour begins, along with Mexican wave instigation and the noble art of streaking.

It has not gone unnoticed by those who study the sociology of modern sport that the contemporary disposition of stadium seating is an almost exact replica of that which the Greeks and Romans invented. A wander round the Coliseum in Rome tells the story. It was in most respects an archetype, a stadium built to a formula reflecting the stratification of classical society. Above all others were the royal boxes and tribunes, antiquity's exact equivalent of the corporate lounges where the elite are treated to the best view. Down below, in the Plebeian sections, the ordinary people would be packed in, often standing, like the great swaying masses who until recently stood at Athletic Park, Lancaster Park or Carisbrook for the privilege of being there.

I suppose it is a sign of progress that much of the terraced areas in rugby stadiums almost everywhere have now gone, replaced by plastic seats, not by any enthusiastic public demand but as a result of the drive to modernise and to maximise revenue from seated patrons who are obliged to pay considerably more for the pleasure of not having to stand. The loss of terraces is widely lamented, particularly in Dunedin where students have traditionally congregated at commendably low cost to provide colourful support for Otago and where there was enough space to burn a couch or two.

There is a theory that rugby stadiums will get progressively smaller rather than larger in order to generate the greatest amount of revenue from the smallest available space and to acknowledge the growing reality that more and more spectators will choose to watch the game on television at home or at some other congenial place. As broadcast technology gets better and better the average punter will increasingly think twice before braving a buffeting while fighting his way to his seat for a distant view of the action and another lengthy battle to get back out again. In another generation most major stadiums will be fully roofed to keep out not just the wind and rain but that deadly dew that diminishes the quality of so many night matches.

Rugby patrons are changing. Gone are the raincoat-clad, trilby-hatted middle-aged men who comprised the overwhelming majority of most big rugby crowds in the past. Now the demographic has opened up. So has the propensity to perform. People turn up in all sorts of oddball outfits almost routinely these days and when the camera is on them they feel obliged to cast off all inhibitions. What is it about the fact that when you suddenly see yourself on the big screen you feel compelled to act like a performing chimp? What is it that drives the desire to start a Mexican wave whenever things get a bit uneventful? Clearly, this is a symptom not of disengagement with what's happening on the field but of an active desire on the part of spectators to be part of the whole spectacle. Is this any better than mutely sitting there, satisfied with what happens on the field? Perhaps it is. Perhaps it is also a subliminal signal to rugby that the game itself isn't enough any longer. Whatever the answer to these questions, the trend is growing stronger. Crowds are growing more impatient, less charitable to losers and undeniably more fickle.

Many more women go to matches these days. Nobody is entirely sure why this is but it is clearly related to the nature of the entertainment dimension. The girls have, of course, always been there in modest numbers but they always looked as if they somehow oughtn't to be there, came by accident, or were dragged reluctantly along by Dad or the boyfriend. Not any more. The girls are there for the fun. They drink every bit as hard as the lads and often behave just as badly. This younger, party-oriented demographic is what makes rugby tick as a spectator sport these days. It is they who the promoters appeal most directly to. It is they who demand music, fireworks, fast food and warm-up acts because they have really only come for the rugby as part of a wider entertainment package. And it is they who have disposable income and are willing to pay for the pleasure.

They are the future. But what happens if the entertainment fails to live up to expectations? With the proliferation of options available on a Saturday night there is a risk that relying on these partygoers may not be the wisest option. But what other options are there? Nude cheerleaders? Instant lotteries? No wonder the marketing costs of rugby keep rising. It is a race between innovation and boredom, and if boredom wins rugby loses.

Under England's Skin

IN THE *Nuremberg Chronicle* of 1493 there is a highly interesting description of the "Antipodean". This was the nether world creature, an object of fear and loathing. The Antipodean was sometimes depicted as an odd, rather ghastly creature, a fanciful dog-headed and one-eyed man with his feet facing backwards. The Antipodes was obviously a very contrary sort of place.

Deep in the psyche of the European there seems to have persisted the notion that those beyond the fringes of the civilised centre of the world were creatures who needed to be subdued, contained and, if possible, remoulded in the European image.

The British, of course, became masters of this particular art. The empire was forged out of a remoulding of all those societies which came under Britannia's very assertive thumb. The British came, saw, colonised and set about converting the locals into something more amenable to their cultural taste. And they did it in a hurry. As James Belich saw it, "Progressive colonisation . . . may well rank as the most rapid form of cultural reproduction — the making of a new people from an old — in human history." And at the crest of that tidal wave of transformation came the team sports, rugby and cricket.

While many in New Zealand, the product of this transformation, came to view their circumstances as a "better Britain", free of the strictures of class and social obligation, the view from the other end wasn't quite as genial. New Zealanders, Australians, South Africans, all those Antipodeans, were not expected to rock the imperial boat in any way. They were, after all, British, even those born in the colonies. "Colonials" was not quite a pejorative term but it was awfully close. Partly because of the fanatical loyalty shown to the imperial cause with Mother Albion at its core, there was general satisfaction among the British as to the worthiness of the colonial peoples. But there was no mistaking the social order. As English writer and administrator John Davidson modestly proclaimed in 1897:

It is with nations as with men
One must be first,
We are the mightiest,
The heirs of Rome.

James Morris, in his monumental *Pax Britannica*, an assessment of the empire at its most exultant, also in 1897, noted that, "A vassal could qualify for respect, if not for power or promotion, if he possessed certain specific qualities the British admired. East was East and West was West and never the twain would meet — but there is neither east nor west, border, nor breed, nor birth, when two strong men stand face to face, though they come from the ends of the earth." He was speaking of the romantic chivalry of "certain subject peoples", those of other races — the Zulu and the Maori in particular. Both were, of course, subdued in the end. The iron fist of colonialism saw to that.

Oddly, it took a Frenchman, André Seigfried, to articulate in 1914 the insidious inference of the word "colonial" as used by the British to describe Australians and New Zealanders: "One must hear the Englishman speak with his air of condescending patronage of the colonial . . . regarding the other citizens of the Empire as, in spite of everything, a slightly inferior class: unintellectual, think the cultured; rather rough, thinks the snob."

This was the environment into which New Zealand rugby first stepped, tentatively, in 1905. It was a circuit-breaking moment, evoking emotions in Britain ranging from delighted surprise to deep resentment. Here were the "Maorilanders", even though all but a couple of the team were Pakeha, demonstrating to the Brits that they were not only better at this quintessentially British game, but faster on their feet and more creative.

That creativity, most notably the use of captain Dave Gallaher as a wing forward, was what generated the resentment. Gallaher became that ghastly "Antipodean" of the *Nuremburg Chronicle*, back to bite the British in the sporting bum. It began a reaction in British rugby which was maintained right through the 20th century. New Zealanders were cheats, exploiters, overly zealous, inclined towards foul play. But most of all, upstarts. The more the All Blacks beat the British the more this attitude became entrenched.

The 1905 team created a sensation in Britain that is difficult to appreciate today. They were that different in appearance, approach and attitude that they became a genuine novelty — a must-see experience.

Not everybody agreed that the New Zealanders were new world supermen. After the loss against Wales, *Punch* magazine, tongue presumably in cheek, remarked that New Zealanders had become a race weakened by the enervating effects of geysers. New Zealand men, said *Punch*, warming to the imagery of the times, were the unwitting victims of the women's rights movement, as witnessed by the recent, revolutionary granting of suffrage to New Zealand women. When the women of a nation had become men, its men, concluded *Punch*, were likely to become women.

Awareness of this new world phenomenon began to spread. The debonair Anthony Wilding's successes at Wimbledon added another dimension to it. In the early 20s it was noted by a prominent London book reviewer that the young New Zealander had begun to appear in British fiction. Long, lean, athletic, olive-skinned and blue-eyed as well as being chivalrous and wealthy, he was, it was observed, at once adorably innocent and miraculously shrewd; in other words, invincible.

But somehow, rugby didn't quite fit this particular identikit image. Our players might have been lean, athletic and olive-skinned but they were also fanatically driven to succeed for the simple reason that New Zealanders had no other options for success among Britain's middle and upper classes unless, like Wilding, Arthur Porritt, Jack Lovelock and others, they folded themselves neatly into British society as local facsimiles first and as Antipodeans only when it came to competing in the field.

The more the All Blacks beat the British the more inclined the British were to treat them as colonials. This edge was still there when we toured Britain in 1963–64. It ushered in the era of the "unsmiling giants", a tag that has dogged every All Black team right up till the advent of professionalism, at which time all teams became equally unsmiling.

Being patronised by the middle and upper reaches of society in Britain can be a galling experience. My introduction to it came as a 19-year-old on my first tour with the All Blacks and I was not well prepared for it. The New Zealanders were the very quintessence of anti-intellectualism and unsophistication in the minds of their upper middle-class hosts. I can remember being furious at some of my team-mates on tours of Britain in the 1960s for sheepishly accepting the cultural put-downs without so much as a murmur. It mystified me that even the most dim-witted member of the English establishment could consider himself superior to any New Zealander.

Things have loosened up in recent years, of course. Much of the old tension has gone. The British class system isn't the primary driving force of society any more and it has certainly lost much of its mojo in sport. All the major cities are now so variegated in ethnic, racial or cultural terms that "Britishness" has frayed at the edges sufficiently for one's particular country of origin to be little more than incidental. The Brits basically don't know who they are any longer and New Zealanders, South Africans and Australians are particularly welcome within British society because of, rather than in spite of, their disrespect for Harrovian hierarchies.

The landscape is shifting. You don't have to be identifiably English to play for England any more. The English team now has black guys with odd names from faraway places but does this cause any angst at Twickenham? Not a bit. No more than our brown guys with odd names from the Pacific, something that rather undermines the accusation that Stephen Jones and other members of the English rugby press persistently parrot that New Zealand pinches talent from abroad. Now, even England does it and the game is all the better for that.

As a result, happily, the old resentment towards New Zealand is being rendered meaningless because the English are even beginning to field New Zealanders in their national rugby team and if there's any angst aroused at Twickenham as a result of that then they certainly don't show it. New Zealand-born Riki Flutey, a Maori, somehow finds a long distant English ancestor after living there for an indecently short time and hey presto he's out there on Twickenham defending the honour of St George.

Good luck to him. Good luck to England. They desperately need players who can sidestep off either foot and, hey, this is the 21st century.

A generation ago that would have been unthinkable. If anybody had said to me even five years ago that Riki Flutey was going to be picked for England I would have assumed they had mixed their medication. But wait, it gets worse. Not only do you not have to be English, you don't even have to play in England to represent England and many English internationals have taken advantage of that. More English players are being poached by the French. It seems that the money being proffered by the likes of Toulon or Perpignan is just that much better than what's on offer at Gloucester or Leicester or Wasps. The market has come back to bite the English.

Anything goes now. Riki Flutey can play for England even though he absconded to a French club. This is the almost unimaginable equivalent of an English player representing the All Blacks even though he has gone off to play in Australia. Are we ready for that in New Zealand? Not quite. But, as and when necessity becomes the mother of invention, we too will be forced to become just as inventive. And who are we to be exclusive? Dave Gallaher's 20th century namesake, John Gallagher, was an Englishman who came to New Zealand, became an All Black in the 1980s and nobody seemed to complain about that. Nor are we complaining about an army of Pacific Islanders who have come to live here and done exactly the same thing with stunning success.

The 21st century is going to be one of intense movement in rugby. Professional players are going to become more and more mobile. Old national identities are bound to dilute and international teams are going to become ethnic and racial kaleidoscopes. But every current creates its counter-current. The more the professional environment responds to globalisation the more we will see localism, what is becoming known in sport as a new tribalism, begin to assert itself. In other words, provincial rugby will become more identifiably tribal in character, by contrast with the hybridised franchises. The local and the global will be at war with each other and nobody knows which will win. All we do know is that, without the local, the global is an emperor with no clothes.

England Expects

IT WAS like a re-run of the Falklands War, the last time that England had won anything substantial. There was ticker-taping, amid vast, adoring crowds down Regent Street, the bands were struck up as soon-to-be-Sir Clive Woodward and his all-white knights paraded around the city. The way the English responded to their countrymen's victory in the 2003 Rugby World Cup was little short of mind-boggling.

All the old tired bulldoggy headlines that made the British tabloid press an international laughing stock at the time of the Falklands War were dusted off. It was "Gotcha!" all over again. Britannia was once more in charge. Stout-hearted men swelled with pride. They strutted around the city with considerably more swagger in the step. Did not the yeomen of England endure a massive siege in Sydney and finally break out of it, and surge on to victory, for Queen and country?

There were fully three-quarters of a million people in Trafalgar Square, outnumbering even the pigeons as the England team were given the freedom of the city of London, whatever that means, and were feted far into the night, and the next one, and the one after that. In the Midlands cities where rugby has its traditional support the celebrations lasted for days. Local Lions were lionised. Phil Vickery didn't just get an MBE. He got the freedom of the city of Gloucester, which provided him with the right to drive cattle through the city centre, something which may have given added stimulus to his business as a cattle inseminator.

The Queen had a brief taste of how her ancestor Victoria must have felt as a vast throng surrounded the palace to cheer themselves silly over another imperial triumph. The England team were given a right royal reception and various gongs were passed about. The Queen had, of course, reminded everybody before the final that she was also Queen of Australia and would cheer for both sides at once, but nobody bought that one. Mrs Windsor even went so far as to have a knee operation as a gesture of solidarity with the England players.

Why all the fuss? Did winning a World Cup really mean all that much to your average Englishman? The answer is really quite simple. The English are thoroughly sick of coming second and their World Cup rugby side was a calculated throw-back to the old imperial belligerence. No more of that soppy stuff about playing the game being more important than winning. This was an assemblage of raw power and it was applied as ruthlessly as the old imperial iron fist.

It was an England none of us had seen before. The old deferential geniality that had marked England's willingness to lose with dignity for so long seemed to have finally gone. Martin Johnson and his flinty colleagues were rulers of the universe. Earlier that year they had beaten the All Blacks in New Zealand with two men in the bin in the grittiest, and tactically smartest, display I had ever seen from an England team. Our psychological dominance seemed to die that night in Wellington.

But what happened next? The following year they were rubbish. What is it with England? With more registered rugby players than Australia, New Zealand and all the Pacific countries put together, they just can't seem to string more than one good season together before lapsing back into the old, familiar bumbling incompetence. One season they're formidable, as in 2003. The next they are absolute rubbish.

England is an oddball rugby nation. It still hasn't quite shaken off its now famous predisposition to be unadventurous. It wasn't always that way. A long time ago it was the other way round. Whenever the All Blacks played England throughout the amateur era the roles were well defined. New Zealand were the unsmiling giants; the grim reapers from down under who ground their opponents underfoot before showing the slightest signs of extravagance.

England, on the other hand, was renowned for its sense of derring-do adventurism, even if it was generally at the worst possible time. The All Blacks would feed voraciously off impetuous England mistakes and the result, almost always, would be the same. Only in 1935, when the English fielded a Russian prince, who was so fast he had to decelerate viciously to avoid tearing over the dead-ball line in scoring his two electrifying tries for England, did they get away with it.

When professionalism came along the roles were strangely reversed. The All Blacks became the adventurous entertainers, concentrating on extravagant flourishes and an ability to score long-range tries with speed and style. England, on the other hand, became drearily button-down. Anything faintly resembling risk was leached out if its game. The English forward pack became a collective menace, a monster from under Darth Vader's cape, grim, ruthless and as unsmiling as any All Blacks team had ever been.

The rolling maul became an English watchword. Games would bed grimly down in the middle of the field as Martin Johnson, Ben Kay, Danny Grewcock, Lawrence Dallaglio, Phil Vickery and the supporting cast of bow-legged yeomen would strangle the life out of their opponents, and the match itself. But you had to hand it to them. They knew how to slow a game down and they learned how to win. The crowds didn't mind a bit. They loved it. Twickenham would cheer on every collapsed maul, every re-set scrum and every loose ruck, confident in the knowledge that their lads would get on top whenever it was an arm wrestle. And win they did. The Sweet Chariot swung low.

But here's the curious thing. In between each bout of physical dominance would be periods of abject, bumbling incompetence. Every now and again the tactical plan would be suddenly abandoned along with England's sense of caution and they would be outrun or outkicked and made to look stupid, just like they used to be in the old days.

Unlike New Zealand, however, they seemed to be able to time their peak performances to perfection when it came to the World Cup. They did well in 1999, then lapsed into a coma. They woke up, mangled Australia to win the Cup in 2003 then promptly produced performances worthy of a Keystone Cops movie. They very nearly did the same routine in 2007. Then they went to sleep again. In 2009 they plumbed the depths. Will, like Rumpelstiltskin, the English awake again in 2011?

Some critics have put this almost pathological inconsistency down to bad coaching. It has little, if anything, to do with coaching. On the whole English coaches are very good. The problem is essentially one of divided loyalties. The players are pawns in a knock-down, drag-out contest between their clubs and their country. It is an ugly war and it won't be won by the Rugby Football Union until it can wrest the legal initiative from the big, privatised clubs. There is every chance that that will never happen, in which case England's chances of becoming the world's permanent rugby superpower are nil.

The English clubs have taken to assembling talent from anywhere they can get it. Their teams now bristle with foreign players on hefty contracts and instant working visas. Some, like Carlos Spencer, are at the end of their careers and are cashing up the accumulated promissory notes from a long, distinguished career at the top. Others, like Carl Hayman, Chris Jack, Aaron Mauger or Luke McAlister are in mid-career with one eye still cocked covetously in the direction of the All Blacks. Australians and Frenchmen abound. And then there is the band of emerging players who come cheaper, often from less prestigious rugby countries like Fiji or Tonga, or Romania, Argentina, Canada or Italy, and who are on the way up.

All this helps the clubs but it doesn't help England because in a number of positions there's hardly an Englishman to be seen in the professional competition. Alarm bells are ringing as England's fortunes slump and one of the key causes of this is the relative lack of experience in several key positions. How do they fix this? Nobody knows. The clubs are businesses. They hold no particular nationalistic candle. A number of them are openly hostile to the RFU and seem almost to go out of their way to obstruct the building and rebuilding of the England squad. The clubs have expanded dramatically in recent years. Vast sums have been invested in larger stadiums. Leicester, Gloucester and London Irish all boast a capacity of at least 15,000 and, until recently, the grounds have been full for the big championship and Heineken Cup matches. Professional rugby has prospered in recent times but that prosperity is now under a dark cloud.

There is a fierce debate in England about the longer term sustainability of the club structure. As the recession of 2008/09 began to bite it started to become apparent that some famous old names might be destined for the receiver. Their particular prosperity began to look rather like that of the many merchant banks of London — built on shifting sand. Clubs like Newcastle, Bristol, Bath, Wasps, Saracens or Worcester are teetering on the brink each year. Leicester is the only club that is genuinely safe. Many of them depend crucially on the personal largesse of their own Lorenzo Medici. Dave Thompson bails out Leicester. Keith Barwell keeps Northampton afloat, Nigel Wray is Saracens' guardian angel, backed by substantial South African dosh, and Cecil Duckworth underwrites Worcester. The salary cap ballooned out to £4.2 million in 2008 and an ever-greater proportion of club funds was hoovered up in player salaries. Players are shopping around and who can blame them? The amount of internal migration is breathtaking. Take the case of England scrumhalf Andy Gomarsall. He began his career with Wasps before spending time at Bedford, Gloucester, Worcester and Harlequins then heading north to play for Leeds Carnegie. And who goes to Leeds for the weather or the scenery?

A big question continually stares English rugby in the face: can any club continue to remain viable if the salaries just keep escalating? And what happens when the benefactor goes bust or simply grows tired of pumping disposable resources into a rugby club that doesn't give him the instant gratification he so obviously needs?

The acid test of sustainability in England will arrive when the British economy recovers and the national competition is expanded into a two-tier one. On the face of it that prospect is an attractive one for the promoters. It means the virtual doubling of the "product" available. It means an expansion of the exposure of pro rugby in a market that is clearly destined for lots more growth, and it means more sponsorship dollars, more television revenue and more security for the clubs. Clubs like Rotherham, London Welsh and Bedford are lining up their sugar daddies in anticipation of all the fruits of exposure in the big league.

It also implies a doubling of the opportunities for foreign players to earn bigger bucks. At the moment there are almost 500 professional contracts in England and a move from a one-tier, 12-team competition to a 20-team, two-tier competition will mean as many as 800 contracts. At the moment about half of the Guinness Premiership players are non-English. Astonishingly, a quarter are actually New Zealanders. The threat to New Zealand couldn't be more obvious. Can something be done to arrest this mass vacuuming up of talent? The clubs won't. The RFU seems incapable of solving it. The IRB is hamstrung. This is the unregulated iniquity of McWorld at work. Not even English xenophobia can be relied upon to come to the rescue.

But expansion has another more sinister implication. It runs the risk of follower fatigue, the disease that has struck the Southern hemisphere. Already there are rugby fans in England crying enough; please, don't give us any more. That signal will be ignored at England's peril.

NZ Rugby Museum

Under two flags. The 1888 “Natives” prepare to invade Britain.

NZ Rugby Museum

Above: The full body suit in 1905. Was this a sign of things to come?
Below: The old and the new. The collarless 1905 jersey and the latest Adidas version. A nod to tradition?

Photosport

Are they singing? The sevens gold medal winners at the Melbourne Commonwealth Games, 2006.

Photosport

All change at Eden Park in preparation for the World Cup.

Photosport

From champ to chump. In 2003 Clive Woodward coached Martin Johnson and his yeomen to beat the All Blacks with two men in the bin, then go on to win the World Cup. Two years later Woodward's Lions ate the humblest of pie in New Zealand.

Photosport

There's a book about it, and a play about it: the day that Munster downed the All Blacks in 1978. As persuasive an argument for the mid-week match as there will ever be.

Photosport

The greyish All Blacks come up short again in Cardiff, 2007. Frenchman Sebastien Chabal thanks Byron Kelleher for the memory.

Photosport

Sometimes history is pre-ordained. Mandela steals the show and the Springboks steal the cup in 1995.

Photosport

Oops, here we go again. Stirling Mortlock flees after an intercept and the 2003 World Cup semi-final is decided.

Photosport

"I'm from the IRB and I'm here to help you." IRB council member Martyn Thomas and Nobby Mashimo, chairman of the Japan RFU, after Japan learned they had won the hosting rights to the 2019 World Cup.

The Beastly Beatitudes of European Union

PEOPLE OFTEN wonder how united are the so-called Six Nations? There isn't an awful lot of love lost among them. The Celtics — the Scots, Welsh and Irish — naturally hate anything to do with England for historical reasons even if they are far too polite to ever say so publicly. The Italians hate the rest of the Six Nations crowd because they always seem to be the poor unwelcome cousin at the party and because Italy can't ever seem to beat any of the others. They also hate the IRB because it never gives them enough money. Hate springs eternal.

The English hate the French, not because they necessarily remain convinced that wogs begin at Calais but because French teams persistently beat them with flair and style — accentuating the very essence of the difference between the two cultures and it grates with the English. The French, naturally, hate the English simply because it is perennially unfashionable in France not to, and why should rugby be any different? Albion remains perfidious in the mind of a Frenchman.

Rugby outside England is very uneven in quality and for a number of years it looked as if the Six Nations was going to be permanently dominated by England and France. After all, that is where much of the purchasing power has been concentrated. Yet, that hasn't happened yet and rugby is much the richer for it. Ireland and Wales have managed, through astute planning, good coaching and a remarkable *esprit de corps* within their teams, to stay with the two heavyweights surprisingly well.

Irish rugby is a delightful blend of middle-class intelligence and raw Celtic anger. Like everything else that is Irish, the surface appearances can be very deceiving. The Irish are always the most welcome tourists wherever they go because they manage to give the impression that they don't take their rugby all that seriously. That is an illusion. It is always easy to be led up the garden path by an Irishman. One doesn't have to be within spitting distance of the Blarney Stone to be fatally vulnerable to that particular enchantment.

I don't know how they do it, but the Irish get away with it almost every time, particularly in New Zealand. Self-deprecation has long been a preoccupation of the more modestly ranked rugby nations. For some, such as the Italians or the Tongans, it is entirely justified. They know, usually from hard experience, that they are in for a whipping and the only question is how severely. The last few times the Irish have come to New Zealand they have arrived echoing the same theme and have nearly got away with a gross case of misrepresentation.

The rebellious nature of the Irish mind should be warning enough. Surely, we should know that regardless of how depleted they may claim to be, they still know full well that they can beat anybody through sheer willpower. And they can; and they do. They put particular energy into their encounters with England, for reasons not unconnected with the spirit of rebellion, and they have done remarkably well lately against this, the most ancient of enemies, cheered on enthusiastically by what seems to be the rest of the rugby world.

The Irish go to considerable lengths to persuade us, with a smile here and a song there, that playing the All Blacks is too much of an honour to get overly combative about. "We haven't really got a chance but we'll give it a go" is the perennial theme song, deliberately designed to lead to underestimation. They did it in Munster in 1978, and it worked. It has nearly worked on so many other occasions that you'd think we would have worked them out by now. We obviously hadn't the last time the All Blacks played Munster in 2008 because New Zealand selected what was more or less a second 15 and won by a margin that would have had difficulty accommodating a cigarette paper. Anyone who has visited Limerick in the rugby season will know how strong a force it is. Alan English, the author of *Stand up and Fight*, a book commemorating Munster's 1978 triumph, said: "It's the only city in all of Ireland where it's a game that's played by . . . all classes and creeds . . . here you have a huge working-class who love rugby." Limerick might be a rather unprepossessing sort of place but Munster is certainly not unprepossessing as a rugby team. It, too, has its share of New Zealand imports. Christian Cullen, Doug Howlett, Rua Tipoki and others have all relished the atmosphere there. They are embraced.

Ireland are unlikely to be easy-beats in the immediate future. The game in the republic is in a hearty state. It is settled, well organised and fairly affluent even if the Irish economy has been more severely buffeted by recession than any other. It isn't at all like the crisis-ridden game of the 1970s, 80s and early 90s when rugby in the republic was heading for oblivion. Immediately before the professional revolution it was just hanging on, waiting for a miracle. But the Irish have always been optimistic in the face of oblivion. They revel in black humour. As Tony O'Reilly used to put it cryptically in the Irish dressing-room at halftime when they were down by 20 points or more, "The situation is critical but not desperate." For that reason they remain capable of beating anybody and everybody.

Professionalism seems to have worked for the Irish. For an intensely tribal people the Irish have absorbed foreign talent with consummate ease. The bigger clubs, Leinster in particular, have prospered mightily from imports and their supporters aren't complaining about a loss of Irish identity. The Irish national team is different, however. Here, there is no sign of dilution, yet Ireland remain fiercely competitive. Their system breeds tough and talented professionals. They will survive.

Scotland, on the other hand, seem to find the going ever tougher. The professional game seems to have been as welcome in Scotland as a fart in a phone box. But let's be honest here. There has always been something mean-spirited and unadventurous about those who run rugby in Scotland. They might have been responsible for arranging the first-ever test match — against England in 1873 — but the record has hardly been a generous one ever since. They refused to cooperate with the 1905 All Blacks, suspecting that this was a bunch of colonial con men, more interested in making money than playing footy. The Scottish union threatened to call off the international ostensibly because of the weather, but in fact because they had arrogantly decided beforehand that the New Zealanders wouldn't be much of a drawcard and had decided to forego any of the financial risk, and with it the gate-takings, which turned out to be considerable.

Scotland refused outright to play the 1924 All Blacks because of the fact that the New Zealanders were paid three shillings a day "expenses". This constituted a horrendous breach of the Protestant perspective of amateurism. That parsimonious attitude persisted, along with a rigid, Protestant approach to amateurism that kept the game locked up in upper middle-class enclaves. The attitudes towards money were as hostile in the 1960s as they were in 1905. I vividly recall a Scottish official searching through the All Blacks dressing-room after a test match in 1967 for one of the match balls which simply had, he said, to be returned to the union.

When Peter Stagg, the giant Scottish lock, tore his sock the union refused to give him a new pair until the next season. They recommended, creatively, that he use boot polish to disguise the hole. The Scottish union insisted that a former captain, Budge Pountney, repay them for a national tie that he gave away to a disabled supporter. The Scots had a reputation for niggardliness and their rugby union has lived up to it enthusiastically.

Even as late as 1983 people who were making money out of the game, no matter how indirectly, were still religiously excluded from any rugby clubhouse and from joining a rugby club. In his autobiography, sports broadcaster Brendan Telfer recalls the time he encountered the great Scottish commentator Bill McLaren at a local club game and invited him into the clubhouse for a nip of scotch to warm the cockles. Bill demurred. He wasn't allowed in. He was a professional according to the rules as applied in Scotland. How daft can you get?

The Scots are only now getting over the nit-picking. They don't have much choice because today's professional players simply don't hang about if they aren't treated like princes.

Scotland just can't quite seem to build support for rugby out beyond the middle classes. It is up against the formidable foe of soccer and that has, in many respects, been its undoing. Scottish clubs remained relatively small and relatively poor right through the 20th century, even if much of their support base was solidly middle-class. When the Heineken Cup was introduced the SRU officials became rightly concerned that modestly endowed Scottish club sides wouldn't be able to compete against the best teams from France and England, or even Wales, and decided to create centrally funded "super-district" teams, rather like the New Zealand franchises. Various attempts to make this work have been tried but these have hardly been a roaring success.

After two seasons, financial difficulties forced the SRU to merge the four teams into two. Edinburgh merged with the Border Reivers to form a team to be known as Edinburgh Reivers. Glasgow merged with Caledonian to form a team to be known as Glasgow Caledonian. Ever since it has been a mishmash of restructuring and name-changing. Even Scotsmen can't keep up.

Many people now ask the obvious question: where is Scottish rugby headed? On the face of it the answer is nowhere. The SRU is near-broke, still paying off the debt associated with the extravagant redevelopment of Murrayfield. All this results in severe disadvantage for Scottish teams from the national side down. Scottish coach Frank Hadden discovered this when in 2007 he sought agreement from Premier League Rugby, the umbrella organisation representing Guinness Premiership clubs, to secure the release of players selected for Scotland two weeks before every test.

The stand-off between the Scottish Rugby Union and leading English clubs came to a head when Sean Lamont, Jim Hamilton and Rory Lawson all sat out a Scotland training session on the instructions of their clubs. The gathering had been called for the "fallow" week of the Six Nations, with no international matches scheduled. Hadden was furious but there was nothing he could do about it.

Premier League Rugby maintained that if the SRU wanted players outside international weeks, they should pay clubs for the privilege. The tactic was in contravention of International Rugby Board regulations, but the IRB said nothing would be done to enforce the regulations unless a complaint was received from a member union.

The SRU was reluctant to take such a course of action, and instead coach Hadden tried to do it the nice way by building a relationship with the affected clubs. He was given the cold shoulder. Premier League Rugby is not in the business of international fairness. It instructed each of its teams not to release players for what was Scotland's first get-together of the next season. Ironically, however, his England counterpart Martin Johnson had no such difficulty as the (English) Rugby Football Union had agreed to pay Premiership clubs for this privilege. It is a privilege that helps explain why England invariably beats Scotland. It is as simple as that. You get what you pay for and if you can't afford it, you lose.

All around Europe the frustration over availability of players for national duty is slowly building up. It seems astonishing that the proprietary rights of the clubs haven't yet been tested in the courts. Surely, the best way to get the issue on the table is to take a test case, the result of which would enable the IRB and the national unions concerned to seek legal clarification of their rights and, if necessary, a change in the restraint of trade laws that would open the way for players who want to play for their country to do so. This is a test of strength that may well determine the future of rugby, not just in Europe but everywhere else.

Whatever Happened to the Hwyl?

"LET'S NOT be intimidated by these New Zealanders," trumpeted the Welsh assistant coach in 2005 in a fit of anxiety-induced bravado before his team was due to be delivered up for its now customary ritual slaughter at the hands of the All Blacks. "They're from a poxy little island in the South Pacific." It was a remark that provoked the obvious temptation, by way of retaliation, to describe Wales as a poxy little principality perched on a dreary wasteland of disused coal pits. That, of course, would be churlish because the assistant coach was, after all, an expat Australian, and his crack was one of those seemingly pointless attempts to gain some kind of psychological upper hand that is so characteristic of the pre-test mental gymnastics these days.

Or was it? Forget about the insult to New Zealand. This was more about Wales than New Zealand. Welsh rugby was at the time, and had been for a decade or more, in a state of acute identity crisis.

The Welsh decline in the last part of the 20th century has been one of the great tragedies of world rugby. There was a time when every man, woman and child in Wales expected their team to deliver up a victory against anyone who came. Some blame it on the refusal among teachers to coach rugby at primary and secondary schools. Others point to the steady pillaging by rugby league clubs, something which is surely over now that rugby union has equalled, if not surpassed, league's player purchasing power.

For a long time rugby was as central to the Welsh psyche as soccer has been in Manchester or Liverpool. A whole society saw itself against the backdrop of those scarlet jerseys. Welshmen ate, slept and dreamed about their game. Everyone had a stake in it one way or another — even those who soared above the rain-sodden principality and became famous for other things.

Take the case of Richard Burton. He was a rugby nut. Burton often reminisced about his rugby playing days in ways that weren't always complimentary of his Welsh countrymen. In 1953 he wrote a short memoir about a particular game he played after making the big-time as a Shakespearean actor. He started the game at flyhalf but had nothing other than utter humiliation. And so he decided: "The thing to do, I told myself with desperate cunning, was to keep alive, and the way to do that was to keep out of the way. After being gardened, mown and rolled a little more, I asked the captain of our team if he didn't think it would be a better idea to hide me deeper in the pack. By the end of the game my face was as red as the setting sun, and the same shape."

We might have had the haka but the Welsh had *hwyl*. This is something that's about as hard to define as it is to spell, let alone pronounce. When I first went to Wales as a naïve 19-year-old All Black, somebody told me that *hwyl* was a kind of national drink, a capricious Welsh potion that produced an explosion of national pride in Welsh players. There was no point in anybody else drinking it, they said, because it only worked if you were Welsh. Somehow, when I learned the truth, it didn't seem to make any difference. *Hwyl* wasn't a drink, but it was real. It was like mojo — hard to define but you knew when it wasn't there. *Hwyl* was potent and it was dangerously volatile whenever Wales played another country.

The Welsh might have had *hwyl* by the bucketload throughout most of the last century but the bucket somehow got holed. The *hwyl* drained out and with it went the engaging jauntiness that accompanied the Welsh game. They lost their confidence along with their coalmines and they have never since been able to recover either.

Yet it wasn't so long ago that the single, constantly echoing chorus of a song that had its origins away back in 1905, was: "Wales'll beat you boyo." And they often did, way back then. The crowds sang, magnificently, in a vast, belligerent single voice, willing you to wilt in the face of its sheer majesty. It is an experience that even the most phlegmatic individual cannot but be affected by.

For many decades the relationship between Wales and New Zealand in international rugby was the one that everybody talked about. There was an almost celestial quality to it. When the two countries clashed it was the tough guys' day out. The flinty valley miner pitted against the hardened southern settler. Irresistible forces and immovable objects. They beat us in 1905, maybe not quite fair and square but, nonetheless, they won and something special began.

Every All Blacks visit after that was supercharged with meaning and purpose. New Zealand finally won at Cardiff in the 1920s but Wales won the next two, in the 30s and the 50s, and they very nearly won again in 1963. Before that match the persistent refrain of "Wales'll beat you" had become a kind of Celtic kapa haka, something the locals just broke into, spontaneously. It was reflex stuff then but we don't hear it any more.

Ever since it's all been one-way traffic with the Welshmen invariably caught, frozen like rabbits in the headlights of the oncoming big black bus before being comprehensively flattened.

In an act curiously symbolic of the way the game sank into the mire in Wales, the players almost provoked a cancellation of a recent tour of Australia and New Zealand by baulking at the payments they were due to receive. Instead of preparing themselves for another pummelling down under, the Welsh players spent most of their pre-tour training camp locked in negotiations with the WRU over the restructuring of salary packages. The Welshmen played Oliver Twist with their increasingly impoverished national union and they got away with it. Perhaps they wanted danger money on top of the normal salary which, itself, was far more than they probably deserved. Most of them would have done better begging in the mean streets of Tiger Bay if their pay had been performance based.

The decline is symbolised in the apocryphal tale of Dai and Gareth, two fanatical Welsh supporters who are trying to decide whether or not to go one last time to the Arms Park in the forlorn hope of seeing something better than farce from the Welsh team. As they make their way through the Cardiff streets Dai suddenly remembers that the local chemist shop sells tickets to the game. "Wait here, Gareth," he says, "while I go in and see if I can get some tickets. I can kill two birds with one stone because I have to stock up on condoms as well."

Gareth appreciates the immutable logic of this economy of effort and settles down on a seat outside the chemist shop to wait for his colleague. He waits, and he waits, and he waits. Finally, minutes before the match is due to start, Dai comes blundering out of the shop red-faced and flustered. "Well," says Gareth, "have you got the tickets then?" "Ah, actually no," blurts Dai. "I got the condoms all right but I was too embarrassed to ask for the tickets."

It's hard to know precisely why or where Wales lost its *hwyl*. Perhaps it became permanently entombed in all those mines that have progressively been sealed off over the years. The great mining town clubs like Neath, Aberavon, Abertillery, Maesteg or Pontypool don't cater for miners any more. Their amateur teams are composed of real estate agents, insurance salesmen and IT experts. But then so are just about everybody else's.

They say that Welsh rugby went soft from the centre and that their traditional comparative advantage — fanatically fit, hard forwards and mercurial runners out wide — has just melted away; gone with the coal.

The old heroes of Welsh rugby found this decline very hard to stomach. A few seasons ago when Wales were at their very worst I asked Gareth Edwards, a player whose sense of ethnic pride pulled him up out of the mud and on to exceptional feats of athleticism in the 1970s, why this collapse had occurred. "Professionalism," he said quite simply. "Now the game isn't owned by the people they are losing interest in it."

Gerald Davies, an equally revered contemporary of Edwards, said much the same. A passionate promoter of the Welsh language and traditions, he wondered what had happened to suck the spirit out of the national team. Was it simply the onrush of global culture, the homogenisation of all things Welsh into the great pool of undifferentiated peoples everywhere? Nobody quite seemed to know.

It seems odd that at the very moment that the Welsh principality was achieving a measure of self-containment under Britain's devolution arrangements its rugby team was slithering down the gurgler of nonentity.

Loyalty to home turf is a delicate flower in the face of financial inducement to cross the border. But what border? Welsh players increasingly see their future in England or France where the big pay cheques are. Their sense of Welshness seems to have been steadily diluted. If you're playing in a team — as many in Europe now are — composed of top players from all over the world, the standard of your own game might go up but your sense of national obligation tends to go down. Even more so when your club says no to your national selectors who want you for test match duty. This is not about national sentiment, or duty. It is about money. A contract is a contract as so many naïve young players, not just in Wales, are finding out.

But hold the obituary notice. The Welsh story has a postscript. As the millennium turned, so, too, did the fortunes of the Welsh national team. They began to win again, not all that often and not always all that convincingly. But there were unmistakable signs of a resurgence of the old passion and pride which had been tragically absent years before. These days triple crowns and grand slams are once again the Welsh watchwords.

What's going on? Is there a new nationalism? There are certainly no outward signs of that. It seems to be more prosaic than that. It's the product of consolidation. Although it is sad to see the demise of so many of the old rugby clubs that have served as such a vital life-force for mining communities up the valleys, or the steel milling towns like Neath or Aberavon, the consolidation of clubs into larger more competitive units has unquestionably strengthened Welsh rugby. The establishment of five regional teams, the equivalent of New Zealand's five Super 14 franchises, has undoubtedly sharpened up the competitive structure in Wales, even if it has caused much angst to many of the 280-odd smaller clubs who wonder about their future.

The line between amateur and professional is being drawn more visibly and the smaller clubs are quietly closing their doors. It is exactly the same concern that we have in New Zealand as the amateur game slides slowly, inexorably, towards extinction and the focus shifts away from the local community to the big, bold, professional franchise. Is this a price worth paying? Unfortunately, it's the only deal on the table.

Is Life Worth Living Without the Lions?

ONE OF the more intriguing traditions to emerge from rugby in Britain — and Ireland — was the willingness to coalesce from time to time to take on the Southern hemisphere juggernauts. The Lions became a central feature of international rugby and the tours they periodically made down under were an irresistible attraction. The Lions are an interesting concept. Originally, they were simply called the British Lions even though they contained players from the Irish Republic. Politics was quite pointedly set aside for rugby which was the only sport that accommodated the English and the Irish together in any capacity without resort to fisticuffs. Now it has become known as the "British and Irish Lions", political correctness having triumphed over pragmatism.

The Celts had their noses put firmly out of joint when they found themselves saddled with an oafish, over the top English management structure in 2005. Clive Woodward and his various assistants insisted on picking too many Englishmen and then tried to use spin in the guise of Alistair Campbell, who was so far out of his political comfort zone that he became a figure of fun. Except, of course, to all those Scotsmen, Irishmen and Welshmen in the squad who had to endure it all.

This, they said, was the big one. This was the moment in which British rugby finally asserted itself, proving that England's win at the 2003 World Cup wasn't just a temporary blip on the radar screen of southern superiority. The 2005 British and Irish Lions team was the greatest expeditionary force of players, coaches, managers, motivators and sundry other specialists that rugby has ever seen. If you add the

Barmy Army, that vast, uninhibited and cheerfully partisan assembly of supporters, we had an invasion force of Iraq proportions with almost as deadly an intent, even if a little short on shock and awe.

Coach Clive Woodward was acutely aware of the fact that history hadn't been kind to the many Lions teams that came to New Zealand. The first thing he said on arrival in Auckland was the fact that his mission was to turn history on its head by somehow defeating the All Blacks on their own territory.

It had only happened once before, in 1971. Although they managed to beat both Australia and South Africa they couldn't overcome the All Blacks again. They came and went in the 1970s, 80s and 90s without success and still suffering from the same essential disunity and managerial ineptitude.

And then along came professionalism and everything changed. New Zealand's critical edge in fitness, basic skill levels, athleticism and dedication was quickly neutralised. Money, and plenty of it, was pumped into the game and the old ethnic and national differences became less relevant. But so, too, it seems, did the rationale for the Lions. The professional season became so congested that there was no room any more for this rather elderly curiosity. But tradition refused to lie down compliantly. After five or more hard, repetitive years of Super 12, Tri Nations, the European Cup and the Six Nations tournaments, those who ran the game realised that this simply wasn't what was wanted. The fans were rebelling against the sudden discarding of the traditional long tour and it became clear that the greatest attraction in Australia, New Zealand and South Africa remained a tour by the Lions.

Now, it's back on the agenda and it's enormously popular as the Lions tour of Australia in 2001, New Zealand in 2005 and South Africa in 2009 showed.

The 2005 Lions crashed and burned and nobody could quite figure out why. Were they over-coached? Were they under-coached? Were there too many of them? Were they simply not good enough against an All Black team that was compact, united and fiercely determined? One thing is indisputable. They weren't happy. As a result of that débâcle the future of the Lions as an entity in world rugby was in doubt.

In 2009, Ian McGeechan, one of the great survivors of British rugby

— and a first-rate coach — ran a much tighter ship, and ran South Africa perilously close. McGeechan is the polar opposite of Woodward. He is modest, canny, universally liked and with a sense of proportion. In effect, he rescued the whole concept of the Lions from oblivion by melding his team into a much more united company. He showed that the Lions could work and were worth persisting with. That is a great relief because the Lions are part of rugby's illogical, oddball character.

The survival of the Lions may in fact help to ensure the survival of rugby itself. The IRB seems to have accepted the fact that life without the Lions is not worth living. As even hardened professional Phil Vickery said at the end of the 2009 tour, this is an experience that goes beyond the day-to-day drudge of the professional circuit. "It's magic," said Vickery, with obvious feeling, and he was right. And the fans agree. If rugby is to survive it has to factor in Lions tours often enough to light up the landscape, but not so often as to debase the currency. That means about once every four years as part of a new, more variegated international calendar. Bring on the Barmy Army. Rugby can't live without the Lions.

Le Beau Jeu to the Rescue

WE SPENT the best part of a century keeping France out of rugby's respectable sanctum and now we need the French to save the game.

Given the fact that France has been invaded, abused, dismembered and humiliated over the centuries, as often as not by the English, it is a bit of a mystery why it ever adopted rugby, the game of the English ruling classes, with such fervent devotion. But it did, and after many years of waiting at the stage door which remained closed to non-Anglo-Saxons for an indecently long time, it is now at centre stage in the world game.

The French are an obdurate lot. They so often seem to be pigheaded and arrogant and acutely conscious of a national ego that seems in need of constant gratification. When A J Hackett bungy jumped his way to folk history off the Eiffel Tower the French people loved it. The French government didn't, however. It was seen in official circles as an act of mockery; a foreigner issuing a calculated insult to the French nation. Collectively, they can be impossible. Individually, they are invariably a delight. They have perplexed many New Zealanders over the years. Katherine Mansfield, during her time in Menton, found them abominable. As she wrote to a friend in New Zealand: "I am very sincere when I say I hate the French. As animals they are interesting monkeys but they have no heart, no heart at all." She was wrong. Katherine was a long way from home and somewhat given to neuroses.

Why has rugby done so well in France? When you think about it rugby isn't a game the French should be naturally good at. Such quintessentially English notions of team spirit, fair play, calmness under pressure, sportsmanship and losing with grace have never really seemed to be among the stronger suits of the French. French rugby has worn its heart on its sleeve. It might seem erratic, irrational, sometimes nasty and often neurotic, but it's infinitely more compelling than English rugby. It has traditionally offered soufflé in contrast to England's suet pudding.

Legend has it that the burghers of Bordeaux borrowed rugby from the English, or rather the English lent it to them in return for quality claret and the French forgot to give it back. But like all legends this one is light on substance. Rugby didn't take initial root in the southwest. It actually got started in Paris, actively promoted by British expatriate sporting clubs in the 1870s.

France had just suffered another of its crushing military defeats, this time against the Prussians, and its national sense of male virility was at crisis point. Amid fierce debates about the moral and physical decrepitude of French society, rugby saw its chance and grabbed it. In these early years a distinctive Parisian style of play was adopted, the same style that the first teams from New Zealand, Australia and South Africa encountered in the first decade of the 20th century. It was known as *le beau jeu*, more notable for its elegance and flamboyance than any real physical grunt. The grunt came later when the game became the social point of difference for small towns in the southwest and the artisans and farmers began to get interested.

Modern French rugby is a curious amalgam of raw power and the distinctive grace of *le beau jeu*. The French have always been able to come up with hardbitten forwards, renowned for their sheer strength, along with many of the most creative and inventive backs in world rugby history. There is an interesting reason for that.

From Paris, the game spread out into the provinces, initially from centres of British influence such as Nantes, Nice, Lyon, Toulouse and, of course, Bordeaux where the British presence was most visible. Slowly it began to invade the southern provinces where it became identified with local, rural notions of machismo, particularly in the Basque country and the tradition of tough, unyielding French forward play was born. Rugby is firmly embedded in the psyche of the southwest and the similarities with New Zealand provincial towns are striking. Tarbes is the Te Kuiti of France. Mont-de-Marsan could be Morrinsville. The rugby club was — and in some of the smaller towns still is — the centre of the town's social life in the southwest. Numerous New Zealanders have found an unlikely second home down south where they love All Blacks.

French rugby never really united as a single force until the 1970s. Provincial or territorial parochialism saw to that. So, too, did the era of shamateurism that began in the 1920s and persisted for decades, resulting in the paranoically amateur Home Unions slamming the door in France's face as a legitimate member of the international rugby fraternity. Rugby was a game of a few francs here, a few francs there, a nod and a wink and a code of silence over player payments. The RFU sniffed at it disdainfully and kept France at arm's length. The French shrugged, and carried right on paying players. Ironically, this meant they were ideally placed to embrace the era of professionalism. Nothing much changed except the size of the payment and, of course, the requirement to pay some tax.

The French might have come onto the international landscape relatively recently but in many aspects of the game they were often years ahead of all the rest of us. They invented the peel off the end of the lineout. They invented the art of lifting lineout jumpers years before it was finally legalised. They invented the miss pass in midfield, the dummy runner and the scissors movement; and, most notably, they invented the head-high tackle — *le cravat* as it was evocatively described.

French club rugby has become a major economic force in recent years. The larger clubs have become enormously powerful, too powerful for their own and the game's good in many respects. French rugby has come to be dominated by a small group of exceptionally wealthy individuals who have bought up clubs, lock, stock and barrel, and who put commercial success ahead of any other consideration.

The professional game in France, as in England, is being held to ransom by these oligarchs. They are driven by the same curious bouts of ego that prompt rich businessmen to buy football clubs worldwide and they have been buying talent from around the world as if there was no tomorrow. Some, too few of them, are rugby devotees but even those few quickly find themselves at odds with the French Federation (FFR) as the demands of club clash with those of country. As things stand, the clubs invariably win and the integrity of the game, internationally, is diminished as a result. It is now the single most important obstacle in rugby's growth to genuine maturity as a world game.

There are signs that the FFR has finally resolved to restrict the foreign invasion and to set about controlling salary levels. André Malraux once said, "France is never France when she fights for herself. The real France is the France of the crusades, or the revolution. When the French fight for mankind they are wonderful. When they fight for themselves, they are nothing." M. Malraux obviously never watched a rugby match at Colombes. When the French fight for themselves on the footy field they can be unstoppable. Ask any All Blacks World Cup player of the last decade.

Yet that same decade has seen France fighting for the wider interests of the game as much as its own. The French are leading the campaign to try to get some order into the relationship between the clubs and the unions. Maybe Malraux was right. When the French fight for everybody they really are at their best.

If France can resolve this issue then world rugby has a future. If it can't, then we will all suffer the consequences. It's time *le beau jeu* came to the rescue.

Finding Gold at the End of the Rainbow

IN SOUTH AFRICA, politics and sport are like two manic depressives shackled together in a small cell. It was like that in the pre-apartheid era, throughout the years of madness and it is the same now in the post-apartheid Rainbow Nation. Somehow the past keeps crash-tackling South African rugby as divergent interests wrestle for control, and it is a miracle that the Springboks are still able to get an agreed team on the field, let alone win the World Cup.

It has always been a mystery to me why the Afrikaners took up rugby. Nobody has ever come up with a truly satisfactory answer to this question. These singular, Protestant people, squeezed out of Holland, France and Germany as the victims of religious intolerance, had every reason to turn their backs on the European world. Indeed, they tried their hardest to do this and very nearly got away with it. Why then would they possibly have been persuaded to adopt the very game of those who conquered them? And to become, with the All Blacks, the hardest in the world to beat. Without an understanding of the Afrikaners' story it is impossible to interpret the current tortured state of the game in that country.

The answer lies in the curious relationship that developed between the great colonial power, its concept of "muscular Christianity" and the options available to the Afrikaner people as the world began to bear in on them a century ago.

Oddly enough, there has been very little objective analysis of Afrikaner society by the outside world. The British encouraged us to ignore and despise them, and we duly did; and apartheid was the consequence. For nearly 100 years they were treated like lepers by the western mainstream and they didn't like it. The only major attempt to peel the onion of the Afrikaner personality was David Dimbleby's celebrated BBC television documentary *The White Tribe of Africa*. Looked at in retrospect, this was patronising and Anglocentric — long on racist rhetoric and short on understanding of the complex forces that shaped South Africa. Dimbleby kept asking himself, "Why can't these people be more like us?"

They weren't. The Afrikaners came from a totally different cultural wellspring and their story is truly romantic. It's the story of a people who were born out of insecurity and a sense of injustice and have been unable to cast that phobia off ever since.

In his marvellous survey of the evolution of the Afrikaner nation, *The Mind of South Africa*, Alister Sparks recognises this as the essential driving force behind all Afrikaner behaviour. He uses the imagery of a Bitter Almond hedge which Jan van Riebeeck, the leader of the first consignment of Dutch settlers, planted in 1660 around his little colony at the Cape to keep out animals and Hottentots, not necessarily in that order of priority. That hedge, the remnants of which are still in evidence at the foot of Table Mountain today, has stood for centuries as a symbol of the attitude of the Afrikaner towards all those who share that land; a metaphor for everything that has happened since. Rugby found itself within the confines of that hedge for far too long.

The story of the Afrikaner emergence is central to the way rugby evolved in South Africa and the way it was pre-empted from the British. It was Albion who started the wars against the Boer republics and it was done purely and simply in the name of avarice. And it was the British who forced the Afrikaner into second-class citizenship from which a burning, and ultimately fatal, nationalism arose.

There has always been something very definite about Afrikaner culture. They have their own language, folklore, traditions, music and literature. It is a distinctive culture: self-contained, unique. All this was, of course, overlaid with a sense of divine Protestant purpose. As Daniel Malan, the new Prime Minister, said after the National Party swept to power in 1948: "The last one hundred years have witnessed a miracle behind which there must be a divine plan." Alas, God's message from there on was catastrophically misinterpreted. Nobody at that moment could have predicted the immense sweep of history that would gather South Africa up and deposit her bumpily into the post-apartheid era.

But while they may have lost their political primacy, Afrikaners still form the backbone of the game in South Africa. A look at any Springboks team list will dispel any doubts on that score.

History has it that the first game of rugby, or something approximating it, was an encounter between British Military and Civilians at Green Point Common in Cape Town in 1862. This was, almost inevitably, an event that was confined to the Anglo-South Africans. There is certainly no record of any Afrikaner taking part. Rugby historian Spiro Zavos reveals that this game was played under the so-called Winchester School rules. Winchester, unlike Rugby School, developed an apparently very different ethos. Whereas Rugby espoused the notion of unity, inclusiveness and the brotherhood of man, Winchester seems to have promoted factionalism, secretiveness and a penchant for sado-masochism. Zavos is convinced that it was Winchester that triumphed in South Africa, attracting Afrikaners and contributing to the exclusive nature of the Afrikaner personality. Perhaps it even provided the essential spark for the subsequent creation of the ultimate secret society, the Broederbond.

Whatever the truth of all this, we don't see much sign of Afrikaner involvement in rugby until the turn of the century. A South African national team was put together to face the first British side to tour the country in 1891 and the South Africans were well and truly walloped. The "nationals" were all Englishmen. It wasn't till 1896 when a second British touring team arrived that there emerged any suggestion that South Africa might be a force to be reckoned with.

By then there were several Afrikaners in the team and they beat the British in the final "test". But this still doesn't explain why the Afrikaner should suddenly grab the Englishman's game and run away with it. Perhaps it was because soccer was the game of the general ranks of the British military — the oppressors — that pushed the Afrikaner into the arms of rugby. Perhaps it was rugby's very roughness, the opportunity to engage in fisticuffs and to batter an opponent into physical submission, that appealed to the Boer republics. Either way, rugby was just the ticket for a people being slowly strangled by cultural colonisation.

Then, of course, war erupted against the British and by the end of it, remarkably, rugby was the Afrikaner's chosen game. On one famous occasion a British commander stationed at O'Kief received a written challenge from General Maritz of the Transvaal Scouting Corps to a cessation of hostilities in order for a rugby match between the warring armies to take place. And it did. And the Afrikaners won, or so folklore has it. Its story can be very elastic in South Africa. The British might have gone on to win the war but at that precise moment they lost their primacy in the game they had transported to the colonies.

Within a very short time the South African Springboks were an almost exclusively Afrikaner team and it stayed that way for nearly a century. Perversely, they even borrowed a Zulu war dance for a while until it became evident to all those who saw it performed that there was more than a little incongruity about the spectacle of an exclusively white bunch of men imitating a black man's ritual.

That was to be the last acknowledgement by South African rugby that non-whites had any part to play in rugby. The shutters came down. Night fell.

By the late 1960s, South African teams were causing untold inconvenience everywhere they toured. Rugby was caught in a divide between liberal and conservative, young and old, and by the early 1990s the die was cast. Apartheid would soon be consigned to the trash can of history and rugby had, after so many decades of infamy, played an important part in the transformation.

Key to that process was Nelson Mandela's realisation, in prison, that he needed to find a unique area of common ground with his Afikaner adversaries. Time was short. A potential race war was looming. His release in 1990 did nothing to stop bloodshed in black townships; it intensified, as white right-wingers talked openly of a coup. Enter the old Afrikaner game as a shapeshifter. The 1995 World Cup furnished the perfect platform. Having persuaded his own people to let the rugby team keep the hated Springbok emblem, the president needed political payback. It came in the form of the Afrikaner players learning to sing the "black" half of the national anthem, "Nkosi Sikelel' iAfrika". Mandela met the squad, and began talking publicly of "my boys", but most of black South Africa remained indifferent. That started to change as the Springboks marched to the final: the excitement of white followers infected the black majority.

When the president made his sensational appearance in a Springboks shirt at the final against the All Blacks, the overwhelmingly white, Afrikaner crowd chanted his name. They were won over. When the team won against all the odds, the whole of South Africa went bananas. Many Afrikaners genuinely believed Mandela had won them the World Cup. When he thanked Pienaar for what he had done for "our country", the Springboks captain replied: "No, Mr President. Thank you very much for what you have done for our country."

New Zealanders were understandably miffed, not least by the belief that the food poisoning suffered by many All Blacks on the day of the final was no accident. But there were bigger things afoot. This was destiny at work. In John Carlin's *Playing the Enemy*, the French player, Abdelatif Benazzi, whose try would have beaten the Springboks in the semi-final, had it been allowed said, after the final, "I knew . . . that something more important was happening . . . than victory or defeat in a game of rugby." He was so right.

But what happened then? Everybody expected South African rugby to be liberated, but little really changed until the government stepped in and started cracking the multiracial whip. For a decade or more chaos reigned. The Springboks began to decline as a world rugby power and there were fears that the game would disappear beneath a rising tide of factionalism, racial discord and compulsory quotas. It was reflected on the field. The Springboks selectors seemed to be at war with each other. They opted for confrontationists one year and mercurial runners the next. They had runners aplenty but, unfortunately, they all seemed to be running in different directions and only occasionally with the ball.

The administration of the game began to imitate the players. Factionalism broke out into the open. Coaches were plucked from obscurity or retirement and after a short string of defeats were summarily dismissed. The government kept asking for more of a black presence in the team and the Springbok administrators kept shuffling their feet. The players became restless and began to demand more money and better working conditions.

The Springboks were sent to an army boot camp to prepare for the 2003 World Cup and the most alarming stories filtered out about various forms of sado-masochism being employed in the hope of turning what had become an unruly, disunited rabble into something resembling a competitive rugby team.

It didn't work. It turned them into an even more surly, resentful and deeply divided outfit. Their performance at that particular World Cup was probably the worst that South Africa had ever delivered up. It looked like it was all over. "Finish and klaar" as the Afrikaners say.

There have always been some who wanted the Springboks renamed the Proteas. The term "Springboks" was still a four-letter word. It still carried all those ugly old connotations from the apartheid era when rugby was politics with a mouth-guard. Players began to flee to the Northern hemisphere for bigger dollars, a strike over pay rates seemed perennially to be just about to start and the administration of the game went completely haywire. Cricket in South Africa, which adapted to the new era with apparent ease, seemed to be light years ahead of rugby and the difference didn't go unremarked.

The SARU story began to read like the script of a Marx brothers movie. There was a succession of administrators who had neither the personality nor the hard qualifications to rise above petty bickering and back-stabbing. Time and again the government meddled with the affairs of the rugby union, issuing threats if more black players weren't brought through to the national team, introducing semi-formal quotas and interfering with the selection of coaches and managers. It was all very unseemly.

Yet, riven by dissent, coaching controversies, arguments over salaries and the availability of European-based players, the Springboks got up off the floor and won the World Cup through sheer application in 2007. Nelson Mandela was suitably chuffed and he didn't have much else to be chuffed about back home by then.

The tortuous business of getting a national rugby team that better reflects the racial make-up of South Africa is going to take a lot longer than people first imagined. Quotas, whether formalised by law or informally imposed by an increasingly impatient government, could quite easily destroy the game.

In spite of everything, rugby remains, by and large, the emotional property of the Afrikaners. There may be no more blacks in the

Springboks team than there were 10 years ago, but South Africa has otherwise been good at cultural compromise. When they couldn't agree on a new anthem they just cobbled together the old and the new. They have done the same thing with the jersey. Nobody could agree whether it should have a protea or a springbok on it; so they did the obvious. They put both on it.

But what lies ahead? If South Africa can remain relatively stable politically then rugby will be sustainable. If it can't then the economy will suffer, sponsorship will evaporate, investment in black advancement will falter, the Afrikaner community will be culturally decimated and rugby will be doomed, once again a political football in a game where nobody will be playing fair. All the signs are that Jacob Zuma's presidency will make or break this remarkable society and the country is currently on a knife-edge.

If South Africa can overcome its awful problems of inequality and lack of opportunity then rugby will prosper. The transformation of the Springboks — from white to brindle and maybe, eventually, to predominantly black — will be part of that and if it actually works then eventually no team on earth will be able to stay with the Springboks. In the meantime it is in the rugby world's interest to concentrate not so much on beating them but helping them find their way home.

Wallaby Wannabe

FOR A very long time rugby union in Australia was a patient in an international casualty ward and New Zealand was the visiting physician. Our people would regularly have to bail out the ARU and New Zealand was under regular pressure to come over and play so that union in Australia could be seen to be competing with league. By and large the Wallabies were the All Blacks' whipping-boy. From the first test ever played in 1903, before 30,000 fascinated and, at times, mystified spectators at the Sydney Cricket Ground, the pattern was established. The All Blacks would pound away up the centre in forward rushes, monopolising possession, while the Australians would desperately look for occasional opportunities to attack through their backs. And New Zealand would win.

They have usually won ever since although the gap has closed somewhat lately. There was a working assumption that New Zealanders were more dedicated, more mean-minded and more pragmatic than their Australian counterparts who tended to be smaller in stature, more middle-class and more debonair in their approach.

There was something of a blithe spirit about Wallabies teams. They took chances. They experimented; they ran just about everything. Part-time poet Peter Fenton conjured up this ethos in this ditty which would often be read out in the Wallabies' dressing-room before a test match:

There's spirit in the Wallabies
mere words cannot describe.
It's as if they are descended
From some legendary tribe.
It's the camaraderie

That's born of valour not of fame.
It's the sheer exhilaration
When you play the running game.

Clunky verse perhaps, but evocative stuff and revealing of the attitude of the Australians. How you played was as important as the result. Needless to say this was in part induced by the overwhelming realisation that the result was more or less a foregone conclusion.

It stayed that way for the next century or so until that great equaliser, the professional game, arrived. The difference between Australia and New Zealand was a significant one. Most Wallabies teams had a relatively high proportion of private school or university-trained players, certainly significantly more than New Zealand.

Wallabies teams have, perhaps as a consequence, always seemed smarter than their All Blacks counterparts. Their game was based on applied intelligence rather than brute force and, at various times over the last century, that has been obvious on the field. In recent times the difference in tactical acumen between the likes of John Eales, George Gregan, Stephen Larkham, Stirling Mortlock and co. and their New Zealand opponents has been palpable and, at times, dispiriting to watch.

Now there is virtually nothing between the two teams. Professionalism has all but eliminated the university graduate from the equation in both countries. The Australians have a better record in World Cup tournaments, partly because of the applied intelligence factor, and the All Blacks are marginally ahead at all other times, largely because of superior natural talent.

For most of the 20th century rugby union in Australia was the skinny guy on the beach who got sand kicked in his face. Everywhere it looked there was the hulking bully — rugby league. League scouts would go to every significant game of union and target the most obvious talent for the great league clubs of Sydney and Brisbane. It was big money. League was king. It was the working man's dream game. Big hits, lashings of machismo and the faint whiff of larrikanism infused the game from top to bottom. It was professional from the get-go and it developed a huge commercial infrastructure in Sydney and Brisbane. Beside the league clubs rugby looked pathetically weak.

The professionalisation of rugby union changed all that. Up stepped union into the ring to square off with its rival and the results of that have been fascinating to watch. Now, if anything, rugby union is ahead on points and league is feeling the pinch. The poaching is heading the other way. Rugby's "teledollars" are outbidding those of league, and league doesn't like having the boot on the other foot at all. But that's business, and rugby is a business. No time for sentimentality.

The absence of sentimentality has also been a feature of the relationship between the two national rugby unions. When John O'Neill took over at the ARU a decade or so ago there was no place for Closer Rugby Relations after all those long years of help from New Zealand. The run-up to the 2003 World Cup showed all too clearly how thin the veneer of filial friendship actually is. We agreed on a joint bid. We jointly won with Australia being the primary host. We set about preparing for the tournament, complying with the IRB's increasingly oppressive conditions, the most onerous of which was that of "clean" stadiums.

The Australians secured a crucial guarantee from their government that it would pick up the tab for any additional costs. We forgot to ask; or at least when the NZRU finally got around to asking, it had become apparent to the government that it would be backing a loser financially, and legally. We began to run into trouble providing an assurance that all stadiums would be clean. The IRB started to stand on ceremony. Tempers frayed. Unpleasant things were said, the personal integrity of Australian and New Zealand administrators was questioned and relations between the NZRU and the IRB/Australian bloc turned to ice.

The IRB's politically elastic chairman, Welsh lawyer Vernon Pugh, gave us a nod and a wink on "clean-ness" and we took him at his word. That was dumb. It implied that we assumed nobody would surely mess with New Zealand, the top rugby nation in the world. John O'Neill, however, began to question New Zealand's ability to comply, dropping timely hints that Australia could go it alone if necessary. It all ended up in a shabby slanging match. The IRB took the sub-hosting rights away from New Zealand, to outrage in this country and O'Neill got to host the whole shebang, making a packet for the ARU. The post-mortems over how, precisely, New Zealand got shafted were long and laborious. The truth of this will always remain a matter of doubt.

That episode marked a low point in trans-Tasman rugby relations. It's better now, but not an awful lot better. Australia did its best to promote Japan's bid over that of New Zealand for the 2011 World Cup, something that really rankled when the news came out.

In some ways, Australian-New Zealand rugby relations have mirrored the wider relationship. It means a good deal more to New Zealanders to win against Australia rather than vice versa. We're bad at losing to anyone but we're particularly bad at losing to Australia. People still go round wearing those T-shirts with the pointed message, "I support New Zealand and any team that's playing Australia." And they mean it.

It's the big brother thing. Australia is bigger, wealthier, better endowed with natural resources, more assertive and more internationally ambitious than New Zealand. New Zealand isn't of much consequence across the Tasman although one suspects that it makes Australians feel more substantial knowing they can beat up on New Zealand whenever they want. Except in rugby. Thus the tension.

One of the most defining characteristics of Australians today is that they pride themselves on being hard-minded businessmen who can foot it in any company. In many respects they can. But when it comes to New Zealand this attitude creates problems. New Zealanders have always expected something more generous, more accommodating when it comes to trans-Tasman cooperation. They are constantly disappointed. Australia treats everybody the same. There is an absence of sentimentality when it comes to business and that absence is reflected in the business of the rugby relationship. John O'Neill, a banker by trade, is a thoroughly engaging individual but he is utterly unsentimental when it comes to the interests of the ARU, as the NZRU found out to its chagrin in 2002.

The truth is, however, that Australia and New Zealand are going to have to work more closely together in the rugby world of the 21st century. John O'Neill and his colleagues need to see the relationship not as a zero sum game but as a core alliance, and his New Zealand counterparts need to get over any lingering resentment about the past and accept that this is ANZAC time. If the two countries want to remain competitive internationally they are going to have to collaborate rather more closely than they ever have before — in Sanzar, in the IRB and in the development of rugby around the Pacific. No matter who has the Bledisloe Cup.

Australia is desperate to enlarge the market for rugby domestically. It has agitated for more Super rugby franchises. It went from three to four, creating a beachhead in Perth and now a fifth, based in Melbourne. Super rugby is the only real way that top-class competition can be gained by Australian players. They are far more dependent on it than New Zealand is and this explains why the Australians have been so desperate to increase the number of professional franchises around the country. A few years ago the notion of professional rugby teams based in Perth or Melbourne would have been unimaginable.

But Australia has a harder nut to crack when it comes to the next tier down, a national competition. With only two viable states — New South Wales and Queensland — along with ACT, there just isn't the scope for a semi-professional, inter-provincial tournament the equivalent of New Zealand's Air New Zealand Cup. Australia tried a new formula in 2007 with its National Championship. This consisted of eight hybrid, mini-franchises spread around the country, drawing on established Super 14 players as a core, but it flopped after a single season, at a loss of $5.5 million. At the time it seemed like a good idea, a natural, market-led initiative that would expand the game's profile domestically and provide a stepping-stone to full professionalism for younger players around the country. It failed because it couldn't generate genuine parochial support. In other words it looked like an artificial add-on and smelt like one too. Suspicions as to its attractiveness were aroused when it became known that, in a remarkable reversal of roles, the ARU actually paid the national free-to-air broadcaster to run it on television.

The ARU is desperate to fill this mid-season gap for its players, even if the players are not desperate to be overloaded with more playing obligations. At the same time there is no particular sign that the rugby public in Australia are crying out for more "product". Quite clearly, they have more than enough to be going on with.

Australian rugby is on the horns of an awful dilemma. It is seeing players being tempted off to the Northern hemisphere, or back to league, and there isn't much it can do about it. The Australians gaze covetously at the national provincial championship in New Zealand and occasionally wonder out loud how they might gatecrash it. Sooner or later they will, and once again it will be a case of New Zealand coming to the rescue.

The Slowly Rising Sun

KOJI TOKUMASU, the secretary of the Japan Rugby Football Union, kept apologising. It was a couple of months before the IRB was due to decide which of three countries — Japan, South Africa or New Zealand — got to host the 2011 World Cup. He was embarrassed about Japan having the cheek to take on the rugby heavyweights. His chairman, Nobby Mashimo, was equally bashful about it all. As we drank tea at the JRFU's modest headquarters in Tokyo there was much self-deprecation. Koji kept saying he hoped I wasn't offended by Japan's presumption. I kept telling him I wasn't. It was almost as if they would rather the whole thing went away. It did. Japan's bid turned into a kamikaze mission.

The Japanese were very committed to that bid. They knew they were better equipped than either New Zealand or South Africa to host a tournament of this size. The stadiums, already in place, were more than capable of coping with the great, affluent expeditionary forces who go to rugby World Cups. So was the accommodation. No need for cavalcades of campervans or itinerant cruise liners offshore to cope with the numbers. Japanese cities have a way of absorbing visitors into small spaces and making them feel particularly comfortable. Japan had had plenty of hard experience in running mega-tournaments. Anyone who doubted this was rapidly referred to the 2002 Soccer World Cup which Japan co-hosted with spectacular success. The Japanese publicity material accompanying its bid resonated with pride over this throughout and it emphasised — no doubt in a dig at South Africa — the other great virtue that Japan offers the visitor: safety. You won't get mugged in Tokyo, Osaka or Nagoya or Kyoto.

The government stated quite unequivocally that it would happily stump up whatever it takes to satisfy the IRB's voracious demands in terms of net income. Money was no object to Japanese rugby because all of the great industrial companies who have their own rugby franchises were in behind the bid too, well aware that a World Cup in Japan would provide them with heaven-sent promotional opportunities on a world stage. The fact that China was hosting the 2008 Olympics acted as a galvanising force for the Japanese. Going for the Rugby World Cup fitted with Japan's foreign policy imperative of forging a new layer of relationships with other Asian countries.

The Japanese even garnered some support from the unlikely personage of Jonah Lomu. Jonah, perhaps naïvely, was simply being honest about what could be done for the game in Asia if the Japanese were to win this particular race. Immediately, the sports shock-jocks fell upon the bemused figure of Lomu who found himself obliged to issue copious clarifications of what he actually said in order not to have his passport cancelled or be regarded as a 21st century Tokyo Rose.

In the end, Japan got shafted. What is more interesting, however, is that there had been some talk a year or so before the Dublin decision that Japan and New Zealand might run a co-host bid. Unfortunately, New Zealand, after announcing that they were actively pursuing it, backed right off. I raised this with Koji Tokumasu. He blushed. He explained, in suitably circumlocutory language, how Japan had never had any real response from New Zealand to the notion of going it together, whether in a World Cup bid or in any other way.

I called my old friend Shiggy Konno, the godfather of Japanese rugby for so many years, to see what light he could shed on it all. He was brutally frank. "I tried to talk them out of this," he said. "Japan's not up to hosting a World Cup. We just aren't good enough on the field. Imagine the shame of the opening match when we lose by a hundred or more!"

Japan has, particularly in the last 30 years, had a number of false dawns. Was this why Japan stumbled at the last hurdle? There was very little evidence of the sort of vote-buying that has turned the IOC or World Soccer into the equivalent of an Iranian bazaar. Japan should have romped home on the grounds of its commercial case.

The answer is more banal than that. Quite simply, there was a crucial missing ingredient from the Japanese bid. Passion. It was all a bit like a multilateral trade negotiation as far as Japan was concerned. Japan Inc. bought into the idea not so much from a desire to celebrate rugby as to turn a yen out there in a world in which sport is no more than a compliant handmaiden of business. Fair enough, but nobody should be under any illusion that a World Cup in Tokyo, Osaka or Nagoya is going to stir traditional rugby juices in quite the same way it would in New Zealand or South Africa.

There are those who maintain that rugby simply doesn't have enough of a grounding in Japan to deliver real excitement. They say it lacks history and tradition. This isn't particularly fair. Anyone who has been on a rugby tour there knows otherwise. The game has a wonderfully colourful history. Its origins date all the way back to the 1890s when an obviously very adventurous Englishman called Edward Clarke, a Cambridge graduate, started it up in Keio University. It has been popular in the universities ever since and was given a major boost in the 1930s when Prince Chichibu, a member of the imperial family, played it and promoted it as the ideal preparation for adulthood. In the pre-war years the Japanese became very interested in team sports that promoted collective endeavour and coordination, something that fitted with the Japanese temperament and a national penchant for doing things in cohesive groups.

A key question in all this is whether or not Japanese rugby is sustainable in its present state. The answer to that is probably not. The IRB has taken some steps to try to integrate Japan into more regular international competition through the Pacific Nations Cup. The Japanese need much more than that, however. Is it possible to foresee a Japanese-based franchise playing in the Super rugby competition in due course? There is a need for incentives for Japanese players to excel on the world stage and the emergence of a superstar Japanese version of Dan Carter to propel the game to the next level.

There are as many registered rugby players in Japan as there are in New Zealand, around 130,000. The game is played at all levels from primary schools upwards but its traditional strength still lies in the universities where it remains a stoutly amateur game. In the past, their matches regularly attracted crowds of 50,000 to 60,000. But support has faltered in recent years, especially since the formation of the Japan Top League;

the best players have been enticed away to the professional game. That sounds eerily familiar to anyone involved in university rugby elsewhere.

On top of all this the Japanese have done what they do best — laid a corporate structure over it all, with a series of independent companies running their own, wholly owned franchises forming the professional side of the game. The teams are company teams, basically because nobody else can afford to pay for the land needed for pitches, training facilities and so on. The players in these teams are usually contracted on an annual basis, but there are some who are hired as regular employees, who are then released from their day jobs to play rugby.

The league is being expanded to 14 teams, but this does not imply that rugby in Japan is in a healthy state. Jean-Pierre Élissalde, the former national coach, regularly complained that Japan was doing badly internationally because the Top League falls far short in quality to the professional game elsewhere. John Kirwan, the current coach, has made much the same point.

Quality might be a lingering problem. Structure is a bigger one. The Japanese Rugby Football Union doesn't have the kind of control that, for instance, the NZRU or the ARU have in calling the shots. Amazingly, the JRFU consists of a couple of dozen employees in a tiny complex adjacent to the Chichibu stadium in Tokyo. Compared to the ballooning casts of hundreds at the NZRU headquarters, or the ARU, or Twickenham or the IRB in Dublin, this is astonishingly modest.

The companies are a law unto themselves, not dissimilar to the larger English clubs. They are on a more secure financial footing than the clubs, however, because they are, effectively, part of the corporate enterprise. The players are employees and many, if not most, of those who play professionally actually have daytime jobs within the company and will stay with the company when they retire from the game.

But Japanese rugby still has three big limitations. First, and most obviously, they just don't have the big guys to compete with the rest of the rugby world. Thus the imports.

Secondly, the schism between the amateur and the professional dimensions of the game means there are few natural escalator systems that enable players to graduate from one to the other. The third weakness, ironically, owes its origin to Japan's greatest asset, its social cohesiveness.

Japanese teams rely on patterns rather than individual flair. They are coached to play to a rigid formula and have great trouble with the notion of improvisation, something that distinguishes rugby from other sports like baseball.

New Zealand, Australia and the Pacific countries see Japan more as a predator rather than a collaborator. Corporate clubs in Japan are prepared to pay a big premium for the sort of ball-playing talent we have in abundance in the Pacific. Stephen Larkham netted $1.2 million to retire gracefully in Japan, raising the bar even further. Today, the real worry is the number of young players who are prepared to do a runner to Japan in the knowledge that they are never going to make the international ranks at home.

This trickle could quickly turn into a tsunami unless we come to terms with the phenomenon of Japan. The New Zealand Rugby Union has, however, been preoccupied with what it thinks are bigger fish and has missed an opportunity to forge an alliance with Japan that could yield profound returns in every sense in the future. John Kirwan has tried almost to exhaustion to get this message across but nobody seems to be listening. Kirwan wants Japan factored into the Australian-New Zealand syndrome in a competition akin to the Heineken Cup, involving New Zealand and Australian provinces together with several Japanese teams and, maybe, a Pacifica team as well. This could ease the problem of New Zealand players disappearing into the rising sunset and being ineligible for the All Blacks. It is an interesting and innovative idea, but it seems to have fallen on barren ground in the NZRU.

When will New Zealand rugby begin to take its relations with Japan seriously? The benefits are so blindingly obvious. We have the players, the coaches, the referees and the role models. They have the facilities, the money, the enthusiasm and the corporate clout to create an unbeatable relationship.

Perhaps the time has come to set up a formal arrangement under the umbrella of New Zealand's bilateral relationship with Japan whereby Japanese coaches and players are brought to New Zealand for intensive training in exchange for Japanese corporate investment in New Zealand rugby, both amateur and professional. In a market-driven sport it seems amazing that we can't think more creatively about strategic partnerships.

New Zealand invested much energy and resources into the international Expo at Aichi in 2005 for the simple reason that we are losing opportunities to work more profitably with the Japanese. Ever since, there has been a suspicion in Tokyo that New Zealand is more interested in China than Japan and that our relations with Japan have been subtly downgraded. That rubs salt into an existing wound. In the post-recession era Japan will become more and more of a focus for New Zealand enterprise. Wouldn't it be nice if a bilateral rugby deal could be part of that effort?

The Japanese now have the certainty of hosting the 2019 World Cup and this will provide them with the confidence to really raise the game's profile. But they won't go much further until they truly engage with New Zealand and Australia. The ball, on this issue, is in our court.

Going Global

IT IS astonishing the way rugby, from its tight little cohort of Anglo-Saxon exclusivity a few short years ago, has exploded onto a world stage and spread its tentacles on every continent. Its ambition is to become a genuinely global game with the capacity to attract global corporate support.

The IRB, bolstered by substantially larger income from various World Cups, has been very busy over the last few years pumping resources into a number of the newer rugby regions. Take Africa for instance. In 2009 they announced a bold new effort to grow the numbers of players and the competitiveness of national teams in Africa. Centred on Kenya, this initiative seems to be paying dividends already. Kenya, in particular, has shot dramatically up the sevens rankings and the 15-a-side game is inevitably going to benefit from this, assuming Kenya is able to get enough real international competition.

Over the next few years the IRB and the Confederation of African Rugby (CAR) will oversee the roll-out of a wide-reaching grassroots development programme aimed at introducing 100,000 primary school children to the sport by 2012.

Much the same is happening in the Gulf states. The existing combined multi-state union, the Arabian Gulf Rugby Football Union, will evolve at the end of 2010 into a number of new unions in the area. The first of these is expected to be the United Arab Emirates, which should become an IRB Member Union by 2010. Given its known purchasing power, Dubai will undoubtedly attract playing talent from all over the world like moths to a spotlight.

Each union will have a direct link to the Asian Rugby Football Union

(ARFU) IRB Regional Association, unlocking IRB assistance in key areas, including technical and administrative support, coaching, funding and new competition structures which will provide a more clearly defined player development pathway in West Asia. If rugby can begin to tap the vast investment reservoir in this area, and it seems that this is on the point of explosion, then it really will have a chance of becoming a genuine world game.

The last great frontier doesn't lie in Asia, however, but in North America and there the IRB really does have a challenge on its hands. Rugby is alive and reasonably well in Canada but in the United States it seems to be forever poised to take off, but never quite does. Like the Wright brothers in the first few years trying to get their odd contraption off the ground, it stutters along waiting for a favourable up-draught. Ironically, it was actually more popular there a century ago than it is now. The Americans, along with France and Britain, managed, remarkably, to talk the IOC into including it as a sport in the Olympic Games. The United States claimed victories in both the 1920 and 1924 Games and remains, perversely, the Olympic champion, even if most Americans have only the vaguest notion as to what rugby is.

But the Americans might yet surprise us all. The game at the higher levels has been reorganised. An American Super League has been founded and the East–West conference-based competition began in 2009. New sponsors have been found. New energy is being injected along with some bounty-hunting foreign players, a sure sign that the game has some attractions. The next step is a fully professionalised system, but that will be much harder to sustain given the total dominance of American football in the mind of Joe the Plumber. It will need serious television support and some really heavyweight sponsorship to get any traction and there are serious doubts about the practicality of these in an already crowded and viciously competitive sports market.

The conventional North American preference is for sub-national professional competitions, with international matches virtually unknown in baseball and football and rare, with the exception of the Olympics and world cups, in ice hockey and basketball. The IRB is, however, determined to break the international ice in the Americas by creating more competition among participating countries. The latest innovation is the Americas Rugby Championship. This new tournament features six teams, including four provincial sides from Canada, joined by the Argentina Jaguars and USA 'A'. The format unites rugby in North and South America in a high performance sub-international structure for the first time. It's a clever experiment. The plan is to gradually expand this into a genuine North–South America competition involving Uruguay, Mexico, Chile and perhaps others.

But everybody knows that the United States is the real pivot to rugby in the Americas. If rugby can gain a secure foothold in the United States who knows what that would do to the game worldwide? The local objective isn't more test matches for the national team, the Eagles, because Americans aren't very interested in watching team sports against other countries. The secret, they say, lies in establishing a domestic competition and selling it to the consumers. The franchise concept was invented in America but, ironically, that seems to be the biggest stumbling block for American rugby.

Could the Americans conceivably host the World Cup sometime in the future? The preconditions may not be in place just yet, but if professionalism can be successfully injected domestically, who knows what might happen. And with the great persuader, Kevin Roberts, in the engine room, anything is possible.

But the geographical expansion of the game is complemented by expansion in other ways. It is now played extensively by women and a women's World Cup is up and running. The IRB announcement that the next but one women's rugby World Cup might take place in Kazakhstan must have come as a bit of a shock to many. Apparently, Kazakhstan is up against Samoa and New Zealand and fancies its chances. I didn't even know they played the game in Kazakhstan. Maybe it's only the women who play. Let's hope Borat doesn't get wind of this.

But wherever it is held it will be a big one. Progress has been so spectacular that the women's game is on a catch-up curve with that of the men. Played by over 200,000 registered players worldwide, across six global regions and 116 Member Unions, women's rugby is growing like a triffid with excessive testosterone.

There is now a Women's Strategic Plan to ensure that their game grows as fast as possible all over the world. Tournaments such as the

2006 Women's Rugby World Cup in Canada, which broke all previous broadcast and attendance records, and the inaugural Women's Rugby World Cup Sevens, hosted in Dubai in 2009, alongside that of the men, have shown that women are closing the gap in terms of international status and support. Nicky Inwood made history by being the first woman to referee an international match — one of the 2007 Women's Six Nations matches. And she made a very good job of it.

It won't be long before the women are refereeing the men's test matches; and why not? They are already doing it in the men's international sevens so the glass ceiling has more than enough cracks in it. Given their proven capacity to keep an eye on several things at once, to multi-task, they might turn out to make a better job of it. The IRB has even appointed a female Development Manager for Women's Rugby to "provide the impetus for the continued growth of the women's game at all levels". Watch out, lads. Here they come.

There has always been a certain squeamishness among males who see women playing rugby for the first time. To many, it just doesn't seem right. We can't quite put our finger on precisely what isn't right about it, but that doesn't diminish the squeamishness. Wasn't this designed to be the ultimate man's game? Wasn't it an accepted wisdom that the kind of nasty collisions that rugby invokes should never be inflicted on women? The spectacle of women belting each other with crash tackles, smashing their way up the field in rolling mauls and rucking each other on the ground also causes quite a few other women some pause for thought as to just what the limits to feminine physicality might be. Maybe there aren't any.

Most other team sports remain totally segregated. International rules prohibit cohabitation. Wouldn't it be odd if rugby, the least likely of all team sports to accommodate men and women together, were to lead the way? That is hardly a hot prospect and, in any case, why would the girls want to invade this particular citadel? They already have their own World Cup. It is sometimes said there is more beauty in the way women play rugby. They rely less on brute strength and therefore more on guile and evasion. Would they bring a more studied feminine dimension to a mixed game? And what would be done about salaries? If other professional sports are anything to go by, rugby would eventually have to pay the women the same and, at the rate their game is expanding, that would mean less money for everyone else.

A more pertinent question is: will women's rugby follow the same organisational path as the men's? Is there any prospect that women's rugby might be able to avoid that slippery slope? To a large extent that depends on the degree to which the women's game is able to compete for sponsorship support and television markets. Logic suggests that there simply won't be enough dosh to go round, but you never know with women. They are considerably more artful in negotiating deals than men. With all that multi-tasking ability the chances are that the women will proceed to make all the same mistakes that men's rugby has made. And, after all, who are we, who have administered the men's game into a box canyon, to offer advice?

But rugby's march forward into the world of politically correct inclusiveness doesn't end at the women's game. In a number of countries there are gay rugby teams openly flaunting what was, and to a large extent still is, the game's great denial. A TV documentary about Ireland's first openly gay rugby team, the Emerald Warriors, inevitably called *Queering the Pitch*, sent a shiver down the spines of traditional rugby unions when it was first shown, but things have moved well beyond that now. New Zealand has the imaginatively named Bold Knights. Argentina has gay teams. So does Australia. They're coming out everywhere. Rugby has always claimed to be an inclusive sport. Now it is obliged to live up to that.

Rugby has, of course, always had more than its fair share of homosexual participants, all of whom, until relatively recently, have been forced to keep their credentials firmly locked in the closet. Rugby and homosexuality may have traditionally been very awkward bedfellows but there are unmistakable signs that it is growing up. The fact that Welsh star Gareth Thomas felt able to publicly reveal that he was gay and that the reaction across rugby circles was simply a shrug of the shoulders as if to say, "So what?" represented a massive leap forward, but there is a long way to go yet.

Rugby is going to need all the infusions from left field that it can get if the amateur base is to have any meaning at all in future. That great kaleidoscopic future will, in a few years, look very different to the monotones of the past, but ironically it will probably have more in common with the past than the rarified air which the professional elite now inhabits.

Conclusion

You cannot solve a problem with the same thinking that created it.
—Albert Einstein

NO DOUBT about it: rugby has a problem. It's a multi-headed problem — of income, loyalty and credibility. The income issue has become one of dependency on the whims of sponsors and broadcasters. It may be solvable with some decisive action to reduce that dependence by trimming expenditure, simplifying some of the more bloated processes and containing the costs of player salaries.

The other two — loyalty and credibility — are rather more intractable. The loyalty of traditional supporters has been stretched to breaking point. They still love the game but they don't like the way it has been wrenched away from its roots by rampant commercialism. Those roots are too deep to blithely accept that amateurism can be shunted aside by the slick new generation of marketers, sponsors and advertising executives. They feel angry and frustrated at the way decisions are taken seemingly without reference to the views and feelings of the great rugby public.

Credibility is a more elusive quality. Rugby's ambitions have run ahead of its means. It wants to be a world game, but it lacks the qualifications to get there. It wants to preserve its precious amateur spirit, but at the same time expand its professional base. It is seriously divided with players, administrators and unions — both nationally and internationally — seemingly in perpetual war with each other.

When I started writing this book, in 2007, the outlook for the game was decidedly overcast. The professional revolution seemed to have gutted it of all inspiration. Within a few short years the professional revolution had all but destroyed rugby's sense of heritage and of fellowship. Rugby clubs all over the world were closing down or being forced to amalgamate. The vast legions of volunteers had all but disappeared. Playing numbers were stagnating except in England and France. Crowds and television audiences in the Southern hemisphere were declining and the baffling complexity of the rules, together with a growing concentration on defence, was stifling imagination and flair. In spite of ever-increasing razzmatazz, rugby was becoming boring, and its pretensions as a global game seemed like a ridiculous pipedream.

The game was seriously out of kilter. Professional players, leading ever more pampered lives, were monopolising an ever greater slice of the financial pie while clubs and provinces had to learn to live with less and less. A new elitism was ushered in, causing sadness and cynicism among those who believed in the integrity of the amateur game. Rugby was being savagely decoupled from its history and those running it either couldn't see, or didn't care about, the damage that was doing. There seemed to be no choice: the game had sold its soul to the sponsors and the broadcasters with both demanding more and more until it became obvious that saturation had been reached.

The IRB had fixed its mind on income generation, creating new tournaments and opening up new frontiers, unable to resolve the more fundamental problems besetting the game. It seemed impossible to secure agreement on a global season into which the many overlapping competitions could be fitted. It seemed impossible to get any real consensus on what rules to change and it seemed equally impossible to achieve a rational measure of international regulation in the face of the commercial imperatives driving the game.

Rugby was, to put it bluntly, in full-blown crisis. But every crisis contains within it the seeds of potential solutions and there are signs that rugby is at last beginning to acknowledge the obvious: that it needs to adapt or die. It is now obvious that however much some people would wish it away, professionalism is here to stay and that the trick is to find ways of accommodating the amateur and professional games alongside each other in relative harmony.

In 2009, some very encouraging trends began to emerge. Tentative agreement was reached on an international calendar, something that had seemed an impossibility a year earlier. This was a significant circuit-breaker because it showed, at last, that all parties recognised that if things continued as they were the game was in grave danger. It brings some welcome certainty to the organisation of both professional and amateur competitions which had been tripping over each other, causing unneccessary antagonism. In England this translated into a promising accord between the RFU, the players' association and the clubs, which may yet open the way to real reform.

In New Zealand an historic agreement on the timing of club, provincial and Super 14 tournaments and the disposition of players between them was reached in December 2009. It means that the NZRU can at last fit the Super 14, the Tri Nations test matches and the two sets of tests against Northern hemisphere countries — in June and November — into a single year. A welcome deal between the players' association and the NZRU, signalling some long-awaited realism from the players, has seen agreement on a significantly lower provincial salary cap and an equally long awaited consensus among the provincial unions on the future shape of the national championship. The new first division championship, featuring 14 teams in two tiers of seven, has the virtue of relative simplicity and, with promotion-relegation incentives, will kick off in August 2011. There remain some doubters among the weaker provinces, but if the salary cap is rigidly enforced, there is no reason why it can't result in real parity among the provinces and feature more local boys and more local pride. Just like the good old days.

It would, of course, be preferable to have a genuinely amateur provincial competition with clear daylight between that and the Super 14, but that is now no longer possible. Commerce has infected provincial rugby too severely for that. Equally sadly, the parting of the ways between the All Blacks and the national championship is now assured. The bloated test match programme has seen to that and the big challenge for the fans is to swallow this bitter pill. If they do, the provincial competition has a future. If they don't, it is doomed.

But the risks don't end there. If rugby is to beat this crisis in New Zealand — and internationally — there is a series of other actions, some of them essential, some desirable, that needs to be taken in the immediate future. The first, and most pressing, is the achievement of an international accord on salary levels. Somehow, the IRB must find the means, both moral and legal, to establish international salary bands, or compensation systems, to arrest the wholesale erosion of talent from the poor to the rich.

Secondly, there needs to occur an all-embracing, bottom-up simplification of the rules, agreed globally, with the single objective of eliminating as many opportunities for the referee to blow his whistle as possible. It is time to stop regional tinkering and start globally simplifying. Rugby has no chance of rising to become a world game while it is weighed down with its current, leaden laws book.

Third, the IRB must be formally mandated to secure an amendment to European law exempting rugby (in concert with other sports seeking the same outcome) from the iniquitous restraint of trade laws that enable European clubs to thumb their noses at national unions when it comes to player availability. This initiative needs to be backed by each of the governments concerned and universally endorsed by rugby nations everywhere. Bernard Lapasset, the chairman of the IRB, has bravely launched the process. He needs every ounce of support he can get. He hasn't yet had that.

Fourth, a fresh look needs to be taken at the so-called "pathway" system by which young players rise to professional status. The current system results in their estrangement from club and even province, and is a major cause of the decline of amateur rugby. That is not a sustainable arrangement. Clubs need to be dealt back into the equation, providing a realistic grounding for young academy players, for their own sake as individuals growing up in an inclusive game, and for the sake of rugby as a whole.

Fifth, the NZRU, working together with relevant government agencies, should pursue a long-term strategic agreement with Japan designed to capitalise on the complementary assets of both countries and the maximisation of bilateral economic opportunities, using rugby as a springboard.

Sixth, New Zealand rugby, together with Australia, needs to develop a set of agreements with the Pacific Island unions, backed if possible by government aid ministries, designed to raise the level of rugby infrastructure in the Pacific. The accords should include rules relating to the movement of players, coaches and administrators within the region. This isn't so much an opportunity as an obligation after decades of unforgiveable neglect.

Seventh, a new deal with the players' association needs to be forged whereby all full-time professionals employed by the NZRU (or the franchises) are deployed to promote the amateur game much more intensively than merely making token appearances at the behest of sponsors or charitable causes. This is the only means by which the professional elite can remain in touch with rugby's community heartland — to which they owe every cent of their income.

Eighth, there needs to be a new approach to the June and November windows in the international calendar which substitutes international tours for the current series of one-off test matches every second or third year. In that way, visiting international teams will be able to play at least a few matches in the provinces, guaranteed to be sell-outs, and provide teams like the Maori XV and New Zealand Universities with an assured programme.

Ninth, and perhaps most important of all, rugby's commentators and fans must come to terms with the fact that the game has no choice but to move with the times. Standing still, let alone hankering back to the past, simply isn't an option any more. Rugby's administrators are going to need all the help they can get to keep the game afloat. The last thing they need is the kind of knee-jerk, vitriolic claptrap that seems to have become the standard retort to any new development.

Is rugby capable of committing itself to a programme of reforms? Do its member countries have the statesmanship to see it through? There is sufficient realisation of the scale of the problem and the threat it poses to the game. Now, rugby needs to find the inspiration to fix it.

Postscript

NOT LONG ago I was invited to an event at which a number of very promising young academy players were being honoured. I got into conversation with one of them, a New Zealand-born Samoan whose ambition was a professional career, wherever it may take him. I asked him what it was about rugby that he liked the best, expecting the reply to be: "The money." Instead, he replied without hesitation, "The friends I make."

All is not yet lost.

Bibliography

Barber, Benjamin R. *Jihad vs McWorld*, Times Books, New York, 1995.

Belich, James. *Making Peoples*, Penguin Books, Auckland, 1996.

Belich, James. *Paradise Reforged*, Penguin Books, Auckland, 2001.

Burton, Richard. 'Richard Burton's Last Match' in Smith, Godfrey (ed), *Take the Ball and Run: A Rugby Anthology*, Pavilion Books, London, 1992.

Carlin, John. *Playing the Enemy: Nelson Mandela and the Game that Made a Nation*, Penguin Books, New York, 2008.

Davidson, John. *New Ballads*, John Lane, London, 1897.

Dawkins, Richard. *The Selfish Gene*, Oxford University Press, Oxford, 1989.

English, Alan. *Stand Up and Fight: When Munster Beat the All Blacks*, Yellow Jersey Press, London, 2007.

Guha, Ramachandra, *A Corner of a Foreign Field: The Indian History of a British Sport*, Picador, London, 2002.

Jones, Lloyd. *The Book of Fame*, Penguin Books, Auckland, 2000.

Keating, Frank. 'It's time the haka posture is put out to pasture', *The Guardian*, 18 November 2008.

Kindleberger, Charles. Address to Saltzburg Seminar on American Studies, Saltzburg, 1977.

King, Michael. *The Penguin History of New Zealand*, Penguin Books, Auckland, 2003.

Laidlaw, Chris. *Mud in Your Eye: A Worm's Eye View of the Changing World of Rugby*, Reed, Wellington, 1973.

Laidlaw, Chris. *Rights of Passage*, Hodder Moa Beckett, Auckland, 1999.

Lasch, Christopher. 'The Corruption of Sports', *New York Review of Books*, Vol. 24, No. 7A, 28 April 1977.

Legrain, Philippe. *Immigrants: Your Country Needs Them*, Princeton University Press, Princeton, 2009.

McConnell, Robin. *Inside the All Blacks*, HarperCollins, Auckland, 1999.

Morris, James. *Pax Britannica: the Climax of an Empire*, Faber, London, 1968.

Owen, Owen Llewellyn. *The History of the Rugby Football Union*, Published for the Rugby Football Union by Playfair Books, 1995.

Paul, Gregor. *Black Obsession: The All Blacks' Quest for World Cup Success*, Exisle, Auckland, 2009.

Patten, Chris. *What Next? Surviving the Twenty-First Century*, Allen Lane, London, 2008.

Patterson, Brad (ed). *Sport, Society and Culture in New Zealand*, Stout Research Centre, Wellington, 1999.

Phillips, Jock. *A Man's Country? The Image of the Pakeha Male*, Penguin Books, Auckland, 1987.

Ryan, Greg (ed). *Tackling Rugby Myths: Rugby and New Zealand Society 1854–2004*, University of Otago Press, Dunedin, 2005.

Siegfried, André. *Democracy in New Zealand*, Bell, London, 1914.

Sinclair, Keith. *A Destiny Apart: New Zealand's Search for National Identity*, Allen & Unwin/Port Nicholson Press, Wellington, 1986.

Slatter, Gordon. *On the Ball*, Whitcomb & Tombs, Christchurch, 1968.

Sparks, Allister. *The Mind of South Africa: The Story of the Rise and Fall of Apartheid*, Heinemann, London, 1990.

Storey, David. *This Sporting Life*. Penguin, London, 1962.

Telfer, Brendan. *A Life in Sport*, Trio Books, Wellington, 2009.

Thomas, Paul. *A Whole New Ball Game*, Hodder Moa Beckett, Auckland, 2003.

Turner, Brian. *Anton Oliver: Inside*, Hodder Moa Beckett, Auckland, 2005.

Wodehouse, P G. *Very Good, Jeeves!*, Herbert Jenkins, London, 1930.

Zavos, Spiro. *Ka Mate! Ka Mate!: New Zealand's Conquest of British Rugby*, Viking, Auckland, 1998.

Zavos, Spiro & Bray, Gordon. *Two Mighty Tribes: A Hundred Years of All Black and Wallaby Battles*, Penguin, Auckland, 2003.

Zavos, Spiro. *Winters of Revenge. The Bitter Rivalry Between the All Blacks and the Springboks*, Viking, Auckland, 1997.

Index of Names

Alatini, Pita 166
Allen, Fred 104
Amin, Idi 40
Anderson, 'Buck'
Ansell, John 31
Ashworth, John 82
Bainimarama, Frank 174
Baldwin, Stanley 86
Barber, Benjamin 19
Barkley, Charles 145
Barnes, Stuart 83
Barron, Jane 45
Barwell, Keith 239
Beckham, David 40
Bedford, Tom 55
Belich, James 19
Benazzi, Abdelatif 265
Bhatnagar, Roger 59
Boric, Anthony 159
Botha, Bakkies 90
Botha, Naas 78
Brown, Olo 165
Brownlie, Cyril 81
Bunce, Frank 166
Burger, Schalk 96
Burton, Richard 248
Campbell, Alistair 250
Carlin, John 265
Carter, Daniel 40, 44, 89, 148, 151, 156, 167, 277
Ceausescu, Nicolae 40
Chesterton, Ray 83
Clark, Helen 191, 196, 211
Clarke, Edward 277
Clarkson, Jeremy 83
Collins, Jerry 108, 146, 165
Cooper, Colin 131
Cowan, Jimmy 92
Cullen, Christian 105, 107, 130, 153, 154, 155–56, 183, 208, 243
Dallaglio, Lawrence 237
Davidson, John 230
Davies, Gerald 83, 250
Dawkins, Richard 51
Deans, Robbie 109–10
Dimbleby, David 262

Douglas, Roger 61
Drake, John 77
Duckworth, Cecil 239
Eales, John 270
Edgar, Eion 226
Edwards, Gareth 250
Élissalde, Jean-Pierre 278
Ellison, T L 181
English, Alan 242
Fenton, Peter 269
Fitzpatrick, Sean 97, 153
Flutey, Riki 232–33
Fox, Grant 77, 166
Gallagher, John 233
Gallaher, David 81, 193, 230–31, 233
Gomarsall, Andy 239
Graham, John 200
Gray, Bill 182
Gray, Wynne 86
Grewcock, Danny 237
Grey, Sir George 180
Gregan, George 155, 270
Guevara, Che 40
Guha, Ramachandra 53
Hackett, A J 257
Hadden, Frank 115, 245
Haig, Ned 205
Hamilton, Jim 245
Hansen, Steve 110, 147
Hart, John 104–05, 108
Hayman, Carl 156, 157, 238
Hemingway, Ernest 39
Henry, Graham 75, 107, 108–10, 124, 127, 128, 137, 147, 162
Hinton, Marc 86
Hogan, Vincent 82
Hoskins, Oregan 65
Howitt, Bob 85
Howlett, Doug 84, 156, 243
Ieremia, Alama 154, 166
Jack, Chris 156, 238
Jacobs, Ron 50
James, Carwyn 103
John, Elton 59
Johnson, Martin 236, 237, 245
Johnson, Tony 77
Jones, Ian 77
Jones, Jerry 219
Jones, Stephen 83, 121
Kay, Ben 237
Kaino, Jerome 165
Kaplan, Jonathan 96
Kearns, Phil 78
Keating, Frank 185, 186, 187
Kelly, Ned 43
Kindleberger, Charles 15
King, Michael 123
Kingsley Jones, Phil 150
Kirton, Earle 104
Kirwan, John 279
Knight, Lindsay 85
Konno, 'Shiggy' 276
Lamont, Sean 245
Lange, David 211
Lapasset, Bernard 17, 290
Lardelli, Derek 187
Larkham, Stephen 270, 279
Lasch, Christopher 149
Lawson, Rory 245
Legrain, Philippe 165
Lewis, Paul 86

Lochore, Brian 93, 104, 108, 153
Loe, Richard 82
Lomu, Jonah 150–51, 153, 154, 171, 208, 276
Lovelock, Jack 231
Mackie, Jem 33
Mains, Laurie 104, 142
Malan, Daniel 262
Mallard, Trevor 114
Malreau, André 260
Mandela, Nelson 55, 123, 264, 266
Mansfield, Katherine 257
Marshall, Justin 10
Martin, Andrew 106
Mashimo, 'Nobby' 275
Mauger, Aaron 156, 158, 238
Mayhew, John 105
McAlister, Luke 238
McCaw, Richie 22, 146, 148
McLaren, Bill 244
McConnell, Robin 47
McGeechan, Ian 254
McLean, Terry 85
Meads, Colin 82, 84
Mealamu, Keven
Mehrtens, Andrew 107
Mencken, H L 189
Mexted, Murray 77, 120
Millar, Syd 17
Mitchell, John 106–07, 108, 142, 156, 168
Montgomery, Percy 157
Morris, James 230
Mortlock, Stirling 270
Mosley, Oswald 40
Mourie, Graham 170
Muliaina, Mils 84, 146
Murdoch, Keith 82, 84
Murdoch, Rupert 60, 73
Namath, Joe 223
Nathan, Waka 177–78
Nepia, George 177, 182
Nichol, Rob 134
Nicholson, Adam 39
Nisbett, Grant 78
Nonu, Ma'a, 44, 146
O'Neill, John 175, 271–72
O'Reilly, Tony 38, 40, 107, 243
Obama, Barack 75, 148
Oliver, Anton 107, 108, 125, 142
Orwell, George 37
Owen, Owen L 181
Paewai, Lui 182
Patten, Chris 74, 206
Paul, Gregor 122, 199
Pearse, Richard 33
Pelé 55
Pope John Paul II 40
Porritt, Arthur 231
Pountney, Budge 244
Pryor, Albie 184
Pugh, Vernon 271
Rabuka, Sitiveni 174
Randall, Taine 88–89
Reason, John 83
Richards, Dean 91
Roberts, Kevin 20, 283
Rudd, Kevin 175
Rush, Eric 208
Ruth, Babe 39
Ryan, Greg 46
Ryder, Jesse 147

Seigfried, André 230
Sella, Philippe 155
Serevi, Waisale 207, 209
Shaw, Mark 82
Skinner, Kevin 82
Smith, Conrad 146, 159, 166
Smith, Jed 33
Smith, Wayne 97, 105–06, 110, 147
Snell, Peter 144
Somerville, Greg 156
So'oialo, Rodney 165
Spackman, Kerry 147
Sparks, Alister 262
Speer, Albert 40
Spencer, Carlos 238
Stagg, Peter 244
Starmer-Smith, Nigel 78
Story, David 213, 215
Stransky, Joel 78
Te Pou, Matt 184
Te Rauparaha 186
Telfer, Brendan 85, 244
Tew, Steve 60
Thomas, Gareth 285
Thomas, J B G 81, 82
Thompson, Dave 239
Tipoki, Rua 243
Tokumasu, Koji 275, 276
Tuqiri, Lote 44
Umaga, Tana 93, 108, 137, 146, 153, 157, 166
Veysey, Alex 85
Vickery, Phil 235, 237, 255
Watson, Eric 60, 173
Webb Ellis, William 33
Wilde, Oscar 30
Wilding, Anthony 231
Wilkinson, Jonny 40
Williams, Ali 44, 108, 146
Williams, Robin 164
Williams, Tom 91
Wilson, Jeff 105, 130, 140
Wodehouse, P G 35, 46, 141
Woodward, Clive 105–06, 235, 253–55
Wooster, Bertie 35
Wray, Nigel 239
Wyllie, Alex 'Grizz' 104
Zavos, Spiro 83, 86, 191, 263
Zuma, Jacob 267